A LEXICON
OF ECONOMICS

A LEXICON OF ECONOMICS

Kenyon A. Knopf

Hollen Parker Professor of Economics, Emeritus
Whitman College
Walla Walla, Washington

ACADEMIC PRESS, INC.

Harcourt Brace Jovanovich, Publishers

San Diego   New York   Boston   London

Sydney   Tokyo   Toronto

Copyright © 1991 by ACADEMIC PRESS, INC.

Academic Press, Inc.
San Diego, California 92101

United Kingdom Edition published by
Academic Press Limited
24–28 Oval Road, London NW1 7DX

Library of Congress Cataloging-in-Publication Data

Knopf, Kenyon A.
    A lexicon of economics / Kenyon A. Knopf.
        p.   cm.
    Includes index.
    ISBN 0-12-416955-4
    1. Economics--Encyclopedias.   I. Title.
    HB61.K57   1991
330'.03--dc20   91-19658
                                                                            CIP

PRINTED IN THE UNITED STATES OF AMERICA
91 92 93 94   9 8 7 6 5 4 3 2 1

CONTENTS

PREFACE

A Lexicon of Economics was written for everyone who wants a handy, clear explanation of the economic terms they hear or read everyday. The idiom of economics is troublesome for two reasons. Primarily, what seems to create the greatest difficulty is the economist's use of a very specific definition for a common word that has many diverse meanings in everyday usage. *Investment* is a good example. When considering the state of the economy, an economist uses the term investment to mean expenditure for new plant and equipment, new office buildings, new housing, and additions to inventories. However, in everyday usage, people also speak of investment as the purchase of some existing asset such as stock on a stock exchange, a 20-year-old home, a lakefront lot, a cattle ranch, or a Cézanne painting. An economic policy that proposes to increase investment during a recession is not aimed at stimulating sales on stock exchanges, in markets for existing houses, or other existing assets (although an increase in such sales might reflect growing public confidence in the prospect for an economic recovery). Rather, the policy goal is the economist's investment, namely more expenditure for new capital goods and inventories. That is what creates new income and employment in the economy.

The second difficulty in trying to follow economic and financial discussions is the frequent use of acronyms and abbreviations for terms that are difficult to understand even when they're spelled out. "RAMs will help the cash-flow of the elderly." To find out that a *RAM* is a reverse annuity mortgage is a first step, but what in the world is a reverse annuity mortgage? What is meant by cash-flow? Then there is GATT, Ginnie Mae, Freddie Mac, M2, and, if you'll pardon the expression, GPDI.

The purpose of this book is to equip people with a ready reference to the definitions of many commonly used economic terms and concepts by furnishing enough detail to make them understandable—even if that requires only two paragraphs or over two pages. I've also tried to provide an up-to-date treatment of the terms. The definition of M1 has changed twice since I started collecting terms for this book. The economist's *accelerator* cannot be understood by most people from an entry of one or two lines. And the *FDIC* isn't what it used to be. Entries reflect the content of relatively new laws (e.g., the Financial Institutions Reform, Recovery, and Enforcement Act of 1989 [FIRREA]), the creation of new agencies, (e.g., the Federal Housing Finance Board [FHFB]), and new terms such as *greenmail*.

This book reflects my understanding of economics, which started with a stimulating introduction to the field by Professor Paul Titus at Kenyon College. I was further influenced by distinguished economics professors at the Harvard University Graduate School of Arts and Sciences just after World War II, by my interchange with colleagues over the succeeding years of teaching, and by all the economists whose writings I have read during more than fifty years of economic study. Obviously, none of the above, nor those identified below, are responsible for any shortcomings in my understanding of economics that might appear in this book.

Two of my colleagues at Whitman College, Professor Gordon A. Philpot and Professor James F. Shepherd, reviewed about two-thirds of the entries (I kept adding more), and I consulted Professor David Stevens on the accuracy of some of the entries in his field of expertise. Marilyn Sparks, the assistant librarian at Whitman College, helped me find some esoteric information, including the origins of the term *bear* as used on stock exchanges. My wife, Siddy, has given me constant encouragement on this project, as with every other aspect of our lives together. Our daughter, Kristin Knopf, a CPA in Seattle, commented on some of the accounting terms and helped with some of my convoluted style. Our daughter, Mary Knopf, an interior space designer in Anchorage, did the fine art work for the illustrations.

Kenyon A. Knopf

Abbreviations, Acronyms, and Foreign Phrases

(with entries in the right-hand column)

AC	Average Cost
AD	Aggregate Demand
ad hoc	(L) For this particular case
ADRs	American Depository Receipts
AFC	Average Fixed Cost or Average Factor Cost, depending on context
AF of L	American Federation of Labor
AFL/CIO	American Federation of Labor/Congress of Industrial Organizations
AID	Agency for International Development
AMEX	American Stock Exchange
APC	Average Propensity to Consume
APS	Average Propensity to Save
AR	Average Revenue
ARM	Adjustable-Rate Mortgage
ARP	Average Revenue Product
AS	Aggregate Supply
ATC	Average Total Cost
ATS Accounts	Automatic Transfer Service Accounts
AVC	Average Variable Cost
BIF	Bank Insurance Fund
BLS	Bureau of Labor Statistics, Department of Labor

C	Consumption expenditure
CBO	Collateralized Bond Obligation
CCO	Commodity Credit Corporation
CD	Certificate of Deposit
cet. par.	*Ceteris paribus* (L), other things equal (unchanged)
CIO	Congress of Industrial Organizations
CPI	Consumer Price Index
COLA	Cost of Living Adjustment
DIDMCA	Depository Institutions Deregulation and Monetary Control Act of 1980
DPY	Disposable Personal Income
EC	European Communities
EEC	European Economic Community
e.g.	*exempli gratia* (L), for example
Fannie Mae	Federal National Mortgage Association (FNMA)
FIDC	Federal Deposit Insurance Corporation
Fed	Federal Reserve Banking System
FHA	Federal Housing Administration
FHFB	Federal Housing Finance Board
FHLB	Federal Home Loan Bank
FHLBB	Federal Home Loan Bank Board
FHLMC	Federal Home Loan Mortgage Corporation (Freddie MAC)
FIFO	First In–First Out
FIRREA	Financial Institution Reform, Recovery, and Enforcement Act of 1989
FNMA	Federal National Mortgage Association (Fannie Mae)
FOB	Free on Board
FOMC	Federal Open-Market Committee
Freddie Mac	Federal Home Loan Mortgage Corporation (FHLMC)
FSLIC	Federal Savings and Loan Insurance Corporation
FTC	Federal Trade Commission
G	Government expenditure
GATT	General Agreement on Tariffs and Trade
Ginnie Mae	Government National Mortgage Association (GNMA)
GNMA	Government National Mortgage Association (Ginnie Mae)

GNP Gross National Product

GPDI Gross Private Domestic Investment

HUD U.S. Department of Housing and Urban Development

I Investment Expenditure

I_g Gross Investment—Part of Gross National Product

I_n Net Investment—Part of Net National Product

i.e. *id est* (L), that is

IMF International Monetary Fund

INV Inventories

L Broadest definition of the money stock

LAC Long-Run Average Cost

Laissez Faire (French) to let do, to let people do as they choose

LDCs Less Developed Countries

LIFO Last In–First Out

LRAC Long-Run Average Cost

M Money

MI Narrowest definition of the money stock, after "currency"

M2 A definition of the money stock

M3 A definition of the money stock

MC Marginal Cost

MEC Marginal Efficiency of Capital = MEI

MEI Marginal Efficiency of Investment = MEC

MFC Marginal Fixed Cost or Marginal Factor Cost, depending on context

MMDA Money Market Deposit Account

MPC Marginal Propensity to Consume

MPP Marginal Physical Product

MPS Marginal Propensity to Save

MR Marginal Revenue

MRP Marginal Revenue Product

MRS Marginal Rate of Substitution

MRTS Marginal Rate of Technical Substitution

MU Marginal Utility

NASDAQ National Association of Securities Dealers Automated Quotations

NE Net Exports (National Income Accounting)

NLRB National Labor Relations Board

NNP   Net National Product
NOW Account   Negotiable Order of Withdrawal Account
NPDI   Net Private Domestic Investment
NY   National Income
NYSE   New York Stock Exchange

OCDs   Other Checkable Deposits
OID   Original-Issue Discount Security
OPEC   Organization of Petroleum Exporting Countries
OTS   Office of Thrift Supervision

P   Price
P/E   Price–Earnings Ratio
PPI   Producer Price Index
PY   Personal Income

RAM   Reverse Annuity Mortgage
RefCorp   Resolution Funding Corporation (RFC)
Repo   Repurchase Agreement (RP)
RFC   Resolution Funding Corporation (RefCorp)
RP   Repurchase Agreement (REPO)
RR   Required Reserves
RTC   Resolution Trust Corporation

S   Savings
SAIF   Savings Association Insurance Fund
SDRs   Special Drawing Rights
SEC   Security and Exchange Commission
SRAC   Short-Run Average Cost
SRMC   Short-Run Marginal Cost

T   Tax Expenditure
T-Bills   Treasury Bills
TC   Total Cost
TFC   Total Factor Cost or Total Fixed Cost
TP   Total Product
TR   Total Revenue
TRP   Total Revenue Product
TVC   Total Variable Cost

VA   Department of Veterans Affairs
VAT   Value-Added Tax

ABILITY-TO-PAY   A principle of taxation which holds that those in society who receive high incomes should provide tax support for the public sector in greater measure than those with low incomes. Usually it is used to support progressive taxation—the higher the income the greater the *percentage* of income paid in taxes. The rationale is that the higher the income, the more fully the necessities of life are met and the larger the proportion of income available for discretionary spending and saving. Therefore, the sacrifice per tax dollar is proportionally less for those with higher income than for those with lower income. Some describe the principle as ''soak the rich.''

Applying the principle is complicated by the problem of defining income and determining when it is received. Also, income is just one measure of ability to pay; there are others such as wealth or assets. See *Income: Disposable Personal Income, Progressive Tax, Proportional Tax, Regressive Tax.*

ABSOLUTE ADVANTAGE   A concept of trade in which one country can produce a quantity of a product more efficiently (with fewer resources of labor, land, and/or capital) than another country. The principle of *comparative advantage* holds that there is a benefit to specialization and trade when there are differences between countries in the *relative* efficiency of producing two products, even though one country has an *absolute* advantage in producing *both* products. See *Comparative Advantage.*

ABSOLUTE INCOME HYPOTHESIS   The view of J. M. Keynes (English economist, 1883–1946) that consumption expenditure is a function of the level of current disposable income seen as the absolute amount of income available to spend. See *Consumption Function, Permanent Income Hypothesis, Relative Income Hypothesis.*

ACCELERATOR   A multiplier used to measure the effect of an initial increase of aggregate demand (AD) in the economy on subsequent AD as the result of induced investment expenditure.

For the logic involved, consider a hypothetical shoe manufacturing industry. The typical firm in this industry uses various machines but the output of one key machine determines the output of the firm. Suppose that this machine produces 100 pairs of shoes per day and the firm has 10 of them. Suppose further that each machine has a useful life of 10 years. The firm grew in size slowly over the years so that one key machine wears out each year. Replacement demand for this shoe firm is one key machine per year which is ordered from the shoe machine manufacturer.

If the shoe industry, of which this firm is a part, is working at optimum capacity, an increase in consumer demand for shoes will result in an increase in the demand for shoe machines. If consumers wish to buy 2000 more pairs of shoes per day, a 10 percent increase in the demand for shoes, and our firm's share of the market increase is 100 pairs, our firm would need to buy one new machine to increase production, plus the usual one machine to replace one worn out. For this firm, a 10% increase in demand for shoes has led to a 100% increase in the demand for shoe machines! This is a typical firm so, for the industry as a whole, a 10% increase in the demand for shoes has resulted in a 100% increase in the demand for shoe machines!

If the shoe machine industry were operating at optimum capacity at the time of this change in the demand for shoes, it would need to engage in a major expansion of plant and equipment to meet the demand for shoe machines, causing another large acceleration in investment expenditure (I), a part of aggregate demand. The total of induced investment expenditure may expand explosively.

However, a problem is immediately apparent. If the demand for shoes remains at the new 10% higher figure next year, and the next, the demand for shoe machines will fall sharply from two for each typical firm (one for replacement and one for the initial 10% expansion in shoe production) to an average of 1.1 machines per year for replacement only.

	SHOES	MACHINES	MACHINE LIFE (yr)	D for MACHINES
Initial year	1000	10	10	1 per year
Second year	1100	11	10	2 this year
Third year	1100	11	10	1.1 this year

A 100% increase in the demand for shoe machines in 1 year is followed by a 45% decline the next year! Only if the demand for shoes were to increase continuously at the same *rate of increase* could the demand for shoe machines (investment expenditure) hold at the new level. *Help, Imelda Marcos!*

The accelerator illustrates the potential volatility of investment expenditure as an important component of AD, with swings of I explosively up, then collapsing down in quantity.

In practice there may be some underemployment of equipment and labor in the capital goods firms when a change in demand for their products occurs. Also, manufacturing plants often can produce beyond *rated* capacity, although at rising unit cost. Therefore, when managers of shoe machine firms estimate that the rate of change in demand is not permanent, a decision not to buy new machines can dampen the swings in I, and hence AD, that otherwise might occur. In addition, the volume of shoe-machine inventories may be large, or the *replacement demand* for plant and machinery may be large relative to the *accelerator-sponsored demand,* so there are many things which may reduce the potential instability of I. Although there may be moderating influences, the accelerator principle describes a potential, and occasionally actual, destabilizing influence on the economy.

ACCOUNTS PAYABLE   Amounts owed by a business to suppliers, normally due within 30 days of receipt of the goods and services. Generally, they are a current liability on a business balance sheet, payable within 1 year.

ACCOUNTS RECEIVABLE   Amounts owed to a business by its customers, usually due within 30 days. Generally, they are a current asset on a business balance sheet, convertible to cash within 1 year.

ADJUSTABLE-RATE MORTGAGE (ARM)   A note signed by a borrower, using real estate as collateral, which specifies the terms of repayment and a rate of interest that is adjusted periodically according to changes in a specified index. Some commonly used indexes are:

1. A cost-of-funds index. Most mortgages are negotiated by savings banks and savings-and-loan institutions, known as "thrifts." Some are negotiated by other financial institutions such as commercial banks and credit unions. The cost-of-funds index is compiled from interest rates that the thrifts pay to their sources of funds, e.g., the rates paid to depositors on deposits and the rates paid for borrowings, such as interest rates on advances from the district Federal Home Loan Bank.

2. A T-bill index. This index is compiled from interest rates established at regular auctions of United States Treasury bills.

3. The prime rate. A rate that banks set for borrowings of their most creditworthy large customers.

Adjustable-rate mortgages sometimes may result in "negative amortization." The interest rate adjusts each month but the size of the payment adjusts only every 6 or 12 months, so the proportion of each payment going to interest and the proportion going to principal may vary from month to month. At times, when the interest rate rises sharply, the amount of the interest may exceed the payment and there is an *addition* to the principal of the mortgage, rather than the usual reduction, until the size of the payment is adjusted. Thus, wide swings in interest rates can change a borrower's equity in the property.

ARMs may be set up to provide for negative amortization in the early years by starting at an interest rate that is below the market rate for ARMs. The difference between interest payments at that rate and interest payments that would occur at the market rate is then added to the principal each month.

The mortgage agreement may provide a "cap" limiting the amount that the interest rate may rise. ARMs that prevent negative amortization have higher interest rates and higher interest caps to offset the greater risk to the lender from fluctuations in market interest rates and the cost of loanable funds. See *Negative Amortization.*

ADMINISTERED PRICE   A price set by the seller with the expectation that demand for the product or service will adjust to the price. Administered pricing occurs where the seller has some market control, such as in monopoly, oligopoly, or monopolistic competition, so that prices do not change immediately in response to market forces. Control in a market can occur because of patents or copyrights, predatory practices, product differentiation through design or advertising, etc. An administered price contrasts with a market price, to which the seller adapts and which is set by the interaction of the impersonal forces of supply and demand, as in a market of pure competition. The seller is a price maker rather than a price taker when administered pricing is possible. See *Monopoly, Monopolistic Competition,* or *Oligopoly.* See also *Atomistic Competition* or *Pure Competition* for contrasting pricing.

AD VALOREM TAX   A tax that is a percentage of the value of a good, rather than an amount per unit, e.g., 1% of the value of an automobile rather than $100 per automobile. (The latter is a specific tax, a flat rate per unit.) An ad valorem customs duty is a customs tax that is a percentage of the value of the imported or exported good, e.g., 4% of the value of a foreign-made television set at the port of entry. Receipts from an ad valorem tax vary with price changes as well as with changes in quantity, while receipts from specific taxes only vary with changes in the quantity of the product. See *Specific Tax, Tariff.*

ADVANCE   1. A loan. In banking, for example, loans from district Federal Home Loan Banks to member thrifts commonly are referred to as advances.

2. A prepayment. An employee may receive an advance from an employer against future earnings, which may be considered a loan without interest because if the employee quits before the advance can be deducted from wages, the balance of the advance is owed to the employer.

A different sort of advance is one an author may receive against royalties from the future sales of books. An author seldom looks upon this as a "loan." If the book doesn't sell and generate enough royalties to pay for the advance, the author seldom is required to pay back the difference.

AGENCY FOR INTERNATIONAL DEVELOPMENT (AID)   A U.S. State Department agency which handles all of the foreign assistance programs of the U.S. except for military assistance, which is handled by the Department of Defense. AID makes loans and grants for economic development in less developed nations and insures such loans made from private sources. For other sources of development funds, see *Export–Import Bank, International Bank for Reconstruction and Development.*

AGENCY SHOP   A firm that requires nonunion employees to pay a fee to the union that represents the employees of that business.

This payment is to help support the union's collective bargaining. The fee usually is equal to that portion of union dues that supports the regular "business" activities of the union and excludes portions that support social or political activities. Its justification is based in the clause in the National Labor Relations Act of 1935 that requires a certified union to represent *all* employees in the designated bargaining unit, not just union members, in dealings with the employer. See *Closed Shop, Open Shop, Union Shop*.

AGGREGATE DEMAND (AD)　In national income analysis, the total demand for goods and services in the economy. Often it is categorized into Consumer Demand plus Investment Demand plus Government Demand plus Net Exports. Aggregate Demand determines the level of output and employment in the economy in the sense that production occurs in response to demand. In Keynesian analysis, aggregate demand determines aggregate supply under conditions of given prices and wages and some unemployment. Under such conditions, firms will produce all they can sell, increasing production if they can sell more and decreasing production if inventories begin to rise involuntarily (i.e., they can only sell less).

In the late 1970s a different view grew in popularity which reduced the emphasis on aggregate demand and increased the emphasis on supply as an active determiner of the level of economic activity. See *Supply-Side Economics*.

AGGREGATE SUPPLY (AS)　In national income analysis, the total output of goods and services produced in the economy during a specified period of time. See *Gross National Product*.

AMERICAN DEPOSITARY RECEIPTS (ADRs)　Receipts that represent claims on foreign companies' shares held in safekeeping by U.S. financial institutions or held in a foreign bank that is an agent of a U.S. bank. ADRs provide a way for American investors to invest in foreign stocks indirectly by buying an ADR that represents shares of a particular foreign company. Such investors avoid having to convert dollars into a foreign currency to purchase foreign stock and then convert back again to dollars upon receipt of dividends or sale of the shares. Buyers of ADRs avoid storing and transferring shares and do not incur the taxes and fees associated with dealings in overseas markets. Instead, their transactions are in dollars and they can trade in ADRs on U.S. markets.

ADRs provide an alternative to the purchase of shares in a mutual fund that invests in shares of foreign companies. ADRs are especially useful to institutional investors who are not permitted to buy and hold foreign securities but who nevertheless want to take advantage of opportunities that appear abroad.

AMERICAN FEDERATION OF LABOR (AF of L)   A federation of national unions formed in 1886 after the failure of the National Labor Union and the decline of the Knights of Labor. The AF of L survived where others failed because its convictions were consistent with the political and economic circumstances of the U.S. in the late nineteenth century and early twentieth centuries. Those convictions involved reliance on goals restricted to improvement of wages and working conditions, the use of economic pressure on employers, and organization of employees by trade or skill.

In particular, the AF of L tenets identified a basic conflict of interest between employees and employers over wages and working conditions. They aimed to control employment conditions by establishing collective bargaining agreements through use of economic pressure rather than by pursuit of general political reform or violent overthrow of the capitalist system. The AF of L shunned political affiliation; instead it pursued a political policy described by its long-time president, Samuel Gompers (1850–1924), as rewarding its friends and punishing its enemies. It tried to suppress dualism by recognizing the exclusive jurisdiction of each national union in organizing employees by trade or skill.

By the 1930s, many of these principles were not suitable to the changed political and economic circumstances. Mass-production industry had grown and spread. The National Labor Relations Act of 1935 opened the way to organization of the new masses of semi-skilled workers by establishing the right to organize by government-supervised secret ballot. It had been difficult to organize semiskilled and unskilled workers and win collective bargaining contracts because they were so easily replaced when they went out on strike.

The new opportunity led to the formation of the Committee for Industrial Organization, composed of unions within the AF of L which had already begun organizing along industrial union lines rather than by trade. Successful organization of unskilled and semi-skilled workers required basic changes in the AF of L beliefs and practices. When the majority of unions in the AF of L held to its position of organization by trade and by exclusive jurisdiction, the Committee split from the AF of L and became the rival Congress of Industrial Organizations (CIO) in 1937. See *Congress of Industrial Organizations, American Federation of Labor–Congress of Industrial Organizations*.

AMERICAN FEDERATION OF LABOR–CONGRESS OF INDUS-TRIAL ORGANIZATIONS (AFL–CIO)

A federation of most national unions in the United States. (Many national unions call themselves International because they have some Canadian locals affiliated.) It was formed by the merger of the AF of L with the CIO in 1955, eighteen years after the CIO had split away from the AF of L because of different organizing philosophies. The AF of L had been a federation predominantly made up of unions organized by craft, while the CIO had been a federation of unions based on plant-wide organization of industries. For example, the International Brotherhood of Electrical Workers, AF of L, tried to organize electricians wherever they worked. On the other hand, the International Union of Electrical Workers, CIO, tried to include in one union the whole gamut of workers from unskilled janitors to skilled machinists, as well as electricians, who worked in factories producing electrical appliances (e.g., General Electric or Maytag plants).

The purpose of the merged AFL–CIO is the same as that pursued by each of the two federations prior to merger: to promote unionism publicly and politically by such means as public relations activities, lobbying federal and state government, and assisting the new organization of groups of nonunion workers. It also attempts to mediate jurisdictional disputes among the member national unions, but has no power, other than expulsion, to impose a resolution. A few national unions were expelled from the federations in the 1950s on charges of communist domination, while the Teamsters union was expelled in 1957 on charges of corruption. A few, such as the United Automobile Workers, have withdrawn from time to time because of policy and leadership differences. The Teamsters rejoined the AFL–CIO in 1988. National unions retain their basic sovereignty, so their relation to the AFL–CIO may be likened to that of nation states within the United Nations. See *Congress of Industrial Organizations.*

AMORTIZATION The gradual reduction of a debt over time by making periodic payments of principal plus interest. Or the gradual reduction over time in the value of a bond for which a buyer paid a premium, so that at maturity the premium has been reduced to zero and the bond is valued at its maturity face value. See *Negative Amortization.*

ANTI-TRUST The legal effort to prevent a variety of business practices and arrangements which reduce competition, such as price-fixing conspiracies, price cutting to destroy competitors, trusts to hold stock of competing firms in order to develop common policies, mergers which would substantially reduce competition, and cartels that are formed to fix prices, allot markets, and control production. Unlawful practices are defined in such antitrust legislation as The Sherman Antitrust Act (1890), The Clayton Antitrust Act (1914), and The Celler–Kefauver Antimerger Act (1950). Many business practices are regulated by such agencies as the Interstate Commerce Commission, the Federal Trade Commission, and the Federal Communications Commission.

Despite the legislation and the creation of regulatory agencies, mergers have continued to occur and rose to a flood in the 1980s comparable to the large number a century earlier. Many of the more recent mergers have skirted antitrust law by joining together firms in different industries. Often the goal has been financial gain because of undervalued capital stock rather than gain from market control or diversity. Also, mergers occur when application of the law changes and when competitive conditions change from time to time, as, for example, when tariffs change or when many national markets become worldwide as foreign producers grow more efficient and create foreign competition in domestic markets. See *Cartel, Conglomerate Merger, Leveraged Buyout, Merger.*

ANNUITY An agreement for the periodic payout of a sum of money over time. The sum to be distributed may be created by an accumulation over time or by a sum paid in a lump. The amount of each annuity payment usually is based on the life expectancy of the recipient as determined by standard actuarial tables and consists of a portion of both the principal and the interest accumulations. A fixed-rate annuity specifies the rate of return to be received over time. A variable annuity may be invested in a mutual fund and the rate of return varies with the performance of the fund. See *Reverse Annuity Mortgage.*

APPORTIONED TAX A tax collected by one governmental entity whose proceeds are shared with other governmental units. Part of a gasoline tax collected by a state may be distributed to county and city governments for local road and street construction. Or, a part of the property taxes collected by a county may be distributed to the state and to cities, school districts, park districts, and television translators, as well as to county services.

An apportioned tax tends to be levied at the level of government which has the greatest ease of collection and flexibility for increases. In the 1970s and early 1980s, public pressure made it difficult for states, and especially local governments, to increase the taxes over which they had control. There were statewide initiatives for ceilings on property taxes and single-issue voting in states and localities against officials who stood for tax increases. The federal government seemed more insulated from single-issue election voting. It collected income taxes to distribute as federal revenue sharing funds to states, which in turn distributed a portion of the funds to cities and counties. These funds could be used for any purpose.

However, the federal government continued to experience large and growing deficits, and the tax revolt was picked up as a major federal issue by Ronald Reagan in his presidential campaign in 1980. The massive federal expansion of the apportioned tax concept was doomed by the Reagan philosophy of lessening the role of government and by the inability to control federal deficits. The collection of federal revenue sharing funds for general purposes was phased out, creating budgetary problems for states, counties, and cities. Instead of revenue sharing, the local levels of government could now ''share the heat'' of a no-win choice: to legislate taxes in order to support public programs or alternatively to reduce the programs. The dilemma for local governments has been moderated only slightly by some growth in revenues resulting from economic growth. See *Revenue Sharing*.

ARBITRAGE   The act of simultaneously buying in one market and selling in another to make a profit on the difference in prices between the two markets. If prices are quoted as delivered, the price difference between markets would have to exceed transportation costs. Arbitrage serves the economic function of keeping prices in different markets in line with one another.

ARBITRATION   A method of handling a disagreement between parties without recourse to a court of law. An outside neutral person hears the matters in dispute and renders a decision. *Binding* arbitration means that the decision is legally binding. Procedures and rules of evidence are more informal and less rigorous in arbitration proceedings than in a court of law, all of which helps to speed up resolution of disputes and reduce costs. Some disputing parties prefer a *board* of arbitrators which might consist of a representative of each of the parties and a neutral third person.

Arbitration frequently is incorporated in collective bargaining agreements between labor unions and management to interpret the agreements and handle grievances under them. Infrequently, arbitration is used to settle labor–management disputes over terms for a new contract.

Occasionally, a commercial contract will call for arbitration of disputes under it in order to provide a less costly, speedier resolution than through suit in a court of law. See *Compulsory Arbitration*.

ARC ELASTICITY The concept of measuring price elasticity of demand or price elasticity of supply when the initiating change in price is a discrete amount. For example, the formula for price elasticity of demand is

$$E_d = \frac{\% \text{ increase in } Q}{\% \text{ cut in } P}$$

where Q is quantity and P is price. The formula is simple to use when price and quantity changes are very small variations about a point on a demand curve (point elasticity). But when the change in price and quantity involves a discrete movement along the demand curve (an arc segment), the elasticity coefficient E_d will be different depending upon whether one divides the increase in Q by the initial Q or the final Q to calculate the percentage change. It is customary to use the average, i.e., $(Q_1 + Q_2)/2$, in order to resolve this quandary. For the same reason, averaging would be used to figure the percentage change in P. The arc elasticity formula, then, is as follows:

$$E = \frac{\dfrac{Q_1 - Q_2}{Q_1 + Q_2}}{\dfrac{P_1 - P_2}{P_1 + P_2}} = \frac{\dfrac{Q_1 - Q_2}{Q_1 + Q_2}}{\dfrac{P_1 - P_2}{P_1 + P_2}}$$

$$= \frac{(Q_1 - Q_2)(P_1 + P_2)}{(Q_1 + Q_2)(P_1 - P_2)}$$

The arc elasticity coefficient here is negative because price and quantity move in opposite directions, but when considering price elasticity of demand economists usually ignore the sign. See *Elasticity of Demand*.

ARM LOANS See *Adjustable-Rate Mortgage*.

ASSEMBLY LINE PRODUCTION A system of production in which the process is broken down into simple steps performed by each worker, such as tightening a bolt or spot-welding a joint. Materials that are to be assembled or processed move on a conveyer from work station to work station as the product is gradually put together from standardized parts.

Assembly-line production originated in the automobile industry, with Henry Ford given credit for its development. In time the system was extended beyond assembly to manufacturing processes. The technique became widespread as scientific management applied time and motion study to minimize effort and increase man-hour output. It is a logical extension of Adam Smith's division of labor concept.

Charlie Chaplin, in his famous 1930s movie, *Modern Times,* caricatured the severe problems created for people doing simple repetitive work on an assembly line. But as processing steps have been reduced to simpler and simpler elements, mechanization of them has become possible. Some of the problems of repetitive work have been mitigated by the growing use of robots to perform tasks more accurately than is possible by humans. Some completely automated plants have appeared.

ASSESSED VALUE   The value placed on a piece of property by a governmental unit, usually a county, for the calculation of property taxes. Assessed value may be based upon 100% of fair market value or some fraction of it, such as 80 or 50%, depending upon the property tax law.

A taxing authority usually develops an expenditure budget and then determines what tax rate will produce that amount of money. If property is taxed at 100% of fair market value, the tax *rate* applied to raise the given sum will be lower than if the assessed value is 50%. One cannot establish whether property taxes in a locality are high or low relative to other communities without studying both assessed valuation levels and tax rates. Appeals of assessed valuation by property owners may question the accuracy of the fair market value level selected by the county assessor, or, more often, the comparability of the appellant's property to those selected for the fair market value standard. See *Fair Market Value.*

ASSETS   Valuable possessions. In economics, assets are things of value owned by persons or firms, such as cash, bank deposits, goods on hand or inventory, accounts receivable, equipment, land, and buildings. Some assets are intangible but nevertheless real, such as the good will of customers or clients built up over the years. In accounting, assets are the entries on the left-hand side of a balance sheet. The term also may be used to include human capital, such as education or the legs of Mary Hart (longtime emcee on the TV program *Entertainment Tonight*), which are insured for $2,000,000.

ATOMISTIC COMPETITION A market form in which market price is determined impersonally by the interaction of a large number of sellers and a large number of buyers, no one of whom constitutes a large enough fraction of the total market to affect price. The wheat market is an example. Buyers and sellers decide to buy and sell in reaction to market price rather than individually setting a price to which those on the other side of the market react. See *Pure Competition*. For a contrasting price-setting situation, see *Administered Price*.

AUTARKY (AUTARCHY) An economic system that is totally self-sufficient, producing all that is consumed and importing nothing from outside. Some countries' leaders have attempted to achieve autarky in order to eliminate any reliance on foreign materials and better defend the society in time of war. Others have pursued autarky together with social isolation to maintain the mores and genetic purity of the native population or to maintain the leaders' control. Such efforts are virtually impossible in today's world of high-tech production and minding one's neighbors' business.

AUTOMATIC STABILIZERS Built-in features that automatically counteract boom and recession, as opposed to ad hoc intervention by governmental action at specific times to try to correct such problems as unemployment or too high or too low a level of aggregate demand. Some examples of automatic stabilizers are (1) The structure of income tax rates. It removes more income from households and businesses during economic expansion, lessening inflation by restricting their spending. It takes less in income tax receipts in recession, cushioning the effect on expenditure from the fall in incomes. (2) Unemployment insurance payments and welfare payments. They rise as national income and employment fall, replacing some of the disposable wage income lost, and they decline as national income and employment rise. (3) Corporation dividend policy. Many firms try to maintain former dividend levels in recessions and in boom times tend to retain a higher percentage of earnings for expansion of plant and equipment. All of these policies help to support household income in recession and slow the growth in disposable income during booms.

AUTOMATIC TRANSFER SERVICE ACCOUNTS (ATS ACCOUNTS) Deposit accounts which provide for automatic transfer of funds between a checking account and an account that bears a higher interest rate whenever the checking account reaches a threshold amount. The service helps depositors to maintain higher interest income than they would receive if they had to maintain larger no-interest or low-interest checking account balances.

Some ATS accounts involve zero-balance accounts which transfer funds into a no-interest checking account from an interest-bearing savings or money market account to precisely offset with-drawals as checks are presented to the bank for payment. The balance in the checking account at the end of each day is zero.

Another type of ATS account will automatically transfer funds from an interest-bearing checking account to a money market ac-count with a higher interest rate whenever the checking account exceeds a designated level (say $2500) and will transfer funds back whenever the checking account falls below that amount.

AUTONOMOUS INVESTMENT In national income analysis, that portion of investment demand that is independent of the level of aggregate demand (gross national product or net national product). It is the opposite of *induced investment,* which is a function of aggregate demand. The sources of autonomous investment are in-vention of new machines, development of new processes and prod-ucts, and other innovative acts. It has been considered a volatile portion of GNP and a prime cause of economic fluctuations. Many economists now believe that consumption demand in economically advanced countries also may be rather volatile and a potential cause of economic instability now that consumer durables and luxury expenditures are a large percentage of consumer demand. See *En-trepreneurship, Innovation, Investment Demand, Gross Invest-ment, Net Investment, Induced Investment.*

AUTONOMOUS VARIABLE A variable whose changes are depen-dent upon forces that are outside of the system in which interrela-tions are being studied. The system is studied by observing, or assuming, a change in an independent variable, and then following the effects of this change, observing or reasoning through the rela-tionships among variables in order to find the resulting effects on dependent variables. The difference between an autonomous vari-able and a dependent variable may be illustrated by the question: What will be the effect of a drought in the U.S.S.R. (autonomous variable) on the price of wheat in the U.S.A. (dependent variable)? See *Dependent Variable.*

AVERAGE COST (AC) Total cost divided by the number of units of output. $AC = TC/Q$. The same as unit cost or average total cost.

It also may be calculated by adding average fixed cost to average variable cost. See *Total Cost*.

AVERAGE COST CURVE A curve illustrating the relation between output and average cost over a range of output. It is U-shaped in the short run because some costs are fixed regardless of the volume of output. Consequently, average fixed cost (a component of average cost) will be high when total fixed cost is divided by a small quantity of output and will fall as that total fixed cost is divided by a larger and larger output. This will cause average total cost to decline also. At the same time average variable cost will be high at low outputs because the low ratio of variable factors of production to fixed factors is not very productive. Average variable cost will fall as output expands from these low levels because each additional unit of the variable factor will increase output by more than the previous variable factor unit. This will reinforce the decline in average total cost caused by falling average fixed cost.

As output continues to expand, the Law of Diminishing Returns tells us that eventually more variable inputs will be necessary to produce each additional unit of output. Average variable cost will rise, overcoming the now slower decline in average fixed cost, and so average total cost rises.

The long-run average cost curve also is U shaped. See *Long-Run Average Cost Curve, Envelope Curve*.

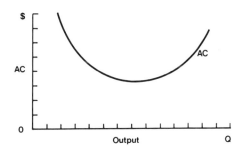

AVERAGE COST CURVE

AVERAGE FIXED COST (AFC) Total fixed cost divided by the number of units of output. $AFC = TFC/Q$. Total fixed cost does not change with changes in output and exists even if output is zero, so dividing it by an ever large quantity of output produces a continuously declining average fixed cost. When AFC is added to average variable cost (AVC) the result is average total cost (ATC). $AFC + AVC = ATC$. See *Total Fixed Cost*.

AVERAGE FIXED COST CURVE A curve depicting the relation between output and fixed cost over a range of output. Because average fixed cost equals fixed cost (a constant) divided by output, as output grows average fixed cost will fall at a declining rate.

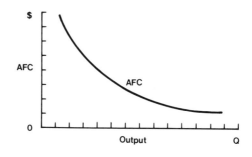

AVERAGE FIXED COST CURVE

AVERAGE PROPENSITY TO CONSUME (APC) In national income analysis, the average propensity to consume (APC) is that fraction of disposable personal income (DPY) spent for consumption (C). $APC = C/DPY$. DPY is either spent for consumption or saved, so $APC + APS = 1$, where APS is the average propensity to save. APC may be used in analysis of either a household or an entire economy.

AVERAGE PROPENSITY TO SAVE (APS) In national income analysis, the average propensity to save (APS) is saving (S) divided by disposable personal income (DPY), or that fraction of income that is saved (not spent for consumption). $APS = S/DPY$. DPY is either spent for consumption or saved, so $APS + APC = 1$, where APC is the average propensity to consume. APS may be used in analysis of either a household or an economy.

AVERAGE REVENUE (AR) Total revenue from the sale of a good divided by the number of units sold. $AR = TR/Q$. AR is equal to price per unit if each unit of the good is sold at the same price. Since $TR = P \times Q$ and $AR = (P \times Q)/Q$, then $AR = P$.

AVERAGE REVENUE PRODUCT (ARP) Average revenue attributable to a variable factor of production. It is equal to total revenue divided by the quantity of the variable factor. $ARP = TR/Q_f$.

AVERAGE TOTAL COST (ATC) See *Average Cost.*

AVERAGE VARIABLE COST (AVC)   Total variable cost divided by the number of units of output. $AVC = TVC/Q$. In the short run, average variable cost equals average total cost minus average fixed cost. In the long run there are no fixed costs, so average variable cost and average total cost are the same. See *Total Variable Cost.*

AVERAGE VARIABLE COST CURVE. A curve representing changes in average variable cost as output changes. The curve will be U shaped. In the short run, at low levels of output there will be too few units of variable factors of production relative to the quantity of fixed factors. The production process will involve an inefficient ratio of variable to fixed factors of production, and output per unit of variable factor will be low; cost per unit of output will be high. As output expands, the relation between fixed and variable factors will become more productive and average variable costs will fall. As production expands further, the Law of Diminishing Returns will come into play and average variable costs will start to rise.

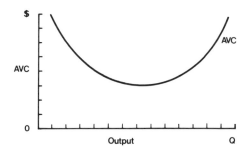

AVERAGE VARIABLE COST CURVE

The long-run average variable cost curve also is U shaped, but it may be flat bottomed for much of the relevant range so that there is not *one* size of plant or level of output at minimum cost, but a range of plants and outputs. In the long run there are no fixed costs, so average variable cost equals average total cost. See *Long-Run Average Cost Curve.*

BALANCE OF PAYMENTS A statement of the money value of all economic transactions between one country and the rest of the world during a period of time. Transactions include purchase and sale of goods and services, gifts, interest payments, and the acquisition or sale of long-term and short-term assets (capital transfers). See *Balance of Trade, Balance on Current Account.*

BALANCE-OF-PAYMENTS DEFICIT An excess of payments over receipts by one country in transactions with the rest of the world for goods, services, gifts, transfers, and *autonomous* capital flows. The deficit is offset and a balance of payments is created by the deficit nation paying out from its stock of foreign currencies and gold, by borrowing largely short-term funds (an accommodating rather than an autonomous capital flow), and/or currency devaluation.

Some economists argue that the term is an oxymoron because "balance of payments" includes *all* transactions between one country and the rest of the world. They draw an analogy with a firm's balance sheet and its "accommodating" entry of net worth, which adjusts to equal the difference between assets and liabilities and keeps the balance sheet in balance. If liabilities exceed assets, a negative net worth entry (net debt) maintains the balance sheet balance (but not the equanimity of stockholders or creditors). In international economics, these economists hold, a country's balance of payments likewise is always in balance because of accommodating private debt accruals, government transfers of foreign currency stocks or gold, government borrowing from agencies such as the International Monetary Fund, devaluation of currency under a fixed exchange rate system, or depreciation of currency in foreign exchange markets under a system of flexible exchange rates.

If we use the concept of a deficit in the balance of payments, the U.S. ran a large deficit through the decade of the 1980s with foreigners holding an ever-growing amount of dollar assets. They were willing to do so because of relatively high interest rates and moderate inflation rates in the U.S., together with the relative safety of the dollar stemming from political stability. Continuous deficits, such as those for the U.S., eventually will lead to satiation of the foreign market for the deficit country's currency. In an era of floating exchange rates (since the international gold standard was abandoned in 1973), depreciation of the currency of the deficit country will occur in foreign-exchange markets as more of the currency is thrown on the market than people want to buy.

The cheaper currency (more dollars per yen, per mark, etc.) will set in motion forces that will tend to reduce the deficit. For example, there will be more purchases of goods and services and more capital investments in the deficit country by countries with a surplus because relative prices are lower in the deficit country. The size of the effect depends upon the price elasticity of demand for the relevant goods and services. An increase in foreign demand indeed happened in the U.S. in 1988–89 following depreciation of the dollar in foreign exchange markets.

The depreciation in the rate of exchange also tends to discourage imports into the deficit country because it requires more of the depreciated currency to buy things abroad. However, higher dollar prices for foreign goods did not seem to inhibit spending by the prosperous and consumption-happy U.S. citizens in the late 1980s, again a matter of the particular price elasticity of demand for many of the goods at that time. See *Balance-of-Payments Surplus, Balance of Trade, Balance on Current Account, Balance on Capital Account, Devaluation.*

BALANCE-OF-PAYMENTS SURPLUS An excess of receipts over payments by one country in transactions with the rest of the world for goods, services, gifts, transfers, and long term assets. The opposite of balance of payments deficit. The surplus will show as a shift of gold stock into the country, a build up of foreign currency and foreign bank account holdings, and/or increases in the holding of short-term debt instruments in debtor countries.

Some economists argue that the term is an oxymoron because "balance of payments" includes *all* transactions between one country and the rest of the world. They draw on the analogy of a firm's balance sheet, in which net worth provides an "accommodating" entry to balance the difference between assets and liabilities. They hold that a country's balance of payments also is always in balance because of accommodating private debt accruals, government transfers of foreign currency stocks or gold, borrowing from agencies such as the International Monetary Fund by the governments with deficits, or a change in the exchange value of currency which can occur quickly under a system of flexible exchange rates.

For some years after World War II the United States had a balance-of-payments surplus even though the *balance-of-trade surplus* was partially offset by large gifts (such as the Marshall Plan) and by substantial long-term investment in other countries. See *Balance-of-Payments Deficit, Balance of Trade, Balance on Capital Account, Balance on Current Account.*

BALANCE OF TRADE 1. The balance of a country's merchandise trade, i.e., merchandise exports and imports. 2. The balance of merchandise trade plus service transactions. Those who limit their definition to merchandise trade would add services plus unilateral transfers to define *current account.* A *favorable balance of trade* refers to an excess of exports over imports, leading in earlier, simpler times to an inflow of gold. An *unfavorable balance of trade* refers to an excess of imports over exports, and an outflow of gold. In modern times, surpluses and deficits in trade are counterbalanced by many different transactions such as gifts, changes in bank deposit balances, transfer of long- and short-term capital assets, and/or exchange rate fluctuations, as well as by the transfer of gold. See *Balance of Payments, Balance on Current Account, Favorable Balance of Trade, Net Exports.*

BALANCE ON CAPITAL ACCOUNT A balance in a country's international transactions between the inflow and the outflow of short-term and long-term capital. Such a balance is rare. The capital account flows added to the current account flows make up the balance of payments in international transactions. If autonomous transactions do not balance, then government transfers, growing foreign-held bank accounts, and/or exchange rate changes will create a balance of payments. See *Balance of Payments, Balance of Trade, Balance on Current Account.*

BALANCE ON CURRENT ACCOUNT Sometimes improperly equated to the balance of trade. The balance on current account refers to the purchase and sale of goods and services by residents of a country in their trade with all other countries, i.e., merchandise trade plus service transactions such as transportation, travel, interest and dividends, banking and insurance services, and government expenditures for embassies, etc., plus unilateral transfers consisting of private remittances and government grants. The balance on current account may exceed the balance of trade by unilateral transfers, or by service transactions plus unilateral transfers, depending upon the definition of balance of trade that is used.

A deficit on current account must be offset by long-term capital flows and autonomous short-term capital flows, or else government fund transfers and/or currency devaluation must occur because of unwanted accommodating foreign-held bank balances. Suppose that, for the U.S., purchases and unilateral transfers out exceed sales and unilateral transfers in. A deficit then arises on the current account. There must be a surplus on the capital account to balance that deficit and achieve a balance of payments. If not, devaluation of the dollar will occur in international currency exchanges, or the Treasury must intervene by selling from its stock of foreign currency, by borrowing from agencies such as the International Monetary Fund, or by transferring gold.

For many years, the U.S. was able to maintain a deficit on current account because foreigners were willing to hold growing amounts of dollar assets in response to a combination of factors such as high interest rates in the U.S., a relatively sound dollar in terms of inflation and political stability in the U.S., and the fact that the dollar has long served as an international medium of exchange. (The Organization of Petroleum Exporting Countries, OPEC, for example, quotes oil prices and carries on transactions in dollars.) But by the mid–1980s autonomous inflows of capital did not keep up with the continuing and growing deficit on current account. Devaluation of the dollar began, which made U.S. exports cheaper in other countries, U.S. imports more expensive, and, given price elasticities of demand, started to reduce the size of the deficit on current account. It also attracted an autonomous inflow of capital as foreigners bought assets in the U.S. with cheap dollars (more dollars per yen, mark, pound, etc.).

A depreciating currency in foreign exchange markets, no matter how appropriate, creates a national embarrassment, especially for a superpower. It raises prices of imports and thus contributes to inflationary pressures. Foreigners now own more property in the U.S. and control more U.S. corporations, for example, than before the devaluation of the dollar in the late 1980s. It is easy to see why a deficit on current account can eventually trigger great concern! See *Current Account, Balance of Payments, Balance of Trade, Balance on Capital Account.*

BALANCE SHEET   A statement of the financial position of a business at a moment in time. Assets are listed on the left side, and liabilities and net worth (or equity) are listed on the right. The two sides are always in balance because net worth (ownership value) is a residual after liabilities are subtracted from assets. When liabilities exceed assets, net worth is negative and the business may be ready for the bankruptcy courts if the condition persists.

BALLOON PAYMENT   A large last payment of the balance owed on a loan whose regular monthly payments were fixed at a lower amount that does not fully amortize the loan. A person's current financial position may not permit as high monthly payments as a fully amortized loan would require. A balloon-payment loan permits lower monthly payments over the life of the loan, with the opportunity to meet the large "balloon" amount owed at the end by refinancing or perhaps by payment from some anticipated change in financial circumstances such as a higher salary or an inheritance. It is used most frequently in real estate contracts and occasionally in loans for other durable goods such as automobiles.

BANK   An ambiguous term applied to a wide variety of financial institutions. Most commonly it has meant an institution which accepts demand deposits and makes commercial loans, that is, a commercial bank. Savings banks historically have had the modifier "savings" always associated with the term "bank." Now, they and savings and loan associations (long known as "thrifts") are often referred to as "banks" because the general populace has used them for transaction accounts since 1980.

The Depository Institutions Deregulation and Monetary Control Act of 1980 permitted thrifts to offer checking accounts and, to a limited extent, commercial and personal loans. Since 1980, some people also may use a credit union as their bank by using a share-draft account as a checking account for their transactions. However, credit unions tend to focus on home improvement loans and personal loans for consumer durables—generally a narrower range of loan categories than used by other transaction account institutions such as commercial banks, savings banks, and savings and loan associations. In 1989, following several years of a high failure rate for savings and loans, legislation tightened limits on the proportion of loans other than home mortgages that S and L's could make.

Banks may operate under either state or federal charter. If state chartered, the bank may become a member of an appropriate federal system such as the Federal Reserve System or the Federal Home Loan Bank System and operate under federal regulation. If not the bank operates under supervision of the state in which it is incorporated although, since 1980, reserve requirements and reserve holdings for *all* banks are controlled by the Federal Reserve System.

Commercial bankers continue to prefer to restrict the term "bank" to institutions which focus on demand-deposit accounts and commercial loans, referring to the others as thrifts, or thrift institutions.

Official government usage often does not require the deposit concept or the loan concept. Investment banks make use of neither, but rather buy large blocks of stocks and bonds for resale in smaller quantities. The Export–Import Bank or the International Bank for Reconstruction and Development make international loans based upon capital subscriptions or the sale of their securities but do not accept deposits. See *Commercial Bank, Savings and Loan Association, Savings Bank.*

BANK CHECKING ACCOUNTS See *Checking Account, Demand Deposits, Negotiable Order of Withdrawal, Share-Draft Account, Transaction Accounts.*

BANK CLEARINGS The dollar amount of claims of one bank against others or all banks against each other that arise from transaction accounts such as demand deposits, NOW accounts, and share-draft accounts. When a check drawn on one bank is deposited by the recipient in another, it "clears" through a clearing house to be presented to the originating bank for payment. The volume of bank clearings may be used as one of several categories of transactions to measure the health of an economy. See *Clearing House, Clearing-House Function.*

BANK CREDIT A bank loan extended to a borrower by creating (or adding to) a checking account against which the borrower may draw, in return for the borrower's note promising to repay the loan with interest. Ninety percent or more of the dollar value of transactions in the U.S. are carried on by payments from transaction accounts which are partly backed by notes receivable rather than backed 100% by currency or official reserves. Thus bank credit has become our principal form of money. About three-fourths of the U.S. money supply (M1) is in the form of transaction accounts, while coins and currency make up about one-fourth. See *Money, M1, M2, M3*.

BANK DEPOSITS   Amounts of money held in banks by depositors who put cash or checks from others into their accounts or who borrowed from their banks with credit entries made into the borrowers' deposit accounts. The deposits are debts of the banks owed to the depositors as creditors. Principal types of deposits are demand-deposit checking accounts, money market checking accounts, negotiable orders of withdrawal (NOW accounts), savings deposits, time deposits or certificates of deposit, and share draft accounts (in credit unions).

BANKER'S ACCEPTANCE   A negotiable instrument drawn by the seller on the buyer's bank to finance the export, import, shipment, or storage of goods. When the bank marks "accepted" on the order to pay, it agrees to pay the draft at maturity, at which time the buyer pays his bank the amount of the draft plus a fee for the bank's guarantee. There is an active international market in banker's acceptances, which allows the seller of goods to receive payment immediately by selling the banker's acceptance.

BANK INSURANCE FUND (BIF)   The federal fund that insures depositors in commercial banks for up to $100,000 of their deposits. Details of the insurance coverage are provided under the *Federal Deposit Insurance Corporation* entry. All federally chartered commercial banks must participate in the BIF, and state-chartered commercial banks may participate. The fund was created in 1989 by the transfer of funds and responsibilities from the Federal Deposit Insurance Corporation (FDIC) fund. The FDIC controls this fund and also the Savings Association Insurance Fund (SAIF) created for savings institutions. (The SAIF funds were transferred from the Federal Savings and Loan Insurance Corporation which then was disbanded.)

The Bank Insurance Fund is built up by premiums from member banks based upon their covered deposit liabilities. The fund is used to pay depositors when the sale of assets of a failed bank does not cover all of the insured deposit liabilities of the bank.

Some states permit state-chartered banks, thrifts, and credit unions to insure their deposits with private insurance companies. The number of such insured institutions usually is too small to spread the risks properly, so that one or a few bank failures will cause the insurance company to fail, leaving depositors uncovered. See *Deposit Insurance* for examples of the problem in Maryland,

Ohio, and Rhode Island. See also *Savings Association Insurance Fund.* See also *Federal Deposit Insurance Corporation* for a description of the insurance coverage.

BANK NOTE A printed piece of paper, issued by banks in various monetary denominations, which is declared "legal tender for all debts public and private," or, historically, when issued by private banks was exchangeable for legal tender upon presentation to the issuing bank. In the U.S., bank notes circulated as paper substitutes for legal tender specie (gold, silver, and copper coins minted by the U.S. Treasury) for carrying on transactions. Many bank notes were issued by state banks during the 19th century until they were taxed out of existence by the National Banking Act of 1863. That Act sought to establish a more uniform currency by permitting paper money to be issued only by the U.S. Treasury (U.S. notes or "greenbacks") or by National Banks when the notes were backed by specified U.S. bonds that were owned and held by the National Banks. All of these bonds were retired in 1935 and no National Bank notes have been issued since then. Bank notes now are issued only by the U.S. Treasury and the Federal Reserve Banking System and are legal tender rather than promises to pay some other specified thing of value. See *Currency, Fiat Money.*

BANK RESERVES All banks are required by law to keep reserves against the funds that are deposited with them. Required reserves for depository institutions must be held in deposits with district Federal Reserve Banks or in vault cash (the latter constituting a minute fraction of the total). Nonmembers of the Fed may maintain reserve balances directly with a Federal Reserve Bank or indirectly as deposits with certain approved institutions which in turn hold deposits with the Fed.

Prior to the passage of the Depository Institutions Deregulation and Monetary Control Act of 1980 (DIDMCA), the amount of required reserves for state-chartered banks was set by state law and supervised by monetary authorities in each state. Bank reserve ranges for nationally chartered banks and savings associations were set by federal law, and particular requirements within a range were set by the Federal Reserve Board of Governors for member commercial and savings banks, by the Federal Home Loan Bank Board for member savings and loan associations and savings banks, and by the National Credit Union Administration Board for member credit unions.

The DIDMCA centralized control of specific reserve requirements for *all* state and national depository institutions that are federally insured or *eligible* for federal insurance. The Act provided for a phase-in period for the achievement of uniform reserve requirements for depository institutions that are not members of the Fed for kinds of accounts that existed prior to 1980.

In pursuit of monetary policy, the Fed has the power to raise and lower reserve requirements for depository institutions within congressionally established limits. The Fed also can change the reserves of banks by buying or selling U.S. government bonds on the open market. The DIDMCA is described in the *Federal Reserve Bulletin* for June 1980. See *Excess Bank Reserves, Federal Open-Market Committee, Fractional Reserve Banking System, Monetary Policy, Required Reserves.*

BANKRUPTCY   A legal protection of a debtor from action by creditors to provide for (1) an orderly liquidation of assets for distribution to creditors by a court of law through a court-appointed trustee under Chapter 7, or (2) a reorganization under Chapter 11. Creditors cannot sue for payment, nor for a lien on assets. Only those creditors at the time of the bankruptcy filing have standing. In the case of liquidation of assets of a person rather than a corporation, the law prescribes a minimum of assets which may be retained by the debtor.

Chapter 11 bankruptcy is designed for reorganization of a business firm under supervision of a court of law. A trustee supervises the reorganization, which is an effort to make a debt-ridden company financially viable. Some companies filed for bankruptcy in the 1980s under this chapter in order to forestall further claims for damages by users of the company's product. Some others filed for Chapter 11 bankruptcy in part because the rules for reorganization permit abrogation of collective bargaining contracts with labor unions.

BANK TRANSACTION ACCOUNTS   See *Transaction Accounts.*

BARGAINING UNIT   A group of workers designated by the National Labor Relations Board as the unit which an employer must recognize and with which the employer must bargain if the group votes for unionization. The designation must occur before the NLRB conducts a secret ballot to determine whether a union will represent the group of workers and, if so, which union.

Which workers to include in a bargaining unit may affect the outcome of an organizational election and, if a union is selected, the bargaining power of the union or the employer. For example, a group of semiskilled workers may feel that their bargaining power is enhanced if the bargaining unit is an industrial union that is plant-wide, including such skilled workers as electricians and tool-and-die makers who are hard to replace. The skilled workers may feel that they can win more if represented by their own separate craft unions. An employer may want some workers included in or excluded from the bargaining unit according to how that might affect the vote for a union or for no union.

Prior to the National Labor Relations Act of 1935 (the Wagner Act) the bargaining unit was determined by the power of a union to sign up workers and to force an employer to recognize it and bargain. If more than one union claimed a group of workers as being in its jurisdiction, the outcome was dependent upon relative union power because the A F of L did not have the ability to enforce its concept of exclusive jurisdiction. Union power is related to its power to interrupt production. The employer often was caught in the middle, not being able to recognize either union without damage to the company from actions by the other union. See *Jurisdictional Dispute, Union*.

BARTER   Exchanging goods directly for other goods or services rather than using the intermediation of money. Under a barter system of exchange a person who wants to acquire some goods may not have for exchange what another person wants in return for his or her goods. Many exchanges may have to occur before a person both disposes of what is available to exchange and acquires what is wanted. Money, however, is a widely accepted common denominator to which the value of everything else is related. It facilitates exchange by eliminating the multiple trading that otherwise may be necessary for a "seller" to receive what he or she wants in return. See *Money*.

BASING-POINT SYSTEM   A pricing system in which the sellers set prices to include transportation charges from a designated "basing-point" location, whether or not the goods are shipped from that place or from some nearer or more distant point. It has been used by some firms to eliminate transportation cost differentials with competitors. Also, it has been used by some industries in the allocation of markets among members of the system.

BASIS POINTS   A measure of interest rate changes in hundredths of one percentage point. 100 basis points = 1%. A financial report, for example, might state that "interest rates on 3-month Treasury bills rose today by 5 basis points, from 7.00 to 7.05%."

BEAR A person who expects stock prices to fall and sells stock that he or she doesn't have for delivery at a future date. When the future date arrives the bear expects to buy in at a lower price to deliver the stock that had been sold under the futures contract at a higher price.

The designation *bear* for such a person appears early in the eighteenth century, first as *bearskin jobber,* which "makes it probable that the original phrase was 'sell the bearskin', and that it originated in the well-known proverb, 'to sell the bear's skin before one has caught the bear.' The associated *bull* appears somewhat later and was perhaps suggested by *bear*" ("The Oxford English Dictionary" (1989). 2nd Ed., Vol. II, p. 19. Clarendon Press, Oxford).

BEAR MARKET A market in which prices are falling or are expected to fall. It is a designation commonly used in securities markets and commodity markets. The opposite of *Bull Market.*

BENEFIT PRINCIPLE OF TAXATION A taxing principle which states that a particular tax should be borne according to the benefits received from the government expenditure of the tax income. For example, to tax people for highways, a gasoline tax collects revenue from users of highways roughly according to the amount of use (benefit). To fit the tax even closer to the amount of benefit, off-road users of gasoline such as farmers receive a refund of the tax that was collected in the pump price. To fund highways with an income tax would depart from the benefit principle and adopt an *Ability-to-pay* principle.

BILATERAL DUOPOLY A market in which two sellers face two buyers and there is a consequent four-way interdependence. See *Duopoly, Duopsony.*

BILATERAL MONOPOLY A market in which a monopolist faces a monopsonist. One seller faces one buyer. See *Monopoly, Monopsony.*

BILL A debt of the issuer which matures in 1 year or less from the date of issue. See *Treasury Bills.*

BILLS PAYABLE. A term used in accounting to identify the value of promissory notes, commercial paper payable, and charges owed to others that are due in 1 year or less. On a balance sheet it is a current liability. Sometimes called *Notes payable,* although "notes" sometimes refers to obligations which mature in 1 to 10 years from date of issue.

BILLS RECEIVABLE. A term used in accounting to identify the value of promissory notes which mature in 1 year or less that are owed to the firm by others and commercial paper received from others. On a balance sheet it is a current asset. Sometimes called *Notes receivable,* although "notes" sometimes refers to obligations which mature in 1 to 10 years from date of issue.

BIMETALLISM A monetary system using two metals, usually gold and silver, rather than just one as a nation's money. Historically, bimetallism was supported by those who felt that the use of just one metal would unduly restrict the supply of money and depress the general price level, at a time when it was considered that money of intrinsic value was the only "good" money. (In that view it is permissible, for convenience, to print paper money so long as it is backed 100% by precious metal.)

An official exchange rate must be established between the two metals, represented by the weight of each metal in coins of the same denomination. When the U.S. was on a bimetallic standard for a time in the nineteenth century, complications arose when the market price ratio for the two metals differed from the official price ratio per ounce as used in coins. It proved impossible to keep both metals in circulation because the market price often differed from the mint price and the dearer coins (in market value of the metal) would be melted down. Hence Gresham's Law: Bad money drives out good. See *Coins, Gresham's Law.*

BLACKLIST A list of people not to be dealt with. The list might consist of individuals, organizations, or nations whose activities or policies are opposed by those creating the list. Blacklist is a term often used in labor relations to refer to a list circulated among employers which identifies so-called troublemakers and thus warns against their employment. It was used against union organizers in the past, but that practice is now illegal under the National Labor Relations Act of 1935 (the Wagner Act). Blacklisting also was used in the 1950s by movie studios against actors and writers who had been accused of being communist sympathizers by people such as Senator Joe McCarthy of Wisconsin. See *Boycott.*

BLACK MARKET The illegal exchange of goods at a free-market price when the product price is set lower by law or when exchange is legally forbidden.

BONDS Certificates which represent long-term debt. U.S. Treasury bonds usually mature 30 years from the date of issue, while many corporate bonds are issued with somewhat shorter maturities. Bonds are issued to raise funds for an organization's activities but, unlike shares of stock of corporations, they are certificates of debt rather than of ownership. The price of negotiable bonds in the bond market will vary inversely with the interest rate. See *Interest Rate, Government Bonds, Collateralized Bond Obligations, Municipals, Treasury Bonds*.

BOOK VALUE 1. For assets, the value of assets carried on a firm's accounting books, for example, original cost less depreciation. If the asset value is carried at replacement cost less depreciation, the book value would equal market value.

2. For capital stock, the value established by dividing the total par (nominal) value plus the retained earnings applicable to that class of stock by the number of shares of that stock outstanding. Book value may differ from market value, which is determined by the trading in that stock on a stock exchange.

BOYCOTT A concerted refusal to deal with a person, firm, group, or nation to punish them or to bring about a change in behavior. See *Blacklist, Consumer Boycott, Labor Boycott, Primary Boycott, Secondary Boycott*.

BROKERED DEPOSIT FUNDS Funds that are placed by brokers who search the nation to find the banks and thrifts with certificates of deposit (CDs) paying the highest interest rate. Risk is eliminated because accounts up to $100,000 are insured by the federal government and the brokers can break up larger amounts into $100,000 units for placement. The process contributed to the thrift debacle at the end of the 1980s. Thrifts near insolvency would offer very high interest rates on CDs to attract funds to loan at high rates to speculative builders and others, in the hope that profit would come in to rebuild capital. Brokered funds made it easier for such thrifts to be found by depositors. When a large number of construction loans went sour, the government was left to pick up the tab with deposit insurance.

BUDGET DEFICIT A situation in which receipts for a budget period are less than expenditures. The deficit becomes indebtedness unless there are sufficient reserves built up in earlier periods from which to draw. In U.S. federal finance, the national debt is the current net sum of all federal budget deficits over the years, counting those occasional surpluses as negative deficits.

Federal deficits may be a form of *fiscal policy* designed to expand economic activity in the economy by providing more government spending when private spending is deemed insufficient. For three decades, however, federal budget deficits continued, and grew, because the Administration and Congress were unwilling to raise sufficient funds by fees and taxation to pay for the expenditures they desired to make. The last federal budget surplus ($0.3 billion) was in 1960. Deficits toward the end of the 1980s had grown to a range of $200–300 billion. The deficits were intended in the sense that they were budgeted, but they were the opposite of appropriate fiscal policy in many years because deficits are inflationary. They made the effort to control inflation by monetary policy much more difficult during the 1980s. See *Crowding Out, Deficit Spending, National Debt, Fiscal Policy.*

BUDGET LINE   In indifference curve analysis of consumer behavior, the line whose points identify all of the attainable combinations of two goods, x and y, given consumer income and the prices of x and y. Suppose that x is priced at $2 each and y at $1 each, while this consumer's income is $10 per day. If the consumer spent all income on x, 5 units would be bought. If all income were spent on y, 10 units would be bought. If the consumer bought 3 units of x, he or she could buy 4 units of y before exhausting income. See *Equilibrium of the Consumer.*

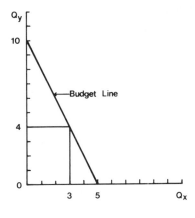

BUDGET LINE

BUFFER STOCK   A stock of goods held by a country or a group of countries to stabilize the price of a product or to raise its price. In the latter case, if quantity supplied exceeds quantity demanded at the target price, a sufficient quantity of goods is bought to maintain the price at the desired minimum price. This stock is stored and available to put on the market should quantity demanded exceed quantity supplied at a target maximum price.

Buffer stocks are possible when goods are storable. Typically, they are used only for goods produced in competitive markets in which producers react to market prices and markets tend to be somewhat unstable. As successive farm programs in the U.S. have shown, minimum prices tend to be set high enough that continued overproduction occurs, and buffer stocks continue to grow beyond the amount necessary to stabilize the market unless effective production quotas are instituted. See *Commodity Credit Corporation, Price Support.*

BULL   A person who expects stock market prices to rise and acts to buy now in order to sell later at a higher price, making a profit on the difference. The origin of the term "bull" is obscure and is believed to be derived from the term "bear." See *Bear.*

BULL MARKET   A market in which prices are rising or are expected to rise. Usually it is applied in auction-type markets such as stock markets or commodity markets. See *Bear Market.*

BUMPING   The exercise of seniority in a firm when the work force is reduced by either temporary or permanent layoffs. In particular, it refers to the exercise of seniority across job classifications. For example, a punch-press operator may have low seniority at that work and face layoff when the line is reduced, but that operator may have high seniority from previous years in the receiving room, so he or she can bump a low-seniority worker there. When seniority is plant-wide there can be a long trail of "bumps" from the initial reduction in force to the persons who are actually laid off.

BUSINESS CYCLES   Fluctuations in the level of economic activity in a country, as measured by real GNP, when the effect of seasonal variations, very long-run (secular) variations, and exogenous forces such as war have been removed statistically. Business cycles are alternating periods of prosperity and depression which have occurred with varying amplitudes and varying periods of duration since the advent of the industrial revolution. Fluctuations in output are accompanied by fluctuations in employment and income. Cycles are not precisely repeated because their causation is complex and variable.

Some students of the business cycle measure cycles from trough to trough or peak to peak. Joseph Schumpeter (1883–1950) argued that this is improper and inconsistent with the historical driving forces. He identified four stages of the cycle: prosperity, representing expansion from an equilibrium to the peak; recession, the decline from the peak to the next point on the trend line; depression, the further fall to the trough; and revival, the expansion from the trough to the next equilibrium on the trend line. He measured the business cycle from equilibrium through the four phases to the next equilibrium. The National Bureau of Economic Research, on the other hand, identifies two phases, expansion and recession, and measures business cycles from peak to peak or trough to trough.

Business cycles are affected by both automatic and ad hoc countercyclical measures which dampen the amplitude of swings in GNP. Unemployment insurance is an example of an automatic countercyclical measure. The insurance payments replace some of the income that workers lose because of unemployment. Spending from unemployment insurance payments helps to maintain production-creating expenditures which otherwise would be lost as unemployment grows. When the economy moves toward recovery, unemployment insurance payments fall as employment expands, which partly counters other expansionary forces.

An example of an ad hoc countercyclical measure is the enactment of legislation increasing road building and repair during a recession to provide employment. It creates employment and production directly. It also stimulates the economy indirectly as the new payments translate into new income which in turn will increase spending for consumer goods according to the marginal propensity to consume and the multiplier. Such measures help to counteract the fall in GNP in a recession. See *Accelerator, Automatic Stabilizers, Gross National Product, Multiplier, Recession, Depression.*

BUYOUTS   See *Leveraged Buyout, Takeover.*

CALLABLE BONDS   Also known as redeemable bonds. Bonds that contain a clause to permit the issuer to "call" or redeem the bonds well before the stated maturity date. Callable bonds are issued by state and local governments as well as by corporations. When interest rates fall well below the rates at which the bonds were issued, the issuers have a clear incentive to refinance them as they become eligible for call even though the refinancing process itself has a cost. Sometimes, as in leveraged buyouts, an acquired firm's cash flow is small enough to strain its ability to meet interest payments, and assets are sold to redeem some of the bonds that are eligible for call. *Convertible bonds,* on the other hand, may be converted into shares of stock in the issuing company on the initiation of the bond holder.

CALLABLE PREFERRED STOCK   Preferred stock specifies a rate of return as a first claim on net profits, and when that appears high, those shares which have a "call" clause may be called for redemption. See *Callable Bonds.*

CALL OPTION   A contract purchased for a fee which permits the holder to buy (call for delivery of) specified securities or commodities at a given price during a specified time period, usually a few months or less. The "call" is exercised at the buyer's option. A call option differs from the purchase of a futures contract in that the call can be exercised *at the buyer's option during the specified time, or not at all,* while in a futures contract the buyer *must buy* *on the maturity date* of the contract. See *Options Trading, Put Option, Futures Market.*

CAPITAL   1. Products that are made to be used in producing other goods and services; a produced factor of production. One of three categories of factors of production, the others being labor and land (natural resources). Capital consists of such things as flint arrow heads in primitive societies; shovels, fishnets, and other equipment; drill presses, road graders, computers, and other machines; factory buildings, roads, dams, goods in inventory, etc. Capital, consumer goods, and natural resources constitute the three broad categories of economic goods. Consumer goods differ from capital in that consumer goods are *end products* consumable by households, such as carrots, T-bone steaks, shirts, skirts, service by a waiter, and the services of consumer durables—automobiles, home computers, and refrigerators—while capital is a *means of production* used to produce other capital goods and consumer goods.

Natural resources are factors of production *as found in nature*, such as a stand of old-growth timber, soil before it is tilled or fertilized, and iron ore in the ground before it is mined.

The term "capital" is one of many words that have multiple meanings in everyday language but which economists use with only one specific meaning for their analysis. This practice can be confusing to noneconomists but may be better than inventing a whole new set of terms, as some social sciences have done. Economists usually restrict the meaning of capital to real producer goods, such as lathes or factory buildings, but must use a money value when developing statistical data about them. For the economist, investment expenditure is made for real capital goods.

2. Businesses may use the word *capital* to refer to *funds* for the purchase of real capital goods, as well as to refer to the real capital goods themselves. Businesses also sometimes use the term to refer to the net worth or ownership share of an enterprise. Sometimes "capital" is used to refer to all assets of a person, a firm, or society. See *Capital Formation, Investment, Consumer Durables.*

CAPITAL CONSUMPTION ALLOWANCE   The value of the capital goods used up in the production process during a year. In national income accounting, it is the difference between gross private domestic investment and net private domestic investment, and it also is the difference between gross national product (GNP) and net national product (NNP). Capital consumption allowance generally stands for the total of *depreciation* of capital goods in the economy during a period of time, usually a year. See *Depreciation.*

CAPITAL FORMATION   The process of constructing capital goods such as new factories, bridges, generators, lathes, etc., beyond the amount needed for replacement of depreciated capital goods. Equivalent to net investment in national income analysis. Capital formation is the substance of economic growth in that resources are used to expand productive capacity rather than for consumables. Variations in the rate of capital formation are one of the important elements in the business cycle.

CAPITAL GAIN (OR LOSS)   In tax accounting it is the increase (or decrease) in the money value of assets that may occur over time. The increase may be caused by general inflation, by a rise in the price of a share of corporate stock in the stock market, by population growth increasing the relative scarcity of fixed assets such as land, by changes in family formation creating a scarcity of housing, by higher world prices for agricultural products increasing the value of agricultural land, and so on.

Capital losses, represented by decreases in the value of assets, may occur from causes that are the opposite of those for capital gains. We see a mixture of meanings for the term "capital" here: it is used to equate with the term "assets" and refers to both real capital goods and securities.

Capital gains are taxed when they are realized, i.e, when the capital good or security is sold. Capital losses, when they are eligible, may be subtracted from taxable income in the year that the asset is sold.

CAPITAL GOODS   A factor-of-production category which consists of man-made products used in the process of production. What the economist means when simply using the term "capital." Examples range from a simple hoe to office buildings, turret lathes, computers, and completely automated chemical plants. Coking coal is part natural resource (or "land," another factor of production), but it also is partly capital since it has been produced (mined) and transported to the coking ovens. See *Capital, Social-Overhead Capital.*

CAPITAL-INTENSIVE PRODUCTION   A high ratio of capital to labor and other resources used in the production process.

CAPITALISM   An economic system in which there is private ownership of natural resources and capital goods. The returns of rent, interest, and profit are paid to private individuals as owners who decide on the use of their natural resources and capital goods.

In practice, an economic system of private ownership has never existed in pure form—some public ownership and some public decision making about the use of the means of production have existed in every society. The term, therefore, refers to economies in which the means of production (natural resources and capital) are *predominantly* privately owned and managed. Examples of rather pure forms of capitalism are Great Britain or the United States of America during the nineteenth century.

As the twentieth century has progressed, governments in capitalist countries have been taking on a growing role in ownership and/or management of natural resources and capital. On the other hand, socialist countries increasingly have permitted their farmers to sell at least part of their produce in markets for their own benefit, and socialist countries more and more have turned toward market direction of production to increase efficiency.

It appeared that countries were moving at varying rates of speed from relatively pure capitalism and relatively pure socialism toward some combination of capitalism and socialism, becoming "mixed economies." However, during the 1980s, the U.S., Great Britain, and France seemed to be moving toward less government ownership in the economy. And in 1989 and 1990, a bloodless revolution occurred in most of the socialist countries of eastern Europe as the people deposed Communist leaders, adopted democratic forms of government, and struggled to begin the shift to market economies with private ownership of the means of production. See *Socialism, Communism, Mixed Economy, Free-Enterprise Economy*.

CAPITALIZED VALUE   See *Present Value*.

CAPITAL STOCK   1. Ownership shares in a corporation, representing the ownership of the residual value of assets of the corporation after all creditors' claims have been deducted. See *Common Stock, Preferred Stock*.

2. The term also is used in economics to refer to the amount of physical capital in a country, the stock of capital goods.

CARTEL   A formal agreement among independent businesses or governments of countries to control production, sales, and/or purchases for the benefit of the members. A cartel is used to regulate markets and fix prices as a monopolist would. Cartels generally are outlawed within the United States by anti-trust legislation, but, at times, U.S. firms have had permission to participate in international cartels, especially in government-sponsored commodity agreements.

The most famous (or infamous) cartel of the 1970s and 1980s is

OPEC, the Organization of Petroleum Exporting Countries, which temporarily succeeded in controlling enough of the total world output of oil to cause its price to rise from $4 per barrel in 1973 to over $24 by 1980. But the success of OPEC has been sporadic because of forces that tend to undermine cartels, particularly international ones. For example, one or more members will find it advantageous to shave price a bit and ignore quotas in order to sell more and reap even greater benefits from prices that are still artificially high. There is not much fear of market sanctions from the other cartel members because the latter have no way of imposing them. Buyers are happy to get even slightly lower prices, and suppliers of equipment are glad to support the expanded output.

Also, over time, artificially high prices will attract new production in areas outside of the cartel, which undercuts output controls and presses down prices. Both of these forces combined with energy conservation measures to cause a substantial decline in oil prices in the U.S. and around the world in the 1980s. See *Organization of Petroleum Exporting Countries, Monopoly.*

CASH FLOW   A statement or chart which shows all cash receipts and disbursements during a period of time. A cash-flow statement may describe a past period or may be a planning estimate for a future period.

Although a business firm may be profitable in terms of an increase in assets over liabilities, it may be in trouble if its cash flow is inadequate to meet contractual obligations such as interest due on outstanding bonds or the principal on maturing bonds and/ or maturing accounts payable.

CELLER–KEFAUVER ANTIMERGER ACT   An antitrust act passed in 1950 to close many of the loopholes in the Clayton Act of 1914 by outlawing mergers "where in any line of commerce in any section of the country, the effect of such acquisition may be substantially to lessen competition, or tend to create a monopoly." Earlier legislation prohibited illegal mergers by acquisition of stock; this act adds the prohibition of such mergers by acquisition of assets. A finding of a *probable* adverse effect provides the federal government with a cause for action to stop the merger. See *Clayton Antitrust Act, Antitrust, Merger, Sherman Antitrust Act.*

CENTRALLY PLANNED ECONOMY   An economy in which basic economic decisions are made by public authorities rather than private persons. The key decisions involve investment in plant and equipment which determines what will be produced. Other decisions usually include how to combine resources and how to distribute the product to households. The productive facilities (natural resources and capital) are held and controlled by the state rather than owned and controlled by private persons. Central planning is a characteristic of socialist and communist economies. The U.S.S.R. and the eastern European countries under its influence have been centrally planned economies, as is the People's Republic of China. The U.S.S.R. and the socialist economies of eastern Europe began to introduce market direction of production in the 1970s on a very small scale to try to overcome inefficiencies in their central planning. The struggle to change intensified in 1989 and 1990 with the peaceable overthrow of Communist governments in eastern Europe. See *Capitalism, Communism, Socialism, Mixed Economy.*

CERTIFICATE OF DEPOSIT (CD)   A time deposit for a fixed sum and fixed maturity date in a commercial bank, savings bank, or savings and loan association. A CD pays a fixed rate of interest that varies with the term of the deposit (e.g., 6 months, 12 months, 36 months) and with the required minimum amount to be deposited (e.g., $1,000, $5,000, $100,000). Smaller CDs (those under $100,000) are non-negotiable. Federal regulations require that a penalty be paid if the depositor holding one of these smaller CDs withdraws any part or all of the sum prior to the end of the specified term.

Originally, when developed by commercial banks, all certificates of deposit were negotiable instruments. Today, only large CDs of $100,000 or more (often $1,000,000 or more) are negotiable. These so-called jumbo CDs usually are issued by major banks for a year or less and are held by businesses, governments, pension funds, and others with large sums available for financial investment and desiring high liquidity.

CETERIS PARIBUS (*cet. par.*)   A Latin phrase meaning "other things remaining the same," or, "other things equal." It is used by economists as a shorthand expression and a sign of erudition. One may study relationships between specific economic variables by holding some independent variables constant, as in a laboratory experiment. The social scientist seldom is able to experiment with people in society and so must carry on "experiments" in his or her mind. Sometimes this can be facilitated by mathematical manipulation of data.

CHECKING ACCOUNT   A transaction account. A bank account held by a depositor which permits the depositor to write a note (check) ordering the bank to pay another party a specified amount on demand. Checks are negotiable by endorsement. The transfer from the check issuer's bank occurs after the check is presented to the receiver's bank for payment and clears through a clearing house. A demand-deposit checking account has no legal limit on the number of checks written other than the amount of money in the deposit account. (However, a bank may impose a fee to cover processing costs when the number of checks exceeds some large amount, such as 40, or when the balance in the account falls below a stipulated amount.) When there are legal limits on the number of checks written, such as three per month for a "money market checking account," the account takes on some of the characteristics of a savings account rather than a demand deposit, and federal reserve regulations covering savings accounts apply.

Until passage of the Depository Institutions Deregulation and Monetary Control Act of 1980 (DIDMCA), only commercial banks were permitted to offer checking accounts (known legally as demand deposits). Authority for various financial activities had been divided among the different kinds of financial institutions to try to prevent a recurrence of the financial problems of the 1930s. Following a few earlier experiments, the DIDMCA authorized negotiable order of withdrawal (NOW) accounts as checking accounts for savings and loan associations and savings banks and share-draft accounts as checking accounts for credit unions. Both kinds of checking accounts may pay a rate of interest on balances. Where interest on demand deposits had been prohibited, it now is permitted on all nonbusiness checking accounts. See *Demand Deposits, Negotiable Order of Withdrawal, Share-Draft Account, Transaction Accounts, Money Supply.*

CHECKOFF A collective bargaining arrangement whereby the employer withholds union dues from workers' paychecks and transfers the funds to the union. It is negotiated by the union to simplify and assure collection of dues. The law requires written permission of the worker for the withholding.

CHURNING More frequent buying and selling of securities on behalf of clients by an unscrupulous broker, trust officer, or fund manager than is warranted by prudent investment practice in order to receive a large payment of commissions on a large volume of transactions.

CLAYTON ANTITRUST ACT A federal law passed in 1914 that bars specific practices which might substantially lessen competition or tend to create a monopoly. Under the act, no corporation can acquire the stock of another competing firm where the effect of such acquisition may be substantially to lessen competition. Other specific practices outlawed are interlocking corporate directorates, price discrimination, and restrictive contracts which force customers or suppliers to deal exclusively with one firm. Also, the Act specifically excludes labor from being considered a commodity, in an effort to prevent applications of antimonopoly law to the formation of labor unions. See *Antitrust, Celler–Kefauver Antimerger Act, Federal Trade Commission, Merger, Robinson–Patman Act, Sherman Antitrust Act.*

CLEAN FLOAT Characterization of an international currency exchange when currency values are allowed to float (change) freely with no governmental intervention in the foreign exchange markets. See *Dirty Float, Flexible Exchange Rates.*

CLEARING HOUSE An association of banks formed to settle claims of each against the others as the result of checks being drawn on one member bank by a depositor and then deposited or cashed in another member bank. Sometimes the function is performed by the regional Federal Reserve Bank or the regional Federal Home Loan Bank. See *Bank Clearings, Checking Account, Clearing-House Function.*

CLEARING-HOUSE FUNCTION A method of transferring sums from checking accounts in one bank to those of other banks without the movement of cash (or, historically, gold and silver). In the course of daily business many checks written against bank A are deposited in bank B, while many written against bank B are deposited in bank A. These may be netted against each other so that only a small remainder need be transferred. If banks A and B both keep deposits in the clearing bank, C, even the small remainder may be transferred by a bookkeeping entry at bank C rather than by a physical transfer. See *Bank Clearings, Checking Account.*

CLOSED-END MUTUAL FUND A mutual fund that sells a *limited* number of shares that trade in financial markets like any other shares. Just as in any mutual fund, the manager invests in a particular portfolio of securities, hoping to do better than the market in total return. It differs from the more common open-end kind of mutual fund, which sells shares to all comers without limit. See *Mutual Fund, Open-End Mutual Fund.*

CLOSED SHOP A labor union agreement with an employer or group of employers that only union members will be hired, so that an individual must join the union *before* he or she can be employed. The closed shop has been attacked with great emotion over the years because it gives a union control over who may be hired. The union controls admission to its own membership, so refusal of admission to union membership means denying the person the right to be considered for a job.

The closed shop has been found most often in the maritime and construction industries, where a worker moves from one employer to another as jobs are completed during the year. The union often provides a "hiring hall" service to employers, organizing a labor market for both employer and employee as other union security arrangements do not.

The Taft–Hartley Act of 1947 banned the closed shop, but because the arrangement benefits both union and employer the ban seldom has been enforced. The Labor–Management Reporting and Disclosure Act of 1959 (Landrum–Griffin Act) in effect legalized the closed shop again in the construction industry. See *Hiring Hall, Agency Shop, Open Shop, Right-to-Work Laws, Union Shop.*

COINS Metallic money. At one time coins contained an amount of metal whose value as bullion would equal the money value designated on the coin. For example, a dime would contain ten cents worth of silver bullion. A silver dollar could be melted down and the silver content sold for a dollar. It was money of intrinsic value.

Obviously, problems could arise because of fluctuations in the market price of the metals used. When the market price of gold or silver rose above the minted value of coins, they would be melted down and sold for bullion and would thereby disappear from circulation. There also was difficulty because of clipping and "sweating" coins to try to remove some of the metal value without losing the money exchange value of the coins.

To keep coins in circulation and in good repair, monetary authorities reduced the amount of valuable metal in coins to a token amount so that the coins would always have more value as a medium of exchange than as a metal.

Coins are included with paper money in the "currency" category by the Federal Reserve System for its statistical compilations of the money stock. See *Bimetallism, Gresham's Law.*

COLLATERAL Assets that are pledged by a borrower to guarantee a loan, a bond, or some other certificate of indebtedness.

COLLATERALIZED BOND OBLIGATIONS (CBOs) Debt instruments that are issued against a pool of other securities, often high-risk securities such as junk bonds. The CBOs might acquire an investment-grade bond rating despite representing junk bonds by, for example, putting $30 million of high-risk securities into a pool that would back a $20 million issue of CBOs. CBOs are similar to mortgage-backed securities issued by or guaranteed by Ginnie Mae, Fannie Mae, or Freddie Mac involving pools that contain insured mortgages rather than bonds. The risk of the mortgage pools tends to be low because of mortgages that usually are of high quality, but especially because of federal guarantees. See *Government National Mortgage Association, Federal National Mortgage Association, Federal Home Loan Mortgage Corporation.*

COLLECTIVE BARGAINING Negotiation over wages and working conditions by representatives of an organized group of employees (a union) and representatives of an employer, or organization of employers, with the goal of a written agreement. Prior to 1935, collective bargaining occurred only when a union had the economic power through strikes, slowdowns, and boycotts to force an employer to bargain. The National Labor Relations Act of 1935 (the Wagner Act) requires employers to bargain "in good faith" with a union if it is certified by the National Labor Relations Board (NLRB) as the representative of the employees after a secret ballot supervised by the NLRB. See *Bargaining Unit, Compulsory Arbitration.*

COMMERCIAL BANK Any banking institution that has demand-deposit liabilities (checking accounts that are limited in number only by the amount of money in the account) and makes short-term business loans. For some time, commercial banks also have provided savings deposits, time deposits, trust services, and mortgage loans. Commercial banks may be chartered by either the federal government or a state. See *Bank, Savings Bank, Savings and Loan Association, Credit Union.*

COMMERCIAL PAPER Negotiable unsecured promissory notes issued by major corporations in denominations of $10,000 and more for short-term maturities. Commercial paper provides an interest income attractive to banks and other financial institutions, pension-fund managers, and other investors. There is an active market which permits easy and quick purchase and sale at prices that reflect the market participants' judgment about the condition of the corporations as well as anticipated movements in interest rates. See *Bills Payable.*

COMMODITY A product such as wheat, oil, natural gas, coffee, copper, cotton, or pork bellies. Commodity markets in the U.S. are dominated by the organized markets in Chicago and New York. See *Hedging, Futures Market*.

COMMODITY CREDIT CORPORATION (CCC) A U.S. federal agency which has provided a method of price support to farmers by making loans at the federal support price, using the crop as collateral. If the market price falls below the support price, the farmer will turn the crop over to the CCC and keep the money. If the price rises above the support level, the farmer will sell the crop and pay off the loan. When market prices for a support crop are low relative to the support price for several years, the government builds up huge stocks of the crop which "hang over the market," preventing price from rising above the support level because of anticipated moves to reduce the stockpile. The process does tend to stabilize prices within narrower margins than a free market would provide.

The system has been criticized for creating artificially high prices for domestic consumers, discouraging foreign buyers, and building huge storage costs. In recent years the support prices have been quite low relative to market prices, even when, for example, the price of wheat fell by 30% in 1990. The CCC continues to make loans, but farmers typically pay them off when the crop is sold rather than letting the crop go to the CCC. The loans seem to be used to ease cash-flow problems and as insurance, but they have not supported prices.

Many critics have recommended a straight subsidy as a cheaper program for the government, and one that does not produce potentially adverse market results. The U.S. Agriculture Department instituted a subsidy system of target prices and "deficiency" payments which runs parallel to the CCC loan program. However, most agricultural markets are international and such subsidies run counter to efforts of the General Agreement on Tariffs and Trade (GATT) to eliminate subsidies that affect international trade. Straight subsidies also undercut our efforts to reduce the subsidies of other countries for products which we feel unfairly compete in our markets. See *Buffer Stock, Price Support, Deficiency Payment, Parity Price: Agriculture, Target Price*.

COMMODITY FUTURES Contracts for delivery of specified commodities such as wheat, cotton, or corn at the stated price on a specified date in the future. The sale and purchase of futures helps to even out commodity price fluctuations due to seasonal production by permitting the market to reflect expectations about future harvests and future changes in demand. Futures also provide a way for processors such as millers to hedge against price changes and avoid the risks of inventory price fluctuations while a commodity is being processed and held in inventory. Commodity futures are traded on a number of markets, including the Chicago Board of Trade, the Chicago Mercantile Exchange, the New York Cotton Exchange, the New York Commodity Exchange, and the New York Mercantile Exchange. See *Futures Market, Hedging*.

COMMON MARKET An economic union among a group of nations to reduce and remove trade barriers among members, to adopt a common trade policy toward the outside world, and to achieve some other types of economic integration. For an example, see *European Community*.

COMMON STOCK Shares of ownership in business corporations. They carry voting rights at annual or special stockholders' meetings at one vote per share. Common stock represents residual ownership of the net worth of a business after all liabilities are deducted from all assets and preferred stock obligations are met. A stock owner's liability for the debts of a corporation is limited to loss of the value of the stock. In some circumstances, common stock may provide for the right to assess stockholders beyond the amount initially paid in to the capital of the corporation or shown as the par value.

The value of shares will fluctuate in stock markets in anticipation of changes in the world regarding war and peace and availability of crucial raw materials and in anticipation of changes in the economy, in the industry, and in the company. The potential volatility of common stock makes it more risky than many other types of financial investment. See *Capital Stock, Preferred Stock*.

COMMUNISM An economy in which capital goods and natural resources are owned and managed by government rather than private persons. Since Karl Marx (1818–1883), it differs from socialism in the belief that the welfare of the worker can only be achieved through revolution and, according to Lenin (1870–1924), a subsequent period (of undesignated length) of authoritarianism on behalf of the worker. Examples of Communist states are the Soviet Union, Albania, and the People's Republic of China.

At the beginning of the 1990s, the U.S.S.R. is struggling to convert to a market system from the centralized Communist economic system it has had for 70 years, but it is making little progress. Other eastern European Communist countries such as Czechoslovakia, Hungary, and Poland experienced bloodless prodemocracy revolutions and replaced their old-line Communist leaders with leaders who also are struggling to introduce market-directed economic systems after their Communist economic systems failed.

Before Marx, many writers differentiated communism from socialism on the basis of principles of income distribution: to each according to need in communism and to each according to contribution to production in socialism. See *Capitalism, Socialism.*

COMMUNITY REINVESTMENT ACT A law passed in 1977 which places an obligation on banks and other insured mortgage lenders to meet the reasonable credit needs of their local low-income communities. It prohibits redlining, which is used to identify properties by areas of a community which are inhabited by racial minorities or low-income groups labeled "poor risks" and hence ineligible for loans, without an individual determination of the creditworthiness of individual loan applicants. The Financial Institutions Reform, Recovery, and Enforcement Act of 1989 mandated access to the ratings of banks on lending and hiring that must be maintained under this act and the Home Mortgage Disclosure Act of 1975. See *Redlining.*

COMPANY UNION An organization of employees who work in one company and are not affiliated with any other labor union organization. Company unions were formed with the assistance of employers to respond to a desire of employees to organize and often to forestall the entry of independent "outside" unions. Many company unions were formed in the 1930s, usually under the strong influence of management if not under its direction. Indeed, many company unions included foremen and other supervisors in their membership, often in leadership roles, and received some funding from the employer.

The National Labor Relations Act of 1935 prohibits employers from forming company unions. It is an unfair labor practice for an employer to dominate or interfere with the formation or administration of any labor organization or contribute financial or other support to it. The National Labor Relations Board created by the law can issue unfair labor practice findings with cease and desist orders to enforce the law. Employer efforts to control a union are further prevented by the power of the NLRB to determine what employees are to be in a collective bargaining unit, exclude those with management responsibilities from it, and hold secret ballots among employees in the designated unit to determine what union they want to represent them, if any. See *Labor Union, Collective Bargaining, Bargaining Unit, Unfair Labor Practices.*

COMPARATIVE ADVANTAGE A principle of trade which shows the advantage for a country to specialize in the production of those things whose production cost, relative to the production cost of other products (the exchange ratio), is lower than the exchange ratio for the same products in other nations.

Suppose nation A could use its resources to produce wheat or cotton or some combination of the two. Suppose further, that nation A can produce both wheat and cotton cheaper (with less resources) than nation B, so that nation A has an "absolute advantage" in the production of both wheat and cotton. Nation A can benefit, nevertheless, from specialization in the production of that product whose *relative* cost is lower and then trade that product with nation B for the other product.

Suppose that in nation A the use of its resources would result in a relative cost of 1 ton of wheat = 10 bales of cotton. If the exchange ratio (relative resource cost) in nation B were 1/2 ton of wheat = 10 bales of cotton, nation A would have a comparative advantage in the production of wheat. It could gain by specializing in wheat. Nation B would have a comparative advantage in the production of cotton and could gain from specializing in the production of cotton. If A divided its resources evenly between wheat and cotton it could produce, say, 1 million tons of wheat and 10 million bales of cotton. However, if it shifted resources out of cotton and into wheat, it could produce another 1 million tons of wheat which could be traded to B for almost 20 million bales of cotton. Both nation A *and* nation B would gain if the exchange ratio between the countries were 1 ton of wheat for less than 10 bales but more than 5 bales of cotton.

Trade would be beneficial here even though nation A had an *absolute advantage* in the production of *both* wheat and cotton, so long as the *comparative advantage* exists.

Comparative advantage arises from the uneven distribution of the world's resources together with the requirement of different proportions of factors of production to produce different commodities and services. Resources in this context include natural resources, capital goods, size and training of the labor force, and technical knowledge. See *Absolute Advantage*.

COMPETITION 1. In common usage, more than one seller in a market or, on the buyer's side, more than one buyer in a market.

2. When the term is used by economists there most often is an implicit assumption of the more rigorous terms of *pure* competition. These include a homogeneous product, so many sellers or so many buyers that no one seller or buyer can affect the market price, and

ease of entry into and exit from the market. See *Pure Competition, Perfect Competition, Competitive Market.*

COMPETITIVE MARKET 1. An economist typically will have in mind the sum of contacts between buyers and sellers of a product or service that conforms to pure competition: There are so many buyers and sellers of a standardized product that no one individual or group can affect price, and buyers and sellers can freely enter or leave the market. Price is determined by impersonal market forces, not set by a seller or buyer, and buyers and sellers react to the market price, deciding how much to buy or how much to produce and sell.

2. Popularly, a competitive market is characterized by rivalry among sellers and/or buyers of a broadly defined product, not necessarily standardized, such as automobiles or fast food. Economists, however, would designate these markets as oligopoly and monopolistic competition, respectively. See *Pure Competition, Duopoly, Oligopoly, Monopolistic Competition, Monopoly.*

COMPLEMENTARY GOODS Goods that are used together so that a change in the price of one good will cause the demand curve of the other good to shift in the opposite direction. For example, a *fall in the price* of beer results in an increase in the quantity of beer demanded and an *increase in the entire demand curve* for the complementary good, pretzels. See *Cross Elasticity.*

COMPOUND INTEREST The calculation of interest on accumulated interest as well as on principal. When the interest return at the end of each time period remains with the principal, the combination becomes the new principal to earn interest in each succeeding time period. Interest may be compounded on a daily, weekly, monthly, quarterly, or annual period. The shorter the compounding period, the greater the yield at the end of a year because of the more frequent calculation of interest on interest.

COMPTROLLER OF THE CURRENCY The federal agency which controls the issuance of charters for national banks based on the need for a new bank's services and the absence of substantial adverse effects on existing banks. The agency, created by the National Banking Act of 1863, provides periodic examination of national banks to test for compliance with rules and regulations, for absence of fraud, and for avoidance of excessive risk. To prevent an unnecessary multiplicity of examinations, the Federal Reserve

System examines only state-chartered member banks and the Federal Deposit Insurance Corporation examines only nonmember insured banks.

COMPULSORY ARBITRATION Arbitration for the settlement of disputes as required by law. Usually it is combined with *binding arbitration,* which requires the parties to accept the arbitration award without further recourse.

Compulsory arbitration often is combined with the prohibition of strikes where continued provision of service is necessary, such as in fire and police protection. It recognizes that independent judicious resolution of disputes is especially needed there because the employer controls the work place and the payroll and can prevail every time when employees lose the power to provide economic pressure through striking.

Many states prohibit strikes by any public employees but provide for a collective bargaining process which includes mediation of disputes and binding arbitration as a final step when issues cannot be resolved. See *Arbitration, Collective Bargaining.*

CONGLOMERATE MERGER The merging of two or more firms which produce different, noncompeting products or services. The number has grown as antitrust laws have made it more difficult for competing firms to merge. There may be a benefit in spreading risks by producing in a variety of markets, some of which might be growing when others are depressed. Or a firm might gain by buying the controlling stock ownership of another firm, whether producing in a different market or not, when the market value of the stock is well below the value of its assets. See *Friendly Takeover, Leveraged Buyout, Takeover, Unfriendly Takeover.*

CONGRESS OF INDUSTRIAL ORGANIZATIONS (CIO) A federation of labor unions in the United States now merged with the American Federation of Labor (AF of L) to form the AFL–CIO. In 1935 eight national unions of the AF of L, under the leadership of John L. Lewis, President of the United Mine Workers, organized as the Committee for Industrial Organization. Its goal was to organize workers on a plant-wide and industry-wide basis rather than on a craft basis.

Organization by craft had left unorganized the semiskilled and unskilled workers who numerically were the bulk of the labor force in mass-production industries. When these workers tried to organize, they generally wanted the skilled craft workers included in a plant-wide union because their skills are harder to replace and therefore add bargaining power to the union. Craft workers, on the other hand, often felt they could get more by bargaining on their own. Conflict developed between the industrial unions and the craft-organized unions over the right to organize the craft workers in manufacturing plants. Craft unions dominated the AF of L, and so the CIO split off in 1937 to form a competing federation of national unions—the Congress of Industrial Organizations. It merged with the AF of L in 1955. See *American Federation of Labor, American Federation of Labor–Congress of Industrial Organizations, Union, Jurisdictional Dispute.*

CONSTANT COSTS As the scale of output of a firm or industry grows, the cost per unit of output (average cost) does not change. Constant costs will occur if there are constant returns to scale and changes in scale do not affect the prices of factors of production. ("Change in scale" refers to a situation in which *all* factors of production are variable.) For example, in a constant-cost industry, the entry of new firms or expansion of existing firms may involve an increase in all factors of production, but that neither drives up nor lowers long-run average costs (LACs) for the typical firm. There are no long-run economies or diseconomies internal or external to the firm in this situation.

In some circumstances, constant costs may not occur at very low or very high levels of output, but may exist for substantial ranges of output in between. In the range of constant costs, Q_1 to Q_2 in the diagram below, long-run *marginal* cost will be horizontal as well because each increase in quantity will increase cost by the same amount as the preceding unit.

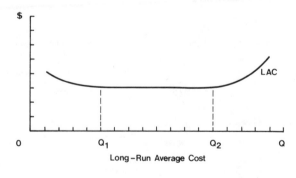

Long-Run Average Cost

CONSTANT COST CURVE

See *Constant Returns, Decreasing Costs, Economies of Scale, Increasing Costs, Long Run.*

CONSTANT DOLLARS   Dollar figures in a time series, such as GNP data, from which inflation has been removed. The monthly, quarterly, or annual data in current dollars of each period is divided by an appropriate price index to remove the effects of inflation and convert the data to constant dollars. One can use constant dollars to compare GNP for 1990 with GNP in 1980 and thereby discover how much better off we have become through growth in "real" output, without mere price increases confusing the picture. The process is known as "deflating" current dollar data to produce constant dollar data. (Use of per capita figures would eliminate population growth and produce an even clearer picture of change in economic well-being.) See *Current Dollars, Deflation, Real versus Money Data.*

CONSTANT RETURNS   As the scale of a firm increases, output will grow in direct proportion to the increase in inputs of the factors of production, i.e., a 5% increase in all factors of production would result in a 5% increase in output. Constant returns may lead to constant costs unless there is an effect on the costs of factors of production when scale changes. A change in scale means that all factors of production are variable, a condition of the long run. See *Constant Costs, Decreasing Returns to Scale, Long Run.*

CONSUMER BOYCOTT   A concerted refusal by a group of consumers to buy products or services from a firm (or group of firms) in order to change its behavior. The desired change might be to lower prices, to stop the sale of objectionable material, to not deal with a particular foreign nation, to recognize a labor union, etc. See *Boycott, Labor Boycott, Primary Boycott, Secondary Boycott.*

CONSUMER DEMAND (C)   In national income analysis, the value of all the goods and services purchased by households in the economy during a period of time. A household is an individual or a group, such as a family or house co-op group of unrelated individuals, that is a decision-making unit for the purchase of consumer goods and services. Consumer demand is a function of the absolute level of household income, the number and age distribution of people in households, their tastes, their preference for present versus future consumption, prices of goods and services, expectations about price changes, expectations about changes in income, the level of personal income taxes, and expectations about their future changes.

Household consumer demand also is affected by the level of its income relative to the income of other families with which it identifies, according to the *relative income hypothesis* of James Duesenberry.

Some of the critical elements concerning expectations have been treated in such theories as Franco Modigliani's *life-cycle hypothesis* and Milton Friedman's *permanent income hypothesis*. Keynesian analysis presumed that most of the determinants other than current income do not change much over short periods of time so that consumption is a function of current income. This is known as the *absolute income hypothesis*.

Aggregate consumer demand, as a summation, depends upon all of the influences on household consumer demand plus the number of households. Consumption expenditure is the largest of the components of GNP or national income (NY). See *Absolute Income Hypothesis, Consumption Function, Permanent Income Hypothesis, Relative Income Hypothesis*.

CONSUMER DEMAND FUNCTION: THE HOUSEHOLD $D_x = f(P_x, P_n, Y, T)$ where D_x is the quantity demanded of product x, f signifies a functional coefficient, P_x is the price of product x, P_n is the prices of all other goods and services, Y is income of the consumer per unit of time, and T stands for the consumer's system of tastes among alternative goods and services. This formulation is based on the *absolute income hypothesis*. See *Consumption Function, Demand Curve*.

CONSUMER DURABLES A category of consumer goods which provide their services over a period of years, such as automobiles, microwave ovens, stereo players, television sets, and washing machines. Most consumer durables involve discretionary spending that can be postponed or sometimes siphoned off into a used-product market. These factors make demand for consumer durables rather volatile. Therefore, expenditure for consumer durables and surveys of plans for such expenditure are important to use in economic forecasting.

CONSUMER GOODS Everything produced for the consumer sector of the economy. The term generally includes *services* such as those of hairdressers, doctors, dry cleaners, and automobile mechanics as well as *things* such as cereal, clothing, and motor boats. Consumer goods often are divided into durable and nondurable. The durable category would include those things that give off their services gradually over an extended period of time such as refrigerators, washing machines, and snowmobiles.

CONSUMER PRICE INDEX (CPI) The weighted average of the prices of a specified set of consumer goods and services known as a "market basket," which is then converted into a time series relating prices of one period to prices of another period. The weighted average price of the base period (say, 1987) is equaled to 100 and prices of other years are related to it as a percentage of the base. A 10% increase in the weighted average price in 1989 over the weighted average price of the base period, 1987, is shown as an index number of 110.

The base year is changed periodically, usually every 10 years, to reflect changes in the goods and services available and changes in their relative importance. The index for 1886 would not include automobiles; the one for 1936 would not include television sets; and the one for 1966 would not include personal computers or compact-disc players.

The Bureau of Labor Statistics (BLS) of the U.S. Department of Labor produces two consumer price indexes for two different market baskets: one for all urban consumers and one for urban wage earners and clerical workers.

The CPI often is called the cost of living index. When wages or Social Security payments are automatically adjusted for inflation, the reference for adjustment often is the CPI. Such agreements are called COLAs, for cost-of-living adjustments. See *Cost-of-Living Adjustment, Price Index, Producer Price Index, Time Series.*

CONSUMER SOVEREIGNTY   The character of an economic system in which consumer decisions to spend will direct what is to be produced and, consequently, direct the allocation of productive resources to the production of the goods and services demanded. A purely competitive market system in its ideal form would be most efficient in solving the allocation problems in a system of consumer sovereignty. If some sellers have market power, output will be lower and prices higher than in pure competition. A real-life competitive market system, although imperfect, may be the least inefficient system of allocation. The opposite of consumer sovereignty would be authoritarianism in a command economy in which a leader or group of leaders would decide what is to be produced for consumption, how it will be produced, and for whom. See *Pure Competition.*

CONSUMER SURPLUS   The excess of value received by consumers over what consumers have to pay for a product or service. It arises from diminishing marginal utility (or diminishing marginal rate of substitution) combined with a uniform price per unit for a product no matter how much a consumer buys.

For most goods the *added* satisfaction derived from consumption of each successive unit in a given time period diminishes (although *total* satisfaction continues to increase to the point of satiation). If a consumer likes orange juice, the first ounce consumed at breakfast will give more satisfaction than the second ounce, the second ounce more than the third, and so on. If the market price is 10 cents per ounce, suppose that our consumer buys 6 ounces each morning because the sixth ounce gives 10 cents worth of satisfaction. If only 1 ounce were available, it would give the consumer, say, 50 cents worth of satisfaction and she would be willing to pay that much for it. Suppose that a second ounce would be worth 40 cents to her, a third worth 30 cents, a fourth worth 20 cents, a fifth worth 15 cents, a sixth worth 10 cents, and a seventh worth 5 cents. The consumer would be willing to pay $1.65 for 6 ounces of orange juice but only has to pay $.60. The difference of $1.05 is consumer surplus. The consumer would not buy a seventh ounce of orange juice when it is priced at 10 cents per ounce because it will only give 5 cents worth of satisfaction.

A monopoly firm could transfer the consumer surplus to itself by making an all-or-nothing offer of 6 ounces of orange juice for $1.65 or by pricing on a sliding scale of 1 ounce for 50 cents, 2 for 90 cents, 3 for $1.20, etc.

Consumer surplus may be seen as the shaded area PAB under the demand curve and above the market price in the figure below.

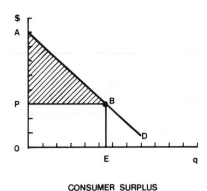

CONSUMER SURPLUS

Consumers are willing to pay an amount equal to the area 0PABE for 0E of the product, but they only have to pay an amount equal to the area 0PBE (i.e., $p \times q$). See *Demand Curve, Diminishing Marginal Utility, Diminishing Marginal Rate of Substitution.*

CONSUMPTION FUNCTION Consumption treated as a function of income. The consumption function is $C = f(Y)$, where C is consumption expenditure and Y is income. The analysis of John Maynard Keynes (1883–1943) focused on the absolute level of current income as the determinant of consumption expenditure. Others have introduced modifications, such as the relative income hypothesis of James Duesenberry, the life-cycle hypothesis of Franco Modigliani, or the permanent income hypothesis of Milton Friedman. Each of these concepts analyzes the relationship between household consumption expenditure and income and then aggregates it for the economy. The following presentation will illustrate the Keynesian concept.

In the diagram below, C is total consumption expenditure for the economy in dollars and DPY is disposable personal income for the economy in dollars. (A similar diagram could represent the relationship between household consumption expenditure and household disposable personal income with appropriate changes in the quantities measured on each axis.) Line CC illustrates the functional relationship between consumption spending and income. The 45° line identifies all of those points where consumption spending equals income. At any particular amount of income, the vertical difference between the associated point on the consumption function and the 45° line measures the amount of saving from that income.

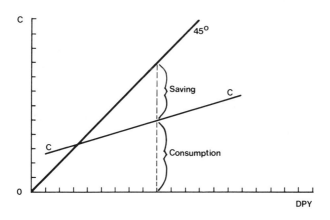

CONSUMPTION FUNCTION

The 45° line also helps to show that a horizontal change in DPY will result in a smaller vertical change in consumption, that is, the marginal propensity to consume (MPC) is less than one, since the slope of the consumption function is less than one. (The MPC is the slope of the consumption function.) At very low income, to the left of the intersection of the CC line with the 45° line, consumption expenditure exceeds income, indicating a net volume of dissaving in the economy. Even though the average propensity to consume ($APC = C/Y$) here is greater than 1, the MPC (dC/dY) still is less than 1.

An autonomous change in consumption expenditure (one caused by something other than a change in the level of disposable personal income) will be illustrated by a shift up or down in the consumption function or a change in its slope.

See *Consumer Demand, Marginal Propensity to Consume*.

CONVERTIBLE BOND A corporate certificate of indebtedness which is convertible to shares of stock that are ownership certificates. Conversion of the bond is initiated by the bond holder under conditions specified on the face of the bond, whereas a *callable bond* is exchanged for money or other securities at the discretion of the bond issuer. Convertible bonds permit the bond holder to hedge against inflation when stock prices rise with inflation.

COPYRIGHT The legal right granted by federal law to an author, composer, artist, or publisher to the exclusive use, publication, reproduction, and distribution of an author's or artist's work.

CORPORATE INCOME TAX A tax on the net income, or profit, of a corporation. Shareholders often complain of "double taxation" because tax is paid on the company's net income and tax is paid again as personal income tax by the shareholders for the part of that same corporate income that is distributed in dividends.

CORPORATION A business organization which receives a charter from a state granting it status as a legal entity which, similar to a person, can hold assets, enter into contracts, and sue or be sued. The charter grants its owners (or shareholders) a limitation on their liability for the debts of the business. Liability usually is limited to the assets of the business so that maximum shareholder loss is the amount paid for shares of stock owned in the business and does not extend to the other assets of the share owner. Shares may be bought and sold without effect on the legal organization of the company. The charter usually is issued for a long period such as 99 years, or in perpetuity, so that a corporation's life is not limited to the lives of the initial owners. See *Common Stock*.

CORRESPONDENT BANK A bank in a large commercial center with which smaller banks (and banks in smaller towns) hold balances.

Alternatively it might be a foreign bank in which a domestic bank holds balances. The correspondent bank transfers funds for depositor banks and often acts as a limited clearing house. The correspondent bank may provide many other services, such as investment opportunities in large financial projects for its depositor banks that have surplus funds, participation in a local project when a depositor bank does not have enough loan capacity to finance the project alone, or the facilitation of foreign sales and purchases by business depositors.

COST–BENEFIT ANALYSIS The evaluation of a proposed project by comparing the present discounted value of all expected benefits to the present discounted value of all anticipated costs. It provides a system for valuing and ranking possible public projects or possible private business investment projects to decide which ones to pursue (which show the greatest net benefit or net return). See *Discounting*.

COST-OF-LIVING ADJUSTMENT (COLA) An adjustment of particular payments (such as wages paid by a firm or Social Security payments to retirees) to compensate recipients for changes in the cost of living occasioned by inflation. A COLA agreement specifies a consumer price index to serve as the basis for adjustments in payments. The one most commonly selected is the consumer price index of the Bureau of Labor Statistics. See *Consumer Price Index*.

COST OF PRODUCTION 1. In economics it is the total amount paid to factors of production plus those amounts implicitly earned by them (such as the imputed salary of the owner–manager of a single proprietorship) for acquiring raw materials, transforming them into finished products, and getting the products into the hands of buyers.

2. In business record keeping the concept does not include implicit costs other than depreciation. See *Costs: Accounting Versus Economic; Implicit Costs*.

COST-PLUS CONTRACT An agreement that calls for payment of the producer firm's costs for the project plus a fixed percentage of that cost for uncovered overhead and profit. It has been used, especially by governments, to purchase products whose development and production costs cannot easily be determined in advance. That uncertainty makes it difficult to agree on a product price in advance of production. Without close supervision there is a tendency for the producer not to try to control costs, resulting in $100 hammers and $800 toilet seats in some Department of Defense contracts.

COST-PUSH INFLATION A descriptive name for a type of inflation which originates with price increases for factors of production that are then transmitted to product prices. A sharp change in some basic raw material, such as oil, may cause a ripple (or tidal wave) of price increases through users such as plastics producers and transport companies who try to pass it on to their customers, and so on. Sometimes negotiated union contracts are pointed to as a cause. Cost-push inflation contrasts with the "demand-pull" type of inflation, which originates in a market reaction to an excess of quantity demanded relative to the quantity supplied. Cost-push inflation originates on the supply side and can occur in a relatively competitive market faced with a noneconomic event such as war which has a major impact on supply, or it can occur in a market characterized by administered pricing. See *Administered Price, Demand-Pull Inflation.*

COSTS: ACCOUNTING VERSUS ECONOMIC 1. Accounting costs focus on what the firm spends for all that it buys, or hires, to produce and sell products and services. These costs are largely explicit amounts paid out to factors of production. The principal exception is depreciation of capital goods.

2. Economic costs, sometimes called "real costs," focus on the cost of resources used up by the firm whether or not they must be paid out to others. Economic costs include accounting costs plus all implicit costs.

Some implicit cost may be found by calculating opportunity cost. For the single proprietor, opportunity cost would be the salary for the best comparable managing job he or she could get. If the firm owns the land on which its plant stands it may not be able to charge the rental value to cost, but an economist would include the rent as an implicit cost.

Implicit cost may be cost external to the firm but yet be a social cost, such as the cost of downstream pollution (the value of recreation foregone or fisheries lost) because of a firm's discharge of effluent upstream. It may be the cost to the surrounding community of foul air from a meat packing plant or paper mill. Environmental concern and legislation are causing some of these implicit "external" costs to be converted into accounting costs as firms are forced by community pressure or law to prevent or clean up pollution. See *Implicit Costs, External Costs, Opportunity Cost.*

COUNTERVAILING DUTIES Import duties imposed as a remedy against subsidies paid by foreign governments on products they export. A subsidy lowers the export price and is considered "unfair competition." The duty offsets the subsidy by raising the price of the product at the port of entry. Sometimes subsidies are created for internal political and economic reasons, but they nevertheless have a spillover export effect. See *Subsidy.*

COUNTERVAILING POWER A concept developed by John Kenneth Galbraith to describe the proposition that the existence of power on one side of a market creates a tendency for countervailing power to develop on the other side. The United Automobile Workers union developed in the labor market to face General Motors and other giant automobile manufacturers. The few powerful auto firms face a small number of very large tire firms in the tire market. Large appliance manufacturers face powerful chain stores in the wholesale appliance market. The development of countervailing power limits market power, and Galbraith considered the result generally to be favorable to the consumer. However, it is possible for the holder of countervailing power to share the fruits of monopoly power with the original holder of power, to the detriment of the consumer. Such an outcome could occur when, for example, a powerful union arises to bargain with firms in a highly concentrated industry.

COUPON The *amount* of interest payable on a bond. The name originated in the coupon attached to bonds that is "clipped" off and sent in for payment of interest when payment was due. A *stripped coupon* is a coupon that is separated from the bond and sold as a separate security from the bond. Coupon differs from "yield" which is the *rate* of interest. See *Deep-Discount Bond, Stripped Coupon, Zero-Coupon Bond, Yield Curve.*

CRAFT UNION A labor union composed of workers with a particular trade or skill, e.g., carpenters, electricians, plumbers, or machinists. Some craft unions encompass several closely allied skills. A craft union contrasts with an industrial union, which is organized by plant or firm, enrolling all nonmanagement workers in the workplace whether they are unskilled, semiskilled, or skilled. See *American Federation of Labor–Congress of Industrial Organizations, Industrial Union.*

CREDIT 1. In accounting, a right-side entry in an account in double-entry bookkeeping. 2. In banking, to "credit your account" means to add the amount to your deposit. 3. "Creditworthy" in banking means an ability to borrow and have the amount of the note credited to your deposit account; creditworthy in business means an ability to "charge" a purchase, or postpone payment as a good credit risk. 4. A "line of credit" is the amount one can borrow, the ability to borrow that amount being an asset. 5. In international trade, a credit is any transaction that involves a money inflow from a foreign country. See *Debit*.

CREDIT UNION   A cooperative savings institution which provides consumer credit and mortgage credit for its members. Usually they are identified by members' employment, such as a federal employees' credit union for a given area, and sometimes they are sponsored by employers. Credit unions are chartered and supervised by the National Credit Union Administration. The Depository Institutions Deregulation and Monetary Control Act of 1980 permitted credit unions to offer interest-bearing checking accounts, known as "share-draft" accounts. The required reserves for deposits are now controlled by the Federal Reserve Board under that act. See *Share-Draft Account*.

CREEPING INFLATION   A continual increase in the price level of perhaps 2 or 3% per year. Some economists believe that such a rate is necessary to provide a reasonable trade-off for lower levels of unemployment. Others believe that creeping inflation feeds on itself and can easily turn into galloping inflation.

CROSS ELASTICITY   The responsiveness of the quantity of one product (x) demanded or supplied to a change in the price of *another product* (y). It is a concept used to measure the degree of substitutability or complementarity of one product with another. If grapefruit (x) and oranges (y) are substitutes, an increase in the price of oranges will cause an increase in the quantity of grapefruit demanded as the buyer substitutes grapefruit for the now higher-priced oranges. If the products are complements, an increase in the price of beer (y) will cause a decrease in the quantity of pretzels (x) demanded as the quantity of beer demanded falls.

   Here it makes a difference in interpretation whether the elasticity coefficient is positive or negative, unlike the case of simple elasticity of demand where the minus sign is ignored. A positive sign for cross elasticity indicates the goods are substitutes, while a negative sign indicates they are complements.

Point Cross Elasticity

$$E = \frac{\frac{dQ_x}{Q_x}}{\frac{dP_y}{P_y}} = \frac{dQ_x P_y}{Q_x dP_y}$$

Arc Cross Elasticity

$$E = \frac{\dfrac{Q_{x1} - Q_{x2}}{Q_{x1} + Q_{x2}}}{\dfrac{P_{y1} - P_{y2}}{P_{y1} + P_{y2}}} = \frac{(Q_{x1} - Q_{x2})(P_{y1} + P_{y2})}{(Q_{x1} + Q_{x2})(P_{y1} - P_{y2})}$$

See *Elasticity, Income Elasticity of Demand, Arc Elasticity.*

CROWDING OUT   1. Large amounts of government expenditure may crowd out (prevent) some private investment expenditure for capital goods. If the federal government has the will to purchase resources, it has the ability to do so through its control of the money supply, ability to borrow, and ability to tax. The federal government, therefore, can outbid private business for resources and divert them to government projects, crowding out private business spending by pushing up prices when resources are generally fully employed or when there are shortages of particular resources.

2. Crowding out often is associated with deficit spending by the federal government and the consequent rise in interest rates. Higher interest rates increase the explicit or implicit interest cost of private investment expenditure. Some kinds of potential private investment expenditure will not provide a rate of return sufficient to cover the higher interest cost and so will not be made.

Crowding out may occur whether it is caused by increased government spending for resources or by federal deficits and higher interest rates relative to the marginal efficiency of capital.

CURRENCY   Dollars, francs, pesos, liras, marks, yen. Paper money, generally. In the Federal Reserve System's definition of currency for statistical compilation of the money stock, coins are included as well as paper money. See *Money, Fiat Money, Federal Reserve Note, Greenback.*

CURRENT ACCOUNT   One of two major categories in the international balance of payments, it consists of merchandise trade plus service transactions (transportation, travel, interest and dividend payments, banking and insurance services, and government expenditures) plus unilateral transfers (private remittances and government grants). The other major category is the *capital account.* See *Balance on Current Account, Balance of Payments.*

CURRENT ASSETS   In accounting, assets shown on a firm's balance sheet that are in hand, such as currency and bank accounts, or assets that are convertible into cash within 12 months or within the firm's current operating cycle if longer than a year, such as accounts receivable, bills receivable, etc.

CURRENT DOLLARS The use of current market prices to measure value. For example, *GNP in current dollars* is the total value of all goods and services produced in the economy during a year *at current market prices* for that year. *GNP in constant dollars* is the total value of goods and services produced in the economy for a year *measured at the prices of a year designated as the base year,* i.e., current dollars deflated by an appropriate price index to remove inflation. See *Constant Dollars*.

CURRENT LIABILITIES In accounting, amounts shown on a firm's balance sheet that are owed and due to be paid within 12 months, or within the firm's operating cycle if longer than a year. Examples are taxes, accounts payable to material suppliers, utilities, etc., plus bills and notes payable.

CUSTOMS DUTY A tax on merchandise imports or exports. It may be a *specific tax* consisting of so much money per unit of the product, or it may be an *ad valorem tax* consisting of a percentage of the value of the product. See *Ad Valorem Tax, Specific Tax*.

CUSTOMS UNION Free trade within a group of states with common tariffs, quotas, etc., imposed on trade with outsiders. The European Economic Community is a modern example of a customs union. There has been an ongoing effort toward further integration beyond the initial steps, and in 1992 the EEC will present a common front in trade with the rest of the world as a full-fledged customs union. See *European Community*.

DEBENTURE BOND   An unsecured bond that is backed only by the general assets of the issuer. A general-obligation bond issued by a city, county, or state against its general revenue is a debenture bond. A debenture bond contrasts with a revenue bond, which is backed by revenue from a specific source such as a sewer district or water district. Business firms also issue bonds that are claims against the general assets of the firm; they do not provide a claim against any specific assets such as an airplane or boxcar. See *Bonds, Revenue Bonds*.

DEBIT   1. In accounting, an entry on the left side of an account in double-entry bookkeeping. 2. In banking, to "debit your account" means to subtract the amount from your deposit. 3. In international trade, a debit is any transaction that involves a money outflow to a foreign country. See *Credit*.

DECILE   A scale for classification of data into ten parts from lowest to highest. The first decile is the lowest tenth, with nine-tenths of the data ranked above it. A student ranked in the ninth decile of her class is in the top 10% with nine-tenths ranked lower. See *Percentile, Quartile*.

DECREASING COSTS   As the scale of output grows in a firm or industry, the cost per unit of output (average cost) decreases. A change in scale involves *all* factors of production being variable, including size of plant and management, as well as quantities of labor, materials, and utilities. Hence, decreasing costs are more precisely named decreasing long-run average costs. Also known as economies of scale. See *Constant Costs, Constant Returns, Decreasing Returns to Scale, Economies of Scale, Increasing Costs, Increasing Returns to Scale, Long-Run Average Costs, Natural Monopoly.*

DECREASING RETURNS TO SCALE In a production process, as all inputs are increased in the same proportion, output increases less than proportionally to the increase in inputs. For example, if all inputs increase by 20%, output increases by less than 20%, say, 15%. Decreasing returns occur because some factors of production are rather specialized and not infinitely divisible. Or, management and communication problems may lead to growing inefficiency after some output level or scale of operation is reached. Decreasing returns to scale will lead to increasing long-run average costs unless offset by other factors, such as reduced prices of inputs as larger quantities are purchased.

"Decreasing returns to scale" is a different concept from "diminishing returns" in the Law of Diminishing Returns. Diminishing returns is a short-run concept and refers to a decline in the addition to total output that eventually occurs as successive units of a variable factor of production are added to a given quantity of fixed factors of production, a matter of *variable proportions*, while decreasing returns to scale is a long-run concept, i.e., there are no fixed factors, *all inputs are variable.* See *Constant Costs, Constant Returns, Decreasing Costs, Diminishing Returns, Economies of Scale, Increasing Costs, Increasing Returns to Scale.*

DEEP DISCOUNT BOND A bond that is issued for a fraction of its maturity face value, the difference being interest accumulation over the life of the bond. It may call for some interest payout before maturity. The firm issuing the bonds benefits in its cash flow because it gets the cash it needs and pays out little or nothing until the bonds mature. The bond holder shifts his or her income from normal semiannual interest receipts to an accumulation, most of which is received when the bond is sold or matures.

Before recent tax reform, much of the income from deep-discount bonds might be treated as a capital gain, which benefited those whose top income tax rate exceeded the capital gains rate. Today, the income generally is treated as ordinary interest income, with an annual tax liability based on the proportion of the original-issue discount (OID) attributable to the bond's increase in value during the tax year, whether or not it was received.

Zero-coupon bonds are the extreme form of deep-discount bonds. They pay zero interest during the life of the bond but pay the face value on maturity, with the difference between maturity price and the deeply discounted purchase price representing the total cumulation of compounded interest. See *Original-Issue Discount Security, Discounting, Zero-Coupon Bond.*

DEFICIENCY PAYMENT A payment from the federal government that is received by farmers when market prices for their subsidized crops are below the "target price." The government sets a target price for each subsidized crop (wheat, corn, feed grains, rice, and cotton). If the average market price falls below the target price, a deficiency check is sent to each farmer in the program to make up for the shortfall in sales receipts. In 1990, calculation of payments was based upon the average market price during the 5 months immediately after harvest, which is favorable to the farmer because prices tend to be lowest at that time of year. Before each crop year, farmers must determine whether to enter the subsidy program. In return for the subsidy protection, the government requires that those who do sign up must restrict their planting, and the program covers only a part (the major part) of the planted acreage. The Acreage Reduction Program announced for 1991 applies to 90% of the average crop base. The reduction for wheat is 15%, and 7-1/2% for other grains. Deficiency payments are part of a subsidy program, which differs from a price-support program in not pushing actual market prices above free-market prices. See *Target Price, Price Support, Subsidy.*

DEFICIT SPENDING Spending more than one's income. It usually refers to a government spending in excess of the amount it receives in taxes and fee payments. The U.S. federal government engages in deficit spending either by borrowing the difference or by creating new money. The cumulated annual federal deficits, adjusted for the occasional surpluses, constitute the national debt.

Deficit spending may be a part of fiscal policy in which the government *plans* deficits in order to stimulate the economy during recession or depression. In prosperity, a balancing fiscal policy would call for a government surplus to retard inflation. The U.S. has not pursued such a balanced fiscal policy. Generally, deficits have occurred in the U.S. because of the unwillingness of Congress and the Administration to face the political heat required to balance the budget, i.e., to raise taxes and fees to pay for the desired expenditures or to reduce the level of spending to coincide with revenues. In fact, the U.S. Treasury has run a budget deficit through prosperity and recession in all but 5 years between 1949 and 1989. The most recent surplus was $.3 billion in 1960. See *Budget Deficit, Fiscal Policy, Monetizing the Debt, National Debt.*

DEFLATION   1. A general, but not necessarily uniform or all-encompassing, decline in prices as measured by a price index such as the Consumer Price Index or the Producer Price Index. The opposite of inflation.

2. For statistical data, "deflation" means the adjustment of a time series to convert data expressed in current dollars to data expressed in constant dollars, thereby removing the effects of inflation. The deflation is accomplished by dividing the "current dollars" series by an appropriate price index. See *Constant Dollars, Inflation, Gross National Product Deflator, Price Index, Time Series.*

DEFLATIONARY GAP   The gap that occurs when aggregate demand at full employment (AD_{fe}) in the economy falls short of aggregate supply at full employment (AS_{fe}) because the amount businesses wish to spend for investment in plant, equipment, and inventories (I) at full employment (I_{fe}) is less than those in the economy wish to save (S) at full employment (S_{fe}). Aggregate Supply = Gross National Product (GNP). The shortfall can occur because businesses reduce the amount of their intended investment expenditure and/or because households increase the amount of their saving (reduce the amount of consumption expenditure).

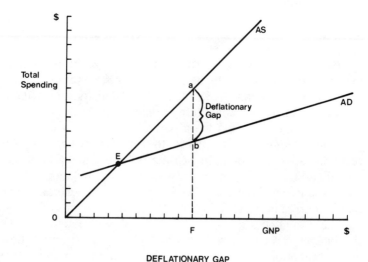

DEFLATIONARY GAP
See: INFLATIONARY GAP

In the diagram (p. 66), the amount of intended spending (AD_{fe}) in billions of dollars is less than the full-employment GNP (AS_{fe}) in billions of dollars. At F (full-employment GNP), there is a shortfall in spending of ab (the deflationary gap) so that the full-employment level of GNP will not be sustained. All that is produced will not be bought and producers will reduce output to the equilibrium at E where AD = AS, at less-than-full-employment GNP. See *Inflationary Gap*.

DEMAND The ability and willingness of buyers to purchase a product or service. The focus of demand analysis usually is on the relationship between quantities demanded and prices of the good or service, *ceteris paribus*. Demand may be expressed as a schedule or curve relating quantities demanded to various possible prices, other elements affecting demand being held constant. (These other elements are described under *Demand for Consumer Goods* and *Demand for Factors of Production*.) In demand analysis, only one of the series of price–quantity possibilities will actually exist at a particular time.

To avoid erroneous conclusions, economists are careful to distinguish a "change in demand" from a "change in quantity demanded." A *change in demand* is caused by a change in some determinant *other than price*. For example, a change in household tastes will change consumer demand, or a change in technology may change a business firm's demand for a factor of production. A change in demand is portrayed by a shift of the entire demand schedule or curve. A *change in quantity demanded*, on the other hand, is caused by a *change in the price of the good or factor itself*. It is illustrated by a movement from one point to another on the same demand schedule or demand curve as illustrated under *Demand Curve*. See *Demand for Consumer Goods, Demand for Factors of Production, Demand Function*. See also *Demand Schedule, Derived Demand, Market Demand Curve*.

DEMAND CURVE A curve illustrating how quantity demanded changes as price changes, *cet. par.* A demand curve is illustrated in panel A (p. 68). It shows a *change in quantity demanded*, that is, a move from a to b along the curve, following a change of price from p_1 to p_2. This curve slopes downward to the right, illustrating that larger quantities are demanded at lower prices, a characteristic that could apply to either household demand for a product or business-firm demand for a factor of production.

Panel B illustrates a *change in demand*, a shift of the demand curve following, for example, a change in tastes for household demand or a change in technology for a firm's demand for a factor of production. See *Demand, Demand Function, Demand Schedule.*

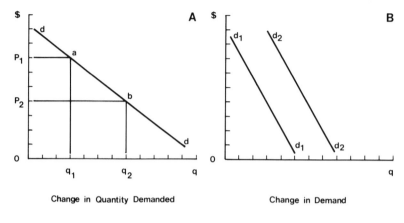

Change in Quantity Demanded   Change in Demand

DEMAND CURVES

DEMAND DEPOSITS   Amounts of money held in commercial banks (the debtors) by depositors (the creditors) subject to withdrawal on demand by the depositors writing checks against the accounts. Also known as checking accounts or transaction accounts (but the latter two terms include other types of deposits).

The Federal Reserve Board ruled in 1978 that interest could be paid to holders of demand deposits (excepting deposits of for-profit corporations) for the first time since the depression of the 1930s. The decision followed experimentation with checkable deposits which carry interest, such as negotiable order of withdrawal (NOW) accounts in federal savings and loan associations and share-draft accounts in credit unions. Today NOW accounts and credit union share-draft accounts usually are called checking accounts and have become indistinguishable from demand deposits of commercial banks in their role as part of the country's money supply. Checking accounts are a major part of the money supply. See *Automatic Transfer Service Accounts, Negotiable Order of Withdrawal, Share-Draft Accounts, Money, M1, Transaction Accounts.*

DEMAND FOR CONSUMER GOODS   Household demand for a product (or service) is a function of the price of the product, the prices of other products and services including the price of money, the income of the buyer, and the buyer's tastes. $D_x = f(P_x, P_n, I, T)$

where D_x is quantity demanded, P_x is the price of x, P_n stands for the prices of other goods and services, I is income, and T is tastes. A demand curve illustrates the relationship between quantity of a product demanded and price of the product, *cet. par.* A change in any of the elements other than price is shown as a shift of the entire demand curve. See *Demand, Demand Curve, Demand Function, Equilibrium of the Firm.*

DEMAND FOR FACTORS OF PRODUCTION   A business firm's demand for a factor of production is a function of the price of the factor, the prices of all other factors of production, input–output relationships (known as the production function), and the price of the firm's product. For example, consider the demand for labor, $D_1 = f(P_1, P_n, I - O, P_x)$, where D_1 is the quantity of labor demanded, P_1 is the price of labor, P_n represents the prices of other factors of production, $I - O$ is the input–output relationships of production, and P_x is the price of the product. A demand curve for a factor of production illustrates the relationship between the quantity of the factor demanded and the price of the factor, *cet. par.* A change in any of the elements other than factor price is shown as a shift in the entire demand curve. See *Demand, Demand Curve, Demand Function, Equilibrium of the Firm: Factor Market.*

DEMAND FOR MONEY   A concept in monetary theories which focuses on the quantity of money demanded in an economy and its relationship to the price of money—the interest rate. The demand for money may be either the *demand for money to hold*, as in the national income analysis of John Maynard Keynes, or the older concept, *demand for money to use* by businesses, consumers, and investors in loanable funds analysis.

1. The *demand for money to hold* consists of a trio of demands. The *transactions demand* for money to hold arises because the timing of income receipts does not coincide perfectly with the flow of expenditures. When receipts occur once a week or once a month some money (which includes checking accounts) must be held for spending through the week or month. Also, businesses must have money in their cash registers to make change. Transactions demand for money to hold will fluctuate with changes in the total volume of income in the economy.

The *precautionary demand* for money to hold arises from the need to respond to uncertain future events, such as a possible tire blowout on an automobile trip, a possible "bargain" in the future, or the possible need to travel because of the death of a close relative in a distant town. It also is a function of income.

The quantity of money held for transactions and precautionary motives has declined as the use of credit cards has substituted for cash or checks in many transactions and has consolidated payments into monthly remittances.

A third category is the *speculative demand* for money to hold. This is the most important demand for money in Keynesian national income analysis. It can be relatively volatile, while transactions demand and precautionary demand tend to change rather slowly over time. If one anticipates that security prices will fall, a person will want to hold assets in the form of money rather than securities. The quantity of money held for speculative purposes depends upon anticipations about the future course of asset prices and the opportunity cost of holding money, that is, the additional interest that money might have earned if the money had been invested in an earning asset other than a checking account. The speculative demand for money to hold is a function of interest rates. The *supply of money* in this analysis is the money stock as determined by the Federal Reserve (the Central Bank). See *M1*.

2. In the traditional *demand for money to use*, or demand for loanable funds concept, demand consists of the amount that consumers want to borrow in order to buy now rather than in the future, plus the amount businesses want to borrow to buy new plant and equipment or to increase inventories. Consumer demand for money to use depends upon how consumers value present consumption versus future consumption, anticipations of the future course of consumer goods prices, anticipations of future income, and the cost of borrowing, i.e., the interest rate. Business demand for money to use depends upon the anticipated rate of profit from the production and sale of goods produced in new plant and equipment or from the changing value of goods in inventory when either is compared with the cost of money (the interest rate). In this analysis, the supply of money consists of the savings that households and businesses are willing to make available at various interest rates plus the bank credit that banks are willing to offer at various interest rates. See *Money Supply*.

DEMAND FUNCTION A mathematical expression relating quantities demanded to those elements which affect the quantity demanded. 1. A household's demand for a product is expressed as: $D_x = f(P_x, P_n, I, T)$ where x is the product, D_x is the quantity of x demanded, P_x is the price of x, P_n stands for the prices of all other related goods and services, I is income, and T is taste. A demand curve, or schedule, is projected on the assumption that P_n, I, and

T remain constant so that D_x varies with changes in P_x, that is, $D_x = f(P_x)$, *cet. par.*

2. A business firm's demand for a factor of production, such as labor, is expressed as: $D_1 = f(P_1, I - O, P_n, P_x)$, where D_1 is the quantity of labor demanded, P_1 is the price of labor (the wage rate), $I - O$ is the input–output relationship among factor inputs and product output (the technological relations among inputs and output, or, the production function), P_n represents the prices of other factors of production, and P_x is the price of the product. A demand curve relating D_1 to P_1 is projected assuming that $I - O$, P_n, and P_x remain constant, that is, $D_1 = f(P_1)$, *cet. par.* See *Demand, Demand Curve.*

DEMAND: INDIVIDUAL DEMAND   The relationship between quantities of a product demanded by a single buying unit (household or firm) and the elements that affect quantity demanded. It usually is expressed as the relationship of quantity demanded to prices of that product, *cet. par.* See *Demand, Demand Function.*

DEMAND: MARKET DEMAND   The relationship between quantities of a product or service demanded and the elements that affect quantity demanded in a market. It usually is expressed as the relationship of quantity demanded and prices of that product or service, *cet. par.,* cumulated for all of the buying units in the market. See *Market, Market Demand Curve.*

DEMAND-PULL INFLATION   Descriptive name for the classic type of inflation. It is used to identify demand-induced inflation, in contrast to the newer concept of "cost-push inflation," which originates from the market power of sellers. Demand-pull inflation is a condition of rapidly rising prices which originates from an excess of quantity demanded relative to quantity supplied in markets where there is no excess capacity, so that demanders, in scrambling for the short supply, bid up prices.

An expanding circle of price increases occurs as rising demand encompasses both resource and product markets. Rising resource prices (from excess demand, not from administered pricing) will increase incomes, which shifts up demand curves for products that resource owners buy, while upward-shifting demand curves for products cause upward-shifting demand curves for factors of production and further increases in their prices (and income).

An "easy money" policy may stimulate the process, as a higher growth rate of the money supply lowers interest cost, which encourages the spending of demanders. Runaway inflation, or hyperinflation, may occur in a frenzy of spending as buyers buy as quickly as possible in expectation of rapid and continuous increases in prices. See *Cost-Push Inflation, Hyperinflation.*

DEMAND SCHEDULE   A numerical representation of the relationship between quantities demanded and prices, when the prices of other products and services, income, and tastes are assumed constant for the household demander. For the business firm, it is the relationship between prices and quantities of a resource demanded, when the prices of other resources (factors of production), input–output relationships of production, and the price of the firm's output are given.

For example:

P ($)	Q
9	1
8	2
7	3
6	5

Note the inverse relationship between price and quantity demanded, which is explained by the Law of Diminishing Marginal Utility or the Law of Diminishing Marginal Rate of Substitution. The inverse relationship also is illustrated by a downward-sloping demand curve. See *Demand, Demand Curve, Marginal Rate of Substitution, Marginal Utility.*

DEPENDENT VARIABLE   A variable element whose changes are caused by changes in other, independent variables within a system. The system describes relationships among independent variables and dependent variables. It thereby identifies the proximate cause of change in the dependent variable. For example, a change in the quantity of wheat demanded (D_w) is caused by a change in the price of wheat (P_w), a change in the price of substitutes or complements for wheat (P_n), a change in household tastes (T), or a change in household income (I). $D_w = f(P_w, P_n, T, I)$. D_w is the dependent variable, while P_w, P_n, T, and I are all independent variables whose changes are caused by factors outside this system. The direction of change and the volume of change in the dependent variable will depend upon the detailed structure of the system, i.e., the specific initiating change in an independent variable and the nature of the functional relationship among the variables. See *Autonomous Variable.*

DEPOSIT INSURANCE   Insurance of deposits in banks, thrifts, and credit unions provided by the Bank Insurance Fund and the Savings

Association Insurance Fund of the Federal Deposit Insurance Corporation and the National Credit Union Share Insurance Fund of the National Credit Union Administration.

In some states, state-chartered banks, thrifts, and credit unions are permitted to insure their deposits with private insurance companies. The population of insured institutions usually is too small for the private companies to survive a large bank failure or several small ones. The result is that depositors are not protected unless the state is willing to step forward to cover the losses. Maryland and Ohio had problems with this in the mid-1980s, and Rhode Island at the beginning of 1991. In the latter case the private insurer was unable to survive one bank failure. The Governor of Rhode Island closed 45 banks and credit unions whose deposits were insured by the company. All but 16 were able to reopen shortly after because they met the standards for admission to federal insurance programs. The 16 that remained closed included some of the larger credit unions. The Governor assured depositors that their deposits would be covered up to $100,000, which could cost the state as much as $1 billion. See *Federal Deposit Insurance Corporation, National Credit Union Administration.*

DEPOSIT MULTIPLIER The multiple by which checking account deposits in banks may increase when the amount in reserve against those deposits increases. It is important for economic policy, particularly monetary policy, because checking accounts are a major portion of the country's money supply; an increase in checking account deposits is an increase in the money supply.

The deposit multiplier is defined as $1/r$, where r is the percentage of bank deposits required as reserves. The money supply can change by a multiplied amount when bank reserve requirements are changed or new money comes into the banking system. Banks must keep a fraction, r, of these checking account deposits as *required reserves* (RR) in vault cash or as deposits at the regional Federal Reserve Banks. Any bank funds kept in these two forms are *legal reserves.* If legal reserves are larger than required, the difference is *excess reserves.* When there are excess reserves, checking deposits in banks holding the excess may expand until deposits equal legal reserves times the deposit multiplier, $1/r$. At that point there is no excess, and legal reserves equal required reserves.

To illustrate how the deposit multiplier works: When loans are made, banks accept notes from the borrowers promising to repay the loans with interest. The loan amount is made available to borrowers by crediting their checking accounts, and the volume of checking deposits (which is a part of the money supply) expands. Banks can expand their loans (and simultaneously their deposits) until their legal reserves equal their required reserves. Banks have an incentive to make personal and commercial loans because the interest rate earned on loans is a major source of bank revenues.

Suppose that the required reserve rate (r) is 10% of checking deposits. The deposit multiplier, $1/r$, then, is $1/0.1 = 10$. If there are excess reserves of $10 billion in the system, banks all together can have new deposits (by making new loans) of $100 billion. If banks expand their loans and acquire $90 billion in new deposits, they still have excess reserves of $1 billion, and checking deposits (money) can still expand by 10 times that amount, or $10 billion.

The simple deposit multiplier, $1/r$, expresses the maximum expansion possible. The *effective* deposit multiplier is more complex because it must account for leakages in the expansion process. Leakages may be caused by a desire for larger holdings of cash as the money supply grows, or by bankers' preferences to hold excess reserves because there are few good credit risks, or by bankers' expectations that interest rates will rise, or by borrowers' reluctance to borrow, or by the flow of some funds into time deposits which have their own different required reserve rate. Estimating each of these leakages involves some uncertainty about peoples' behavior, so that the effective deposit multiplier formula is more complex *and* more difficult to quantify than a simple referral to the required reserve rate would suggest.

The Federal Reserve Board (the Fed) can affect excess reserves, hence the money stock, by changing reserve requirements within the range established by law, by buying or selling Treasury securities in the open market, or by varying the Fed discount rate, which can encourage or discourage the borrowing of reserves by banks. The discount rate has been used more frequently in recent years as a tool to affect the level of excess reserves. The financial community takes a change in the discount rate as a signal that the Fed desires some change in economic activity and reacts accordingly.

If monetary policy calls for expansion of the money supply, an increase of bank reserves by the Fed may not produce the full expansion possible because of the leakages described above. The Fed must calculate the complex deposit multiplier and account for currency and traveler's checks in order to determine the amount that reserves must change to produce a target change in M1. Additional adjustments are necessary if the target is a change in M2. If policy calls for contraction of the money supply, the Fed holds enough Treasury securities to be able to eliminate excess reserves and force contraction by putting them on the market. It may be easier to force contraction than to encourage expansion, but calculation of the change in reserves necessary for a desired reduction in the money supply still is complicated and uncertain. See *Money Multiplier*.

DEPRECIATION   The reduction in value of capital goods due to wearing out, or due to obsolescence because of technological change, or due to a shift of demand away from the product produced by the capital goods. Businesses take into consideration uncertainty associated with such things as technological change and the business cycle when estimating the life of an asset. Depreciation sometimes is referred to as write-off. It is a cost of production representing the using up of a factor of production, capital, over time. For national income accounts, depreciation is called the capital consumption allowance. Economists use reported business accounting figures for depreciation when measuring the capital consumption allowance. See *Capital Consumption Allowance*.

DEPRECIATION OF A NATION'S CURRENCY   1. A fall in the value of one currency in terms of other nations' currencies in trading on foreign exchange markets. Today, with freely fluctuating exchange rates, when foreigners wish to hold fewer dollars the value of the dollar will fall in international currency markets, i.e., the price of the dollar in terms of other currencies will fall as foreigners on balance try to sell more dollars. A dollar then buys fewer marks, francs, or yen. Sometimes, as in mid-1989, there is agreement among the monetary authorities of several nations to enter currency exchanges and sell dollars that they hold in order to prevent a rise in the value of the dollar on foreign exchange markets when the rise is seen as a destabilizing influence on trade. See *Dirty Float*.

   2. A second meaning of "depreciation of a nation's currency" is largely internal to a particular country. A fall in the value of a nation's currency results when *inflation* reduces the amount of goods and services that each unit of money, say a dollar, will buy. Each dollar is not worth as much in terms of domestic goods and services as it was before the price increases. See *Devaluation, Dollar Surplus*.

DEPRESSION   The bottom, or trough phase of the business cycle when that bottom is unusually low. Some, such as Joseph Schumpeter (1883–1950), reserve the term for the phase of the cycle from trend line to trough, with the other three phases being revival from trough to trend line, prosperity from trend line to peak, and recession from peak to trend line. Today the term generally is reserved for a state of the economy which has very substantial unemployment of labor, many factories idle or producing well below capacity, and strong downward pressure on prices. The period from 1929 to 1933 in the U.S. is an extreme example of depression.

Less severe downturns in economic activity are called recessions, a label that is not as scary and so might be less likely to cause further constriction in spending by households and businesses. Such sensitivity toward possible adverse psychological effects was evident when, at the end of 1990, Federal Reserve Chairman Alan Greenspan even avoided use of the term "recession" and instead spoke of "a meaningful downturn in aggregate output." See *Business Cycles, Recession.*

DEREGULATION   The reduction or elimination of governmental controls and rules regulating the behavior of firms in an industry. Deregulation and regulatory reform developed momentum in the U.S. in the Nixon administration and continued apace in the administrations of Ford, Carter, and Reagan. The deregulation that occurred during those years has been referred to as *economic deregulation* because it involved returning to a reliance on competition in markets to control prices and quantities rather than reliance on laws and commission rules. At the same time that economic regulation was declining, a new regulatory movement was under way in the form of *protective regulation,* designed to protect people from the social consequences of production with legislation to provide clean air, clean water, occupational safety and health, equal employment opportunity, consumer products safety, etc.

Deregulation, primarily in the form of reduced regulation rather than its complete elimination, occurred in a wide variety of industries, including airlines (the favorite example of proponents in the years immediately following the deregulation), banking and especially thrifts, broadcasting, natural gas, railroads, stock brokerage, telephones, and trucking. The apex of the deregulatory "supply-side" movement perhaps was reached in 1980 with major regulatory reform legislation affecting such industries as trucking, railroads, and banking, and with the agreement to break up the American Telephone and Telegraph Company under court supervision.

The Motor Carrier Act of 1980 provided easier entry by independent truckers and reduced rate, route, and backhaul regulation. The result was a huge influx of new truckers (11,000 in 3 years), price and service benefits for shippers, and low profits or bankruptcy for many trucking firms. The Staggers Rail Act of 1980 loosened the regulation of railroad freight rates, which moderately increased intraindustry competition and, with the Motor Carrier Act, realigned traffic between rails and trucks with rates more closely reflecting costs.

The Depository Institutions Deregulation and Monetary Control Act (DIDMCA) provided for the gradual elimination of interest rate regulation, opened up new kinds of liabilities available to thrifts such as negotiable orders of withdrawal (interest-bearing checking accounts), and freed thrifts to some extent in the types of loans they can make (assets they can hold). That act plus the Garn–St. Germaine bill of 1982 introduced new and complex kinds of activity to thrift management and attracted a number of shady operators looking for the "fast buck." Some thrift managers, while honest, did not develop staffs with enough expertise to perform well in the newly available activities. Reduced appropriations for bank examiners despite the expanded need for them and pressure by some Congressmen on regulators to ease up on some campaign contributors together provided further opportunity for the disaster that materialized in the thrift industry debacle at the end of the decade.

Some deregulation occurred in the telephone industry prior to 1980 as competitors were permitted to enter the long-lines (long-distance) service and produce telephones and private exchange equipment. The culmination in the process of opening up competition came with the 1980 agreement between AT&T and the Justice Department to break up the Bell System into 7 independent regional organizations of some 22 member telephone service companies. The AT&T breakup stimulated competition in the manufacture of phones and other terminal equipment, in the provision of long-lines service, in data transmission, and in directories with "yellow pages." The result has been cheaper equipment, lower long-distance rates, higher local rates, and more directories than the average householder wants.

The airline industry has lost some of its luster as the epitome of deregulation. Airline ticket fares fell with the entry of many new competitors and have become complex with a wide variety of special fares. Many airlines have failed and the consolidation of lines progresses. Prices for travel between a few major terminals are lower, while those boarding at small airports often pay higher fares. Flight frequency has improved, while service on the planes has deteriorated, producing a kind of hidden inflation.

Deregulation in this era has had mixed results as noted in the examples presented above. Results are similarly mixed in other industries than those considered here, yet it is clear that, even where some "reregulation" may be needed, there continue to be areas where the market does or would do a better job of controlling business practices than government regulation has done.

DERIVED DEMAND   1. The demand for factors of production is derived from the demand for products and services. Business firms demand factors of production only because there is an anticipated demand for what the factors produce. See *Demand, Marginal Physical Product, Marginal Revenue Product, Total Revenue Product.*

2. The demand for one good which is derived from demand for another good. For example, the demand for pretzels is derived (partly) from the demand for beer. The demand for gasoline is derived from demand for transportation by automobile. The demand for diesel fuel is derived from the demand for shipment of goods by truck, the demand for farm produce whose production uses tractors, etc. (themselves a derived demand), and the demand for highways whose construction uses earth movers, graders, etc. (and whose demand also is derived). See *Complementary Goods, Cross Elasticity.*

DEVALUATION   1. A reduction in the value of one nation's money in terms of other nations' money, which is caused by a governmental declaration of the reduction under a fixed exchange-rate international monetary system. When the dollar, for example, is devalued it buys fewer francs, marks, pounds, yens, etc. When countries were on the gold standard devaluation would occur by a government declaring an increase in the price of gold. In 1933, Congress and the President of the United States declared that one ounce of gold was worth $35 rather than the previous $20. All other currencies related to gold were now worth more dollars (per franc, mark, or yen) than before. Conversely, the dollar would buy fewer units of the foreign currencies. See *Gold Standard.*

2. A reduction in the value of one nation's money in terms of other nations' money caused by governmental action under a floating exchange-rate system. For example, when the government of the U.S. enters a foreign exchange market to sell dollars, that will increase the supply of dollars and tend to reduce the value of the dollar in terms of other nations' currency. It is an action that might be taken to correct a trade imbalance by encouraging imports and discouraging exports. See *Depreciation of a Nation's Currency, Dirty Float, Flexible Exchange Rates, Run on the Dollar.*

DIFFERENTIATED OLIGOPOLY   A market characterized by a small number of interdependent firms whose products are not identical with one another but are relatively close substitutes. A firm in this type of oligopoly constantly tries to increase the real or perceived differences between its product and the similar products of other firms in order to increase its sales. Some price differences may be maintained when product differentiation is successfully established. Examples are the automobile industry, the cigarette industry, or the tire industry. See *Differentiated Product, Oligopoly, Homogeneous Oligopoly, Nonprice Competition.*

DIFFERENTIATED PRODUCT A product that has real or imagined differences from other similar products in a market; the products are not homogeneous. Firms use design, ''secret'' ingredients, packaging, and advertising to try to increase the perceived differences among products in a market. A large proportion of the advertising industry is devoted to identifying or creating these differences for products that are highly substitutable for one another. The goal is to create consumer loyalty and thus maintain or increase the demand for the advertised product. Differentiated products may be found in an oligopoly market such as that described above under *differentiated oligopoly* or they may be found in markets characterized by monopolistic competition. Examples of the latter are cold remedies, many household items, and services in convenience stores, drug stores, etc., in large cities. See *Differentiated Oligopoly, Monopolistic Competition.*

DIMINISHING MARGINAL RATE OF SUBSTITUTION A ''law'' in the indifference curve theory of consumer demand, which uses the substitution of one good for another to illustrate that each additional unit of a product will be of less value to a consumer than the previous unit. Starting with a small amount of good x and a large amount of good y, the consumer is asked how much y he or she would be willing to give up for one more unit of x to provide a new combination of x and y that would maintain the same level of consumer satisfaction as the old combination. A whole array of xy combinations is established which provide equal satisfaction—the consumer is ''indifferent'' as to which combination he or she has.

As an individual substitutes successive units of product x for quantities of product y, he or she will be willing to give up smaller quantities of y for each additional unit of x as the substitution of x for y progresses. This reflects the *diminishing* marginal rate of substitution of x for y. Investigators discover that when a person has a large amount of y relative to x, there is a willingness to give up a rather large amount of the plentiful y to get another unit of the scarce x, while holding the total level of satisfaction constant. As substitution of x for y progresses, the person will have larger and larger amounts of x and smaller and smaller amounts of y. For the subject to maintain the same level of satisfaction, one expects an unwillingness to give up as much y for each added unit of x, as y becomes more scarce and x more plentiful.

Of course, the analysis relates only to goods and services that are to some extent substitutable. It would not work for goods that are complementary to one another nor when one of the goods is disliked. An addictive good might show an *increasing* marginal rate of substitution.

Diminishing marginal rate of substitution is illustrated as the slope of the indifference curve and is expressed by its convex shape. It provides the reason for the downward slope of the demand curve, illustrating that more of a product will be demanded only if price falls. See *Diminishing Marginal Utility, Indifference Curve, Marginal Rate of Substitution.*

DIMINISHING MARGINAL RATE OF TECHNICAL SUBSTITUTION In analysis of the firm, an isoquant curve illustrates the substitution of two factors of production, say, labor (l) and machines (m), that is possible from a technical or engineering perspective, while holding output of the product constant. Generally, as l is substituted for m in successive combinations of the two factors of production, the firm will be required to give up less and less m for each additional unit of l in a new combination of l and m that will provide the same level of total output as the previous combination. The isoquant curve is convex. This is the Law of Diminishing Marginal Rate of Technical Substitution. See *Isoquant Curve, Marginal Rate of Technical Substitution, Isoquant–Isocost Equilibrium.*

DIMINISHING MARGINAL UTILITY This "law" in the marginal utility theory of consumption states that as an individual consumes more and more of a good in a given time period, the satisfaction derived from each additional unit will be less than the satisfaction from the preceding unit. This reasoning provides the basis for the downward slope of the demand curve, illustrating that more of a product will be demanded only if price falls. Introspection tends to support this diminishing satisfaction at the margin. A major exception to the law is an addictive drug such as heroin, cocaine, or "crack." The law would hold for a disliked product in that an increase in dissatisfaction as more is consumed constitutes a decrease in satisfaction.

The difficulty of empirical verification and quantification associated with trying to measure changes in amounts of satisfaction led to the development of the law of diminishing marginal rate of substitution, which also has some difficulties of empirical verification. See *Diminishing Marginal Rate of Substitution, Marginal Utility, Indifference Curve, Paradox of Value.*

DIMINISHING RETURNS This "law" in the analysis of production, sometimes known as the law of variable proportions, states that as more and more units of a variable factor of production are added to a given quantity of fixed factors, a point will be reached where the addition to total output attributable to each added unit of the variable factor will be less than the output from adding the preceding unit of the variable factor. If the law did not operate, it would be possible to feed the world simply by adding more seed, labor, and fertilizer to a plot of land of fixed size, say, Yankee Stadium. In the diagram below, diminishing returns commence at point A with the addition of the nth unit of labor. Note that each unit of labor beyond $0n$ continues to add to output until the xth unit of labor, when the additions to output become negative and the stage of negative returns is reached, beyond B.

See *Increasing Returns to Scale, Marginal Physical Product.*

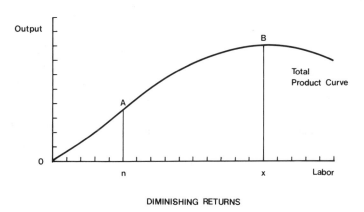

DIMINISHING RETURNS

DIRTY FLOAT An international exchange system which involves freely floating currency values in the foreign exchange markets, but governments step in occasionally to stabilize the value of their currency so that the float is not entirely free. A clean float exists when there is no intervention in the market. See *Clean Float, Flexible Exchange Rates.*

DISCOUNTING The process of reducing the value of an amount of money to be received in the future to its present value. The present value is lower because money in hand now can earn interest over the period between now and the time of a future receipt. If the interest rate is 6% per year, $100 today would be worth $106 in a year. Likewise, $106 to be received in 1 year is worth only $100 today. Because of interest on interest, compounded annually, $112.36 to be received in 2 years is worth $100 today at a 6% annual rate of interest. Discounting is used for cost–benefit analysis and for marketing loans and other debt instruments. It is the opposite of compounding. See *Compound Interest, Cost–Benefit Analysis, Discount Rate*.

DISCOUNT RATE 1. An interest rate which reduces the amount provided to a borrower below the face value of a note by the amount of interest. A person would want to receive more than $100 a year from today in exchange for $100 today because of the interest that could be earned with the money. If the interest rate is 6% per year, $100 in hand today could earn $6 in interest over the next year, becoming $106. Therefore, $106 to be received in 1 year is worth only $100 today. A bank in these circumstances would loan a customer $100 in return for a note promising to pay the bank $106 in 1 year. This process discounts a future receipt by the interest rate (the discount rate) in order to establish its present value.

2. "*The* Discount Rate" refers to the rate of interest at which loans from the U.S. Federal Reserve System to member banks are discounted. It is one of several monetary policy tools that may be used to try to stimulate or slow down economic activity. If the rate is raised, banks are discouraged from renewing loans or contracting new loans from the Federal Reserve. This restricts members' reserves against checking accounts which in turn restricts loans by the member banks that create checking account money. The raising or lowering of the Discount Rate has become an important signal of the Fed's monetary policy position to bankers and others, especially foreigners, interested in the behavior of the U.S. economy. See *Monetary Policy, Checking Account.*

DISINFLATION A synonym for deflation. See *Deflation.*

DISINTERMEDIATION The withdrawal of deposits in a depository institution to seek higher interest rates when rates on deposits are controlled. It occurred to some extent when the Federal Reserve's Regulation Q permitted higher rates for time deposits in savings institutions (thrifts) than for time deposits in commercial banks. During the inflation of the late 1970s, disintermediation created a crisis for savings institutions because savings accounts were their major source of funds for home mortgages. Deposits were with-drawn from federal savings and loan associations, where interest rates on deposits were limited by law, in order to invest funds directly in treasury bills at higher interest rates. Funds also flowed into money market mutual funds which grew rapidly because their interest rates also were not restricted. This disintermediation inhib-ited the flow of funds into housing. The loss of funds was offset in part when the Federal Home Loan Bank System became a major source of funds, making a larger amount of advances (loans) avail-able to its member savings institutions.

The Depository Institutions Deregulation Act of 1980 provided for the gradual elimination of limits on the maximum rates of interest and dividends that may be paid on deposits and accounts of deposi-tory institutions.

DISINVESTMENT   A decline in the total stock of capital goods in an economy. This negative net investment occurs when gross invest-ment expenditure is less than replacement investment so that the economy is not fully replacing the machines and buildings that are wearing out and/or the inventory that is worked off. See *Capital Consumption Allowance.*

DISPOSABLE PERSONAL INCOME   In national income accounting, disposable personal income (DPY) is the amount received during a period of time by households, which they then have available to spend or save. It may be determined by subtracting from Net Na-tional Product (NNP) all indirect business taxes, social security taxes, corporate profits taxes, personal income taxes, and retained earnings of corporations and then adding government transfer pay-ments.

DISSAVING   Spending more than one's current disposable income, as many red-blooded Americans do with their multiple charge cards, car loans, recreational vehicle loans, etc. Dissaving results in draw-ing down accumulated savings, or creating net debt. See *Disposable Personal Income.*

DISTRIBUTION   1. In economics, the allocation of the product of society among the factors of production in the form of wages, interest, rent, and profit. Distribution is one of three categories of activity studied in economics, the others being *production* and *consumption.* A more precise name is "functional distribution."

2. Measurement of the proportion of total income in a society going to each percentage of the population, ranking the population

from poorest to richest. For example, in one society the poorest 10% of the people receive 2% of society's total income, while the richest 10% receive 30% of the income. A measure of the equality or inequality of income distribution of society. See *Lorenz Curve*.

3. In business, distribution may refer to the channels through which goods move from manufacturer to consumer. In some cases, retailers deal directly with manufacturers. In other cases there are intermediaries, including brokers and wholesalers, who stand between producer and consumer.

DISUTILITY A characteristic of a good whose consumption produces a negative reaction. Some goods, such as poison ivy, may have an innate disutility. Other goods have utility when consumed in moderate amounts, but disutility for those units consumed beyond the point of satiation, such as the fifteenth dill pickle eaten in a day (or for some, only the second). See *Utility, Marginal Utility*.

DIVERSIFICATION 1. The characteristic of a business firm which offers for sale a variety of goods whose seasonal and cyclical sales patterns are different, so that net income tends to be stabilized over time for the enterprise as a whole.

2. Holding a variety of securities of business firms and governments in an investment portfolio to try to stabilize income and reduce risk of loss over time.

DIVIDEND An amount of net earnings (profits) periodically distributed by firms to their stockholders. Often the distribution is quarterly. A dividend usually represents a portion of recent net earnings, the remainder being held by the company as retained earnings (undistributed profit). Occasionally, a firm will pay out 100% of net earnings for the past period. Sometimes a firm will distribute more than 100% of recent profits when it wishes to maintain its image by paying a steady dividend amount even though profits are negative (a euphemism for losses) for the period.

Some stocks carry no dividend. All profits are plowed back into the company to finance growth. The value of assets that each share represents will increase, which may or may not be reflected in the market price of the stock. See *Stock*.

DIVISION OF LABOR The breaking down of a job into more and more minute parts and motions so that a worker can repeat the simplified act more skillfully, with less waste motion, and with less interruption in moving from one production step to the next. Labor-hour output increases and it becomes easier to conceive mechanization of the process. It is one of the sources of increased efficiency identified by Adam Smith (1723–1790), who saw division of labor as an outgrowth of increases in the size of markets and consequent growth in the size of production units. It is identified as a cause for "economies of scale."

DOLLAR SURPLUS   A situation in which the amount of dollars offered for sale in foreign exchange markets exceeds the amount of dollars demanded at existing prices. Thus other currencies rise in price in terms of dollars; more dollars are required to buy a pound, mark, or yen. Conversely, each pound, mark, or yen will buy more dollars. A dollar surplus may be caused by a deficit in the balance of payments of the United States and/or a reduced willingness of foreigners to hold assets in dollar accounts because of expected inflation in the U.S., or expected decline in interest rates, etc. See *Balance-of-Payments Deficit, Devaluation, Depreciation of a Nation's Currency.*

DUMPING   In international trade, the sale of goods abroad at prices below the cost of production and/or below domestic prices. It may occur to invade markets that have been difficult to enter. Or, it may be used to discourage the development or continued production of the goods in another country. Or, it may reflect an effort to lower the cost of production by expansion of output where there are economies of scale and thereby increase profits on domestic sales. In this latter case it may be marginal cost pricing, but marginal cost is below average cost until output can expand.

Producers in the dumpee country will try to retaliate by pressing for tariffs, import quotas, and other prohibitions aimed at the dumper.

DUOPOLY   A market consisting of two rival sellers who, consequently, are interdependent; i.e., an action by one firm will so affect the other firm that it will tend to react. For example, a price reduction by one firm will tend to cause a price reduction or an increase in advertising expenditure by the other firm in an effort to avoid losing customers. The actual or potential instability in such a market would lead the two sellers to seek ways to cooperate to achieve monopolylike profits without running afoul of antitrust action by the government. See *Bilateral Duopoly, Duopsony.*

DUOPSONY   A market consisting of two rival buyers who, consequently, are interdependent; i.e., an action by one buyer will tend to elicit a reaction by the other in self-protection. See *Bilateral Duopoly, Duopoly.*

DURABLE GOODS Goods that have a life extending more than 3 years. Capital goods such as buildings, machines, and many types of equipment are examples, as are many consumer goods, such as automobiles, dishwashing machines, video cassette recorders, and ovens. Durable goods usually wear out gradually and can be kept in service by growing amounts of maintenance and repair, so that decisions about their replacement can be postponed or speeded up. A secondhand market increases the flexibility of decision making about maintenance versus replacement or about a large expenditure for a new unit versus a lower expenditure for a used unit. Variation in expenditure for new durable goods is an important contributor to business cycles. See *Depreciation, Obsolescence.*

DURABLE POWER OF ATTORNEY A legal document which entitles another person to act on one's behalf on legal and financial matters. It is durable because it continues on if one becomes physically or mentally incapacitated.

EARNED INCOME   Income from work in the form of wages and salaries. All other kinds of income—interest, rent, and dividends from profits—are unearned income by omission. This is a U.S. Internal Revenue Service definition, perhaps the only occasion when the IRS agrees with socialists and communists. The designation causes some to gnash their teeth because "unearned" seems synonymous with "undeserved." Perhaps to avoid the implication, some businesses prefer to use the term "net earnings" as more respectable than "profits." Some senior citizens are irate because "earned income" from work reduces Social Security receipts until age 70, while "fat-cats" receiving interest, rent, and dividends are not penalized. Earned income is the source of Social Security tax revenue collected from employers, employees, and the self-employed.

ECONOMIC DEVELOPMENT   The process of increasing output per capita, hence potential improvement in economic well-being. It is potential because well-being depends upon what the greater productivity is used for. Given the land area of a country, economic development can occur with increases in the quality and quantity of capital goods and the quality of the labor force. Education and technological change are great driving forces of economic growth.

   Less developed countries can experience great strides in economic development by acquiring more and better capital goods as well as by more education and training of the labor force. They usually lack social-overhead capital, such as efficient transportation and communication systems, and need more as a prerequisite for growth. Economically developed countries already have a substantial capital base and tend to rely more upon invention and discovery, translated into innovation, as the sources for further development. See *Economic Growth, Innovation, Less Developed Countries, Social-Overhead Capital.*

ECONOMIC GOOD   Any good or service that is scarce and that can satisfy wants directly as a consumer good or indirectly as a good in the production process. If a good is desirable and scarce, it will have a market value as compared to a *free good* such as the air we breathe. Even air may become an economic good. Sometimes air is foul and must be cleaned, or it is the wrong temperature and must be heated or cooled. See *Free Good.*

ECONOMIC GROWTH   The process by which an economy increases its ability to produce goods and services as measured by output. Immediate causes of economic growth are (1) an increase in the quantity of capital goods, and (2) the introduction of new techniques of production and new kinds of machines. Long-run causes of growth are research and invention, population growth, and improved education. Population growth may increase total output, but the other causes also increase productivity (labor-hour output) and provide the potential for increases in *per capita* growth, hence economic well-being. Numerous theories of economic growth include those by Adam Smith, Karl Marx, Joseph Schumpeter, Roy Harrod, E. D. Domar, and Franco Modigliani. See *Economic Development.*

ECONOMIC RENT   A payment above the supply price or opportunity cost for the use of a resource that is fixed in supply. The payment, therefore, is above the minimum amount necessary to assure the continued supply of that factor of production. *Pure* economic rent is the price of a factor of production whose supply is perfectly inelastic. The price, then, is completely a function of demand, i.e., "what the traffic will bear." Because the supply exists and cannot be increased, there is no effective current cost of production. The *Mona Lisa* painting by Leonardo da Vinci is singular. There will never be another. Its supply price is a vertical straight line at unit 1 on a supply diagram. Its price is determined by where that line is crossed by a demand curve. In the figure below, the vertical axis measures price in units of $200,000, while the horizontal axis measures the number of Mona Lisa paintings, namely one.

The limitation of supply may be temporary or permanent, so the ability to extract economic rent also may be temporary or

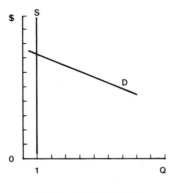

PURE ECONOMIC RENT

permanent. Economic rent may be identified for land in limited supply, a capital good in limited supply, or a particular quality of labor in limited supply. A portion of the income of a superstar athlete may be considered economic rent as it stems from a limited supply of rare natural ability. See *Rent, Quasi-Rent*.

ECONOMICS The study of the way society allocates scarce resources for the production, distribution, and consumption of goods and services. It is concerned with how societies answer the basic economic questions of (1) what goods and services to produce, (2) how to produce them, and (3) for whom in society the goods and services are to be produced.

ECONOMICS: THE DISMAL SCIENCE Economics was called "the dismal science" by the Scottish historian Thomas Carlyle (1795–1881). Parson/economist Thomas Malthus (1766–1834) had expounded his theory of population, and its implications for wage theory and standards of living were accepted by prominent economists of the time. Malthus believed that there is a tendency for population to grow at geometric rates (for example 1, 2, 4, 8), while the food supply grows at arithmetic rates (1, 2, 3, 4). The population tends to outgrow the food supply, so that periods of economic growth which raise living standards above subsistence are temporary because population will grow to absorb the increased sustenance. Wars, pestilence, and especially famine serve ultimately to keep population in check.

Economists used the population theory as the basis of a theory of wages which held that wages tend toward a subsistence level. In the economy, falling wages as population grows and rising food prices as more people try to buy food will keep the population at the margin of subsistence. The science that discovered this dismal outcome was labeled the dismal science. There are some countries today that sadly seem to bear out the theory. But there are other countries where the population has lived well above subsistence for a very extended period of time.

Carlyle also considered economics the dismal science because of other long-run constrictions, such as David Ricardo's (1772–1823) projection of declining profits and the projection of declining economic growth by both Ricardo and John Stuart Mill (1806–1873).

Today some would call economics the dismal science because, contrary to the popular belief of the 1960s that we can have it all, choices are indeed necessary in the face of relative scarcity. And economics identifies the need to choose among "bads" as well as among goods. For example, to solve the federal budget deficit problem in the U.S., it will be necessary for Congress and the President either to reduce federal expenditures for goods and services provided to constituents or to raise revenues by raising taxes or fees that people pay. Polls have shown neither choice, nor any combination, to be popular. Only in the long run would encouragement of economic growth, a good, possibly help to solve the budget problem, a bad. There is no free lunch.

ECONOMIES OF SCALE   Decreases in average costs as manufacturing plants and firms grow larger, i.e., falling long-run average costs when all factor inputs are increased. This situation may occur because some kinds of equipment are very large in their minimum efficient size. Or, different and more efficient arrangements and techniques of production may be utilized as the plant or firm grows larger. Adam Smith identified specialization and division of labor as causes of economies of scale. See *Division of Labor, Increasing Returns to Scale, Long-Run Average Cost.*

EDGE ACT CORPORATIONS   Federally chartered corporations authorized by the Edge Act of 1919 (an amendment to the Federal Reserve Act of 1913). Edge Act corporations may engage in financing international trade and investment with fewer restrictions than apply to federal commercial banks engaged in domestic banking. For example, the restrictions on branch banking are relaxed to permit U.S. banks to have a subsidiary in another state to carry on international banking. Subsequent legislation permits foreign banks to set up Edge Act corporations and expands the powers of U.S. Edge Act corporations.

ELASTICITY   Usually refers to price elasticity, which is a measure of the responsiveness of quantity demanded, or supplied, to a change in price. It is expressed as a percentage change in quantity relative to a percentage change in price.

The formula for price elasticity is:

$$E = \frac{\text{percentage change in } Q_x}{\text{percentage change in } P_x}$$

or:

$$E = \frac{\dfrac{Q_2 - Q_1}{Q}}{\dfrac{P_1 - P_2}{P}}$$

By working with percentage changes, it is possible to compare different products for their sensitivity of demand (or supply) to price changes. Percentage change also avoids the distortion that can occur from choice of different quantity units (pounds versus ounces per dollar) or different price units (cents versus dollars per pound). The coefficient for elasticity of demand is negative because the relationship between price and quantity is negative, but in this instance economists usually ignore the sign.

The elasticity formula shown above applies to *point elasticity*, i.e., to price and quantity changes that are infinitesimal variations about a point on a demand or supply curve. But, when the price change is a discrete amount, selection of the initial P for the denominator in the price section of the equation will produce a different elasticity coefficient than if the second P is chosen. A similar problem may exist with the choice of Q for the denominator in the quantity section. For these cases of *arc elasticity* (rather than point elasticity), economists have adopted the convention of averaging the P's and the Q's for the denominators, so that:

$$E = \frac{\dfrac{Q_2 - Q_1}{\dfrac{Q_1 + Q_2}{2}}}{\dfrac{P_1 - P_2}{\dfrac{P_1 + P_2}{2}}} = \frac{\dfrac{Q_2 - Q_1}{Q_1 + Q_2}}{\dfrac{P_1 - P_2}{P_1 + P_2}}$$

$$= \frac{(Q_2 - Q_1)(P_1 + P_2)}{(Q_1 + Q_2)(P_1 - P_2)}$$

Mind your P's and Q's!

See *Arc Elasticity, Cross Elasticity, Income Elasticity of Demand.*

ELASTICITY OF DEMAND   The sensitivity of quantity demanded to changes in price. More precisely, the percentage change in quantity demanded relative to the percentage change in price. Price elasticity of demand is negative because the relationship between price and quantity is negative, that is, a reduction in price results in an *increase* in quantity demanded, while an increase in price results in a *decrease* in quantity demanded (except in the limiting case of perfectly inelastic demand). Economists assume the reader's knowledge that the relationship is negative and use the absolute value, ignoring the sign when considering price elasticity of demand. (Elasticity of supply is a *positive* relationship.)

Price elasticity of demand provides a guide to what happens to total revenue when price changes. When the elasticity coefficient is greater than 1, the percentage change in quantity exceeds the percentage change in price. The quantity demanded is relatively sensitive to price changes, or elastic. A price reduction will increase total revenue for the firm, and a price increase will reduce total revenue.

When the coefficient is less than 1, quantity demanded is relatively insensitive to price changes, or inelastic. A price increase will *increase* total revenue and a price decrease will *decrease* total revenue.

When the percentage change in quantity demanded equals the percentage change in price, the elasticity coefficient equals 1. This is called *unit elasticity*, and total revenue to the seller (or total outlay for the buyer) will not change with a change in price.

Whether a price change is good for the firm's profit depends upon the change in total cost when quantity changes as well as the price elasticity of demand and its effect on total revenue.

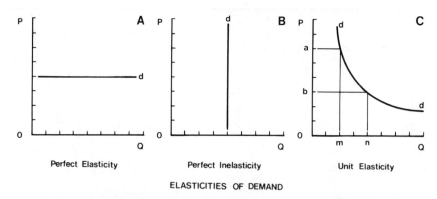

ELASTICITIES OF DEMAND

Perfectly elastic demand, at one extreme, may be illustrated by a demand curve that is a horizontal straight line from the vertical price axis at the market price (panel A above). The total possible quantity available will be demanded at the going price, so a price reduction could not elicit greater demand. A slight increase in price would cause demand to fall to zero. Perfectly inelastic demand, at the other extreme, may be illustrated by a demand curve that is a vertical straight line at the fixed quantity (panel B) indicating zero change in quantity demanded along the horizontal axis when price changes along the vertical axis. A demand curve of unit elasticity is a rectangular hyperbola (panel C) i.e., the area of the rectangle lying below each point on the curve is the same as the area of rectangles described under every other point.

ELASTICITY OF SUPPLY The sensitivity of quantity supplied to changes in price. More precisely, the percentage change in quantity supplied relative to the percentage change in price. Price elasticity of supply is positive because an increase in price leads to an increase in quantity supplied except in the limiting case of perfectly inelastic supply. Perfectly inelastic supply may be illustrated by a vertical straight line (panel A below), indicating that there is no change in quantity supplied when price changes. This will hold true for a price increase when in the short run it is not possible to increase output, as in a local market for fresh vegetables. In the longer run, when output can adjust (or vegetables can be brought in from afar), price increases will lead to some increase in quantity supplied.

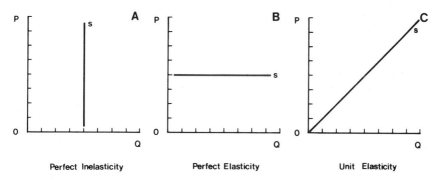

ELASTICITIES OF SUPPLY

Perfectly elastic supply is illustrated by a horizontal supply curve (panel B) showing that within the range of possible output all will be supplied that can be provided. An increase in price cannot elicit more, and a slight reduction in price will cause quantity supplied to drop to zero. Unit elasticity of supply is illustrated as a straight line from the origin bisecting the quadrant at 45% (panel C).

Elasticity of supply depends upon the character of the cost of production and distribution of a product as output changes.

EMBARGO A prohibition on the movement of goods. It might be a governmental prohibition such as the U.S. embargo on the shipment of arms and certain high-technology goods to the Soviet Union. Or the United Nations embargo in 1990 of oil shipments and other goods out of Iraq and all but minimum food shipments into Iraq following its seizure of Kuwait.

A private embargo occurs when, for example, members of the Teamsters union refuse to cross another union's picket line to pick up or deliver goods.

ENDOGENOUS CHANGE A change that originates within an economic system and causes other changes within the system. An example is the failure of a large financial center bank because of falling real estate values when the economy is on the brink of recession. The failure might be sufficient to plunge the economy into the recession as repercussions flow into the production side of the economy through substantial financial center reactions. For example, credit might tighten as other banks review their credit policies to look more carefully at the risk factor in prospective loans and write off a larger amount of their poorly performing loans. The result can be an adverse effect on business investment expenditure. The opposite of *Exogenous Change*.

ENTREPRENEUR An introducer, developer, or organizer of new methods and new things in the economy, as distinguished from the manager of an established routine business. A person who performs creatively by organizing production in new ways or introducing new products, services, tools, machines, and so on into the production process. An introducer rather than inventor, although one person might do both. An entrepreneur might provide some of the needed funds or might rely entirely on others for funds. In the economist's theory of income distribution, an entrepreneur earns profit. Managerial activities of routine supervision and direction earn wages or salary. Providers of funds (lenders) earn interest. Owners of scarce resources earn rent.

ENTREPRENEURSHIP A fourth factor of production added to labor, land, and capital. Introduced by J. B. Say and adopted as a key concept by Joseph A. Schumpeter for his theory of economic development, entrepreneurship is responsible for much of what is dynamic in an economy. It is the identification of the economic promise of something new, plus the marshaling of funds and productive factors to put the new thing or method into production. See *Innovation, Technological Change*.

ENVELOPE CURVE   See *Long-Run Average Cost Curve*.

EQUILIBRIUM   A balance of forces in an economic system which will continue the existing relationships and results until a change is introduced from outside the system. A state of no change over time. For example, an equilibrium market price is one which tends to remain the same until other variables in the market, such as tastes or technology, change to disturb the equilibrium. The system, hence the equilibrium, may be partial, involving a part of the economy such as a firm or household or market. Or the system may be general, encompassing an entire national economy.

A stable equilibrium is one toward which the system will move if it gets away from equilibrium for some reason. An unstable equilibrium is one that involves movement farther away from the equilibrium once it is jarred away from equilibrium for some reason.

The concept of equilibrium is used to try to understand relationships among variables in a system. An economic system, whether a firm, a market, or an entire economy, is bombarded by changes from outside, so economists must engage in mental experimentation and mathematical manipulation to try to track the process of change from one equilibrium to another. One equilibrium may not be achieved before forces from outside push the system in another direction.

To analyze equilibriums and arrive at unique solutions, economists generally build their theories on several maximizing and minimizing assumptions such as, for example, that business firms will try to make as much profit as they can, that resource owners will try to receive as much income for the use of their resources as they can, that consumers will try to spend or save in ways that will give them as much satisfaction as they can get, and that firms and households will try to minimize costs.

EQUILIBRIUM OF THE CONSUMER   A situation in which the consumer maximizes satisfaction, given the consumer's income and tastes and the prices of products and services. Presented below are two of the methods economists have developed to analyze equilibrium of the consumer.

1. *The Marginal Utility approach.* In order to maximize utility, the consumer adjusts spending until the ratio of marginal utility to price (MU/P) of each product and service equals the MU/P of every other product and service. Marginal utility is defined as the addition to total utility (or satisfaction) from the consumption of one more unit of a good or service.

$$\frac{MU_A}{P_A} = \frac{MU_B}{P_B} = \frac{MU_C}{P_C} = \ldots = \frac{MU_n}{P_n}$$

If $\dfrac{MU_A}{P_A} > \dfrac{MU_B}{P_B}$, that is, the marginal satisfaction from A per dollar spent exceeds the marginal satisfaction from B per dollar, the consumer can increase total satisfaction by withdrawing expenditure of dollars from B and spending more on A. The increase in satisfaction from another dollar's worth of A exceeds the reduction in satisfaction when a dollar less is spent on B. Because of the Law of Diminishing Marginal Utility, as less B is consumed, its MU will rise, and as more A is consumed, its MU will fall, until the MU/P ratios are equal. At that point, the consumer cannot increase total satisfaction by shifting expenditure. The consumer is in equilibrium. See *Diminishing Marginal Utility, Marginal Utility.*

2. *The Indifference Curve approach.* A consumer is in equilibrium, i.e., maximizes satisfaction, by consuming goods so that on his or her indifference map, the marginal rate of substitution (MRS) of any good (A) for all other goods (n) on the highest attainable indifference curve is equal to the ratio of the price of A and the combined prices of n on the consumer's budget line. The $MRS_{An} = P_A/P_n$.

The indifference curve approach can be illustrated by the diagram below. It compares various combinations of A and n, on a map of indifference curves, with combinations of the two on the consumer's budget line, BL.

Each indifference curve represents all of the combinations of good A with all other goods (n) which will give this consumer equal satisfaction. The slope at each point on the curve represents the marginal rate of substitution of A for n, for that combination of A and n. The marginal rate of substitution is the rate at which a consumer will substitute quantities of one good (A) for all other goods (n) while maintaining the same level of satisfaction.

The indifference curves on the map, I_1, I_2, and I_3 may be likened to contours on a geographic map: each successive curve from the origin out represents a higher level of satisfaction than the previous curve.

The budget line, BL, represents all of the combinations of A and *n* that can be purchased given the consumer's income and the prices of A and *n*; all income is spent on *n* (all other goods) at the intersection L on the horizontal axis and, alternatively, all income is spent on A at the intersection B on the vertical axis. Point E depicts consumer equilibrium where the consumer reaches the highest level of satisfaction given consumer tastes, income, and the prices of goods. There the ratio of prices (the slope of the budget line) equals the MRS_{An} (the slope of the highest attainable indifference curve, I_2.) The consumer will buy OY of good A and OX of all other goods *n*. Any other attainable combination would place the consumer on a lower indifference curve, such as I_1, and produce less total satisfaction. A higher indifference curve, such as I_3, is unattainable because no combination of A and *n* on it can be purchased with the available budget.

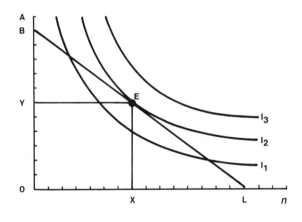

CONSUMER EQUILIBRIUM
The Indifference Curve Approach

For reasons of easier conceptualization, the indifference curve analysis usually is introduced by comparing choices among combinations of two goods, A and B. However, to arrive at consumer equilibrium among all goods and services in a two-dimensional illustration, any one good (A) is compared with a combination of all other goods (*n*). See *Budget Line, Diminishing Marginal Rate of Substitution, Indifference Curve, Indifference Map.*

EQUILIBRIUM OF THE FIRM   The general postulate of this equilibrium is that the business firm will try to produce where its marginal cost equals its marginal revenue (MR = MC) and the MC curve intersects the MR curve from below, because that is the position of most total profit or least loss.

The reasoning for the product market equilibrium runs as follows: Profit equals total revenue minus total cost. Marginal revenue is the change of total revenue when output changes by one unit. Marginal cost is the change in total cost when output changes by one unit. If marginal revenue at a particular level of output exceeds marginal cost, the firm can add more to its total revenue than to its total cost by expanding output. When marginal revenue is less than marginal cost, the firm can reduce its total revenue less than it reduces total cost and thereby increase profit or reduce loss, if it produces less. The firm cannot improve its position if MR = MC (although it may go out of business in the long run if this "best" position involves losses, that is, average cost exceeds average revenue). For illustrations and the effect of particular market characteristics, see: *Equilibrium of the Firm: Pure Competition, Equilibrium of the Firm: Monopoly, Equilibrium of the Firm: Monopolistic Competition, Market Equilibrium.* For application to the firm as buyer of factors of production, see *Equilibrium of the Firm: Factor Market.*

EQUILIBRIUM OF THE FIRM: FACTOR MARKET The business firm will try to buy that quantity of factors of production for which the marginal revenue product of each factor (MRP_F) equals its marginal factor cost (MFC). That is the position in the factor market which produces the greatest total profit or the least loss. If the MRP of a factor exceeds its MFC, the last added unit of the factor will add more to total revenue than its cost. The firm will add to its profit by adding units of the factor so long as $MRP_F > MFC$. When another unit of the factor adds more to cost than to total revenue ($MFC > MRP_F$), the firm will not want to employ it. The firm will have no incentive to change—it will be in equilibrium—at the factor quantity where $MRP_F = MFC$.

In panel A (p. 99), the firm is in a factor market in which it can buy any amount of the factor (F) it might want without affecting the price. It is a competitive market. $MFC = P_F$ (factor price) and the MFC curve is a straight horizontal line at the going market price. Point E identifies the equilibrium quantity Q_1 where $MRP_F = MFC$.

In panel B, below, the firm will have to pay a higher price to attract the factor, the larger the quantity of the factor (F) it wishes to buy. The firm's demand is a large part of the factor market, so the firm has market power as a buyer. Here, the MFC is greater than P at each possible quantity of the factor. Price of the factor (P_F) equals average factor cost (AFC). The MFC curve lies above the AFC curve. This reflects the situation that, for a continuing operation, if the firm must pay a higher price for an additional unit of a factor, it must pay the higher price for all of the previous units of the factor, too. Equilibrium of the firm is at point E, where $MRP_F = MFC$. The equilibrium quantity of the factor is Q_1, but the price for that quantity of the factor is lower than point E; it is at P on the vertical axis.

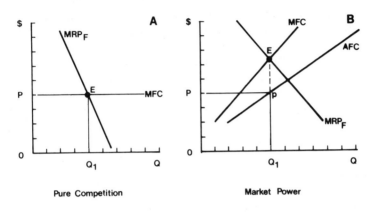

Pure Competition   Market Power

EQUILIBRIUM OF THE FIRM: FACTOR MARKET

EQUILIBRIUM OF THE FIRM: MONOPOLISTIC COMPETI-TION

Firms in a market of monopolistic competition, like firms in other markets, will try to produce at that output where marginal revenue equals marginal cost (MR = MC), because that is the output for maximum profit. For the rationale, see *Equilibrium of the Firm*.

In monopolistic competition, the product of the firm is similar to, but differentiated from, the products of other firms in the market, so that a price increase by this firm will cause some but not all of its customers to shift to competitors. It must lower price to sell more. The situation is illustrated by a downward-sloping demand curve as shown below.

Marginal revenue for the firm in monopolistic competition is less than price because the firm must lower price to sell more and, in a continuing operation, the firm must reduce price on all of the identical units of output. (Over time, the firm cannot just reduce price on the last unit of output that can be sold because of the lower price.) The additional revenue, then, is less than the price of the additional unit sold; it is less by the amount of the price reduction on all of the units that could have been sold before the price reduction, multiplied by the number of those units.

$MR_n = P_n - [(P_{n-1} - P_n)(Q_{n-1})]$, where MR_n is the marginal revenue of the nth unit, P_n is the price per unit when n units are sold, P_{n-1} is the higher price without the nth unit, and Q_{n-1} is the quantity that could have been sold at the higher price of P_{n-1}.

The marginal revenue curve therefore lies below the demand curve (which measures price at various levels of output), and MR intersects the marginal cost curve at a value less than price (P).

Average cost, for the economist, includes a return to those providing funds that is sufficient to assure a continued flow of funds, i.e., a normal rate of return on the balance sheet. If average cost (AC) exceeds price, firms will tend to leave the industry in the long run, raising the demand curves of the remaining firms.

If AC is less than P, there is an above-normal rate of return, and new firms will be attracted into the industry. The entry of new firms will lower the demand curves and marginal revenue curves of the firms already there. That is, the new firms will take away some of the sales of the existing firms because of product substitutability. In addition, long-run average cost for an existing firm may increase because of the added pressure on resources or increased advertising expense as the existing firms fight to keep their customers.

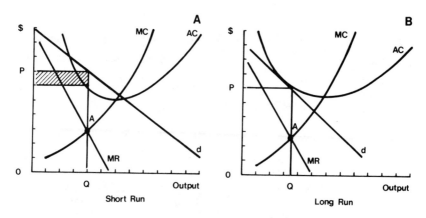

EQUILIBRIUM OF THE FIRM: MONOPOLISTIC COMPETITION

The equilibrium is determined at point A in the illustrations above, where MR = MC. P is the equilibrium price and Q is the equilibrium quantity. In the short run (panel A), above-normal profit is shown as the shaded area. In panel B, the long-run equilibrium price equals average cost because firms will enter or leave until there are no excess profits or losses, i.e., the rate of return equals the going interest rate, and is included in AC as an opportunity cost, as a cost of maintaining the flow of resources. Existing firms are receiving a normal rate of return and new firms are not attracted by the opportunity to earn greater-than-normal returns.

See *Monopolistic Competition*.

EQUILIBRIUM OF THE FIRM: MONOPOLY Monopolists, like all other firms, try to produce at that output where marginal revenue equals marginal cost (MR = MC) in order to maximize total profit. For the rationale, see *Equilibrium of the Firm*.

Monopoly is defined as a market in which a single seller controls the supply of a product, there are no close substitutes, and entry of other sellers into the market is restricted. The firm's demand curve is the market demand curve. It slopes downward, illustrating that in order to sell more of the product, the firm must reduce price. In a continuing operation, the firm must lower price on all units produced, not just the last added unit. (There are exceptions where price discrimination is possible.) The addition to total revenue from selling another unit of the product (marginal revenue) will be less than the price of the new unit because the price of all units falls, not just the price of the new unit. Since the demand curve represents price–quantity relationships, the marginal revenue curve (representing MR–quantity relationships) will lie below the demand curve.

Note that the equality of marginal revenue and marginal cost (MR = MC) determines price (as well as quantity) even though MR does not equal price. The short-run equilibrium and the long-run equilibrium are the same because, unlike pure competition or monopolistic competition, other firms cannot enter the industry. There are barriers to entry: patents which prevent others from entering production or natural monopoly characterized by decreasing long-run average costs.

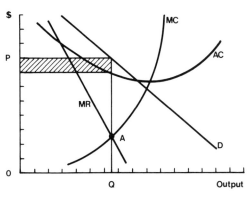

EQUILIBRIUM OF THE FIRM : MONOPOLY

The equilibrium is determined at point A in the illustration (p. 101), where MR = MC, producing an equilibrium price of P and an equilibrium quantity of Q. Profit above a normal rate of return on invested capital is shown by the shaded area. That profit will persist as long as cost and demand conditions remain the same, because a condition of monopoly is that new firms cannot enter the market to compete away the abnormal rate of return.

A monopolistic firm that is not publicly regulated can charge any price it chooses, but it cannot sell all it wants at that price. The quantity sold depends upon the willingness of buyers to buy at that price. See *Monopoly*.

EQUILIBRIUM OF THE FIRM: PURE COMPETITION Competitive firms, like those in other kinds of markets, try to produce where marginal revenue equals marginal cost in order to maximize profit. For the rationale, see *Equilibrium of the Firm*.

In pure competition, a firm is such a small part of the total market for a homogeneous product that it cannot affect price even if it were to withhold all of its product from the market or if it were to put its entire output on the market. The firm is a price taker rather than a price maker. A wheat rancher is an example of a competitive firm in such a market.

The demand curve facing such a firm appears to be a horizontal line at the market price. The firm cannot sell more by lowering price, and sales fall to zero if the firm asks more than the market price. Every time the firm increases output by one unit, total revenue will increase by the price of that unit. Marginal revenue equals price. MR = P.

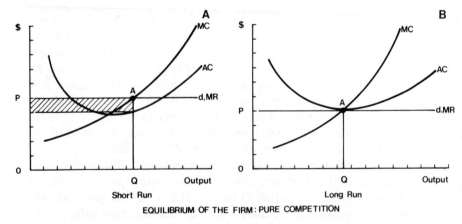

EQUILIBRIUM OF THE FIRM: PURE COMPETITION

In the illustrations above, MR = MC at point A, with an equilibrium price of P (determined by the market) and an equilibrium quantity of q. Average cost (AC) includes a normal rate of return just sufficient to maintain the flow of capital resources to the firm. It is calculated as an opportunity cost. If there is a higher-than-normal rate of return in the short run (the shaded area in panel A), new firms will enter until falling market price and/or rising costs reduce the rate of return to normal for the long run (panel B). In the wheat market, new production might come from uncultivated arable land, but more likely it will come from ranchers entering the wheat market by shifting from barley or hay production.

EQUILIBRIUM OF THE MARKET: MONOPOLISTIC COMPETI-
TION In monopolistic competition, the concept of a market may be an oxymoron because the product of each firm is slightly different from the products of all of the other firms. However, a market is identified because the products, while different, are close substitutes for one another. Product differentiation prevents use of "a" market demand curve or "a" market supply curve. Instead, economists refer to *group* equilibrium and show it through changes in the equilibrium of a typical firm.

In pure competition, on the other hand, a market equilibrium can be shown by market demand and market supply curves which are found by horizontally adding the demand curves of the individual buyers and the supply curves (marginal cost curves) of the individual firms producing the homogeneous product.

Relative ease of entry and exit in a market of monopolistic competition means that above-normal rates of return to firms will attract new competitors, while below-normal rates will cause firms to leave. If price exceeds average cost (including a normal rate of return on capital funds), new firms will be attracted to the industry. Because the product of each firm is a close substitute for the products of the other firms, the entry of new firms will reduce market shares of the existing firms, lowering the demand curves of the latter. New firms might also bid up the prices of resources and thereby push up average costs, depending upon the tightness in resource markets. Then again, new firms might cause increases in average costs in all firms by initiating large advertising expenditures, which existing firms feel compelled to emulate. Monopoly profits may persist for some members of the "group" because of successful product differentiation.

In panel A (p. 104), a typical firm has a higher-than-normal rate of return in the short run. Price exceeds average cost (P > AC) at the most profitable output Q (where MR = MC at point A). AC in both illustrations includes a normal rate of return sufficient to maintain the flow of capital resources to the firm, calculated as an opportunity cost. In panel B, new firms have entered, lowering the

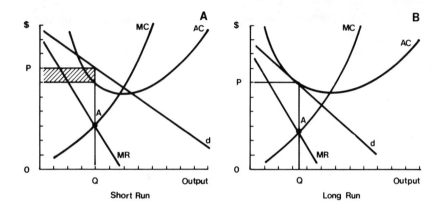

MARKET EQUILIBRIUM IN MONOPOLISTIC COMPETITION AS
SHOWN THROUGH ADJUSTMENTS IN A TYPICAL FIRM

demand curve of the typical firm and raising its average cost curve. A long-run equilibrium is produced where P = AC, and there is no abnormal profit at the output where MR = MC.

See *Equilibrium of the Firm: Monopolistic Competition.*

EQUILIBRIUM OF THE MARKET: PURE COMPETITION Market equilibrium is determined by impersonal market forces involving large numbers of buyers and sellers of a standardized product who react to market price. Profits above a normal rate of return on the funds invested in factors of production will be competed away by the ease with which buyers and sellers enter and leave the market.

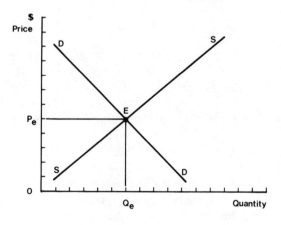

MARKET EQUILIBRIUM: PURE COMPETITION

Market equilibrium for pure competition is illustrated by market supply and demand curves. The market demand curve is found by horizontally adding the quantity demanded from the demand curves of individual buyers at each possible market price; the market supply curve is found by horizontally adding the quantities supplied from the supply curves of individual sellers.

In the diagram (p. 104), the equilibrium is shown as the intersection of market supply and demand curves at E. If price is higher, the curves show that a larger quantity will be supplied than demanded. Price will fall as sellers in the aggregate accept a lower price and buyers in the aggregate buy more, until the quantity buyers demand equals the quantity sellers want to sell and the market is cleared. Equilibrium price is P_e and equilibrium quantity is Q_e. If price is below equilibrium, the diagram shows that quantity demanded exceeds quantity supplied and buyers will bid up the price.

EQUILIBRIUM PRICE 1. For a *market*, equilibrium price is that price which equates the quantity buyers wish to buy with the quantity sellers wish to sell, so that the market is cleared of the product. The price will tend to persist so long as tastes, income, and prices of related goods remain the same for buyers, while technology and factor costs remain the same for sellers. See *Equilibrium of the Market* (for various types of markets).

2. For a *firm*, equilibrium price is that price at which marginal cost equals marginal revenue. See *Equilibrium of the Firm* for the explanation.

EQUITY 1. The ownership value of the firm calculated as total assets minus total liabilities. In a corporation the claims of the owners are represented by capital stock at par value, additional paid-in capital, plus the annual profits retained by the firm (retained earnings). Equity is distinguished from debt of a firm, which instead is represented by notes or bonds as alternative ways of funding the firm's operations.

2. That portion of the value of a property (e.g., a home) or a product (e.g., an automobile) being purchased on time that has been paid for and is owned by the purchaser.

ESCROW Money, a bond, or a deed for property that is placed in the hands of another, usually an escrow department of a bank or trust company, for delivery to a third person upon completion of specified conditions, such as final payment on a loan or completion of a project.

EURODOLLAR   A dollar held in a bank office located outside the United States. Offshore dollar deposits become attractive when the Eurodollar interest rates exceed the rates on domestic deposits by more than enough to compensate for the additional costs, inconveniences, and risks of holding dollar deposits abroad. They are called Eurodollars because the first formal market arose in Europe. Markets for Eurodollars have multiplied, and brisk trading has developed in such dollars.

Eurodollar deposits may be held in foreign branches of U.S. banks or in foreign bank offices outside the U.S. Only overnight Eurodollars issued to U.S. residents by foreign branches of U.S. banks are included in the U.S. money stock "M2" totals. The money supply concept "M3" adds term Eurodollars held by U.S. residents at foreign branches of U.S. banks and all United Kingdom and Canadian Banks. See *M2, M3*.

EUROPEAN COMMON MARKET   See *European Community*.

EUROPEAN COMMUNITY (EC)   Also known as the European Communities. An economic union among 12 Western European democratic countries formed to integrate their economies by reducing and removing trade barriers among members, by adopting a common trade policy toward the outside world, and by providing for the free movement of labor and capital within the group. The EC has a Council of Ministers, a Commission, a European Parliament, and a Court of Justice.

The EC is moving toward even more economic integration than the goals above suggest. There now is agreement to merge into a single trading block in 1992. Businesses in countries outside the group anticipate that it may become more difficult to enter the EC market and are actively developing branch or joint production facilities within it as well as searching for ways to export into it.

The European Monetary System is an organization whose members agree to hold their exchange rates in a relatively fixed relation to the currencies of the other members. Not all of the EC members have joined this monetary system, but even so, the EC members are discussing how to achieve a single Eurocurrency and a European central bank.

In addition to economic integration, the EC has an ultimate goal of political union.

The EC members are Belgium, Denmark, France, Great Britain, Greece, Ireland, Italy, Luxembourg, Portugal, Spain, The Netherlands, and West Germany. The EC was founded as the

European Coal and Steel Community by France, West Germany, and the Benelux countries—Belgium, The Netherlands, and Luxembourg—in 1951. The European Economic Community (EEC, also known as the Common Market) and the European Atomic Energy Community (EURATOM) were merged with the Coal and Steel Community in 1967 to form the European Community. See *Common Market*.

EUROPEAN ECONOMIC COMMUNITY (EEC) See *European Community*.

EXCESS RESERVES Vault cash and Federal Reserve deposits held by banks that are in excess of the minimum reserves against deposit liabilities that are required by law. They represent a loan potential for banks that is a multiple of the excess reserves, because banks usually make loans by creating or crediting deposits, and expenditures from these deposits usually find their way into other bank deposits in the system when checks are deposited, which is the basis for the deposit multiplier. For example, if required reserves are 10% of deposits and there are $500 million of excess reserves in the banking system, banks could make loans up to $5 billion and still meet the legal minimum reserve requirement.

The Federal Reserve Board of Governors can attempt to expand economic activity by lowering the reserve requirement, and thereby creating excess reserves. Or the Fed can attempt to slow economic activity by raising the reserve requirement, which restricts the ability of banks to make loans. The Fed also can create or soak up excess reserves by the purchase or sale of government bonds by its Open Market Committee.

Banks have an incentive to eliminate excess reserves because they make profit by making an interest return from loans. However, that incentive may be offset by the poor quality of potential loans or anticipation of being able to charge higher interest rates in the near future. See *Required Reserves, Deposit Multiplier, Monetary Policy*.

EXCHANGE CONTROLS Regulations controlling the use of a country's money in international trade and finance to protect the international exchange value of the currency, to protect foreign exchange reserves, to direct imports and exports into governmentally desired channels, or to reduce a deficit in the balance of international payments. Exchange controls regulate the use of domestic currency for the purchase and sale of foreign currency, which in turn may control what is imported or exported. An extreme of control might require that all foreign exchange from exports be sold to the central bank and all purchases of foreign exchange for imports be bought from the central bank.

EXCHANGE RATE   The ratio of the value of one country's money to the value of another country's money. It is expressed, for example, as dollars per pound sterling, or francs per dollar, or yen per franc. When the world is on a fixed standard such as the gold standard, each currency is related to gold by law, e.g., the U.S. declares that one ounce of gold equals $35, and France declares that one ounce of gold equals F175. Thus each currency is related to others by a legal ratio to gold (which is $1.00 = F5 in this example). If trade imbalance were to create a surplus of dollars relative to what the French want to hold, francs would be used from the U.S. stabilization fund to purchase dollars, and ultimately gold would flow from the U.S. to France in exchange for remaining surplus dollars. The exchange rate might vary from the legal rate slightly, depending upon the cost of gold shipment.

   When the world is on a fluctuating exchange-rate system, each exchange rate is established by the buying and selling of currencies in the world's money markets and can change over a very short period of time, even second by second when markets are open. See *Fixed Exchange Rates, Flexible Exchange Rates, Gold Standard.*

EXCHANGE-RATE DEPRECIATION   A fall in the value of a nation's currency in world money markets relative to other currencies and gold. It then takes more of the nation's currency (say, dollars) to buy the currency of another nation (say, Swiss marks) or to buy an ounce of gold.

   Under a fixed exchange-rate system, such as the gold standard, exchange-rate depreciation is prevented by the country under pressure selling gold to soak up the excess of its currency. *Devaluation* may occur by a country declaring that an ounce of gold equals more of its currency than before, when the deflationary forces are inexorable. See *Dollar Surplus, Depreciation of a Nation's Currency, Devaluation.*

EXCHANGE RATIO   The rate at which one product exchanges for another. If 1 ton of structural steel has the same value (sells for the same price) as 1 ton of soft white winter wheat the exchange ratio is 1S = 1W; if steel were twice as valuable the ratio would be 1S = 2W. The value of each may vary from region to region and country to country. It is a function of the value of the resources used in production, methods of combining the resources, and market demand. See *Terms of Trade*.

EXCISE TAX   A tax levied on the manufacture, sale, or consumption of specified goods such as gasoline or automobiles. When levied on cigarettes and alcoholic beverages it often is called a "sin tax."

EXOGENOUS CHANGE   A change that occurs outside the economic system which in turn causes some change within the system. Examples of exogenous change are war, hurricanes, floods, or drought. If the system under consideration is a single market, the exogenous change might be a change of buyers' tastes or the invention of a new machine for the production process. See *Endogenous Change*.

EXPLICIT COSTS   Those sums that are paid out to or legally due other firms and individuals, plus the internally calculated cost of depreciation of plant, equipment, and inventories. Costs that must enter into business accounts, unlike the opportunity costs of owner-provided capital or labor that constitute implicit costs. See *Implicit Costs*.

EXPORT CREDITS   Loans at favorable rates to foreign buyers of a country's goods. A mechanism to expand exports. Export loans are made by specialized agencies such as the U.S. Export–Import Bank, or loans may be guaranteed by them. See *Export-Import Bank*.

EXPORT–IMPORT BANK   Created in 1934, it is the U.S. example of a government agency whose purpose is to encourage exports by making loans to foreigners at favorable rates for the purchase of U.S. goods.

EXTERNAL BENEFITS   Some kinds of production will produce side benefits that recipients may not have to pay for if is too difficult or costly to collect for them. If a new business locates in a small town, the influx of a number of well-educated management-level employees will increase the level of civic leadership with effects in service clubs, city government, public school education, etc. If a utility firm creates a lake when damming a river system to produce electricity, many people may benefit from the recreational opportunities incidental to the production of electricity. Thus economic welfare may exceed market value. See *External Costs, Externality*.

EXTERNAL COSTS Some kinds of production will produce undesirable side effects which are costs to society for that production even if they do not enter into the firm's calculation of its costs and its prices. Examples are smoke from a steel mill, odor from a meat packing plant or paper mill, or pollution of a lake by the discharge of industrial waste into it. Laws requiring firms to control these side effects result in cost calculations and pricing by firms that include the social costs. Economic welfare may be less than market value because of external costs that do not enter firms' cost accounts or their pricing. See *Externality*.

EXTERNAL ECONOMIES Economies that are outside of the cost and revenue considerations of the firm or industry. An example is the creation of a pool of skilled labor in Akron, Ohio, when tire production there grew from low levels at the turn of the century to very large volume in the 1920s. See *External Benefits*.

EXTERNALITY Refers to spillover effects of economic activity. When certain things are produced and sold, some people are required to incur costs for which they are not reimbursed or may receive benefits for which they do not have to pay. In these cases, prices do not reflect all of the social costs or benefits which are involved in the economic activity.

A positive externality is the same as an external benefit. A negative externality is the same as an external cost.

See *External Benefits, External Costs, External Economies*.

FACTORS OF PRODUCTION   Resources which enter into the production of goods and services, usually classified into the categories of labor, land (or natural resources), capital goods, and sometimes entrepreneurship.

FAIR MARKET VALUE   The price at which a property can be sold by a willing and able seller to a willing and able buyer. It is determined primarily by reference to recent sales prices of comparable property in the vicinity. The comparison might be flawed if there are very few recent sales, because one sale can involve special circumstances such as sale to a relative or a sale where one party is a poor negotiator. If there are few recent sales, one such special price can have a substantial effect on the typical or average price that is selected as the standard.

   The fair market value of a property may bear no relation to the *list price,* which is the price at which the property is listed with an agent, nor to the *asking price,* which may differ from both. *Assessed value,* which is the value placed upon the property for tax purposes, may vary from fair market value if the law calls for it to be set at some fraction rather than at 100% of fair market value. See *Assessed Value.*

FAIR-TRADE LAWS   See *Resale Price-Maintenance Agreements.*

FALLACY OF COMPOSITION   In economics the whole is often more than the sum of its parts. For example, an individual may decide to save more and consume less, and succeed; but if many people in the economy decide to save more, they may altogether save less because of the adverse effect of reduced consumption expenditure on national income. See *Paradox of Thrift*.

A farmer may decide to produce more wheat in order to increase the family income. But if a large number of farmers plant more wheat, the price of wheat may fall and, because of inelastic market demand for wheat, the total revenue received by farmers will fall. (Of course, if one farmer fails to increase wheat planting while others do increase it, that farmer will experience an even greater drop in revenue.) See *Elasticity*.

FANNIE MAE See *Federal National Mortgage Association*.

FAVORABLE BALANCE OF TRADE An excess of merchandise exports over merchandise imports. A designation applied to that loose body of political and economic writings of the sixteenth and seventeenth centuries known as *mercantilism*, when rising nation states sought the importation of gold and silver bullion as payment for the excess of exports. Gold and silver often were synonymous with money and were the "common denominator" for international trade. Gold and silver were desired to pay for standing armies and for goods useful to strengthen nations.

A favorable balance of trade also is known more neutrally as a trade surplus. Many modern countries are proud of a trade surplus as a sign of power and prestige (a national superiority complex?) and are worried by a trade deficit (an attitude transferred from one's personal accounts?). However, most economists focus on the net value of goods and services received and capital flows that increase welfare, and they are less concerned about the prestige or degradation felt about creditor-debtor conditions as such. See *Balance of Trade, Net Exports*.

FEATHERBEDDING The establishment of make-work rules which purposely use inefficient tools, materials, or techniques, which employ more workers than actually needed, or which provide pay for work not actually done. Workers attempt to impose featherbedding rules in order to resist the loss of jobs or the reduction in the value of skills when technological change occurs. Featherbedding promotes employment at the expense of economic efficiency. The Taft–Hartley Law (enacted in 1947 as an amendment to the National Labor Relations Act of 1935) attempted to make many forms of featherbedding illegal by making it an unfair labor practice to exact payment "for services which are not performed or not to be performed." However, courts and the National Labor Relations Board have found some rules lawful (though opponents charge they are "make-work") if there are some specified duties assigned to the employee and he/she is present for some time on the job site.

FEDERAL DEPOSIT INSURANCE CORPORATION (FDIC) A federal government agency which insures deposits at banks and thrifts against losses due to bank failure. The FDIC controls two separate insurance funds: the Bank Insurance Fund (BIF), which insures the deposits of banks that are members of the Federal Reserve System, and the Savings Association Insurance Fund (SAIF), which insures the deposits of thrifts. Each fund consists of premiums paid in by its member financial institutions. The FDIC is governed by a five-member board of directors consisting of the Comptroller of the Currency, the director of the Office of Thrift Supervision, and three private citizens nominated by the President and confirmed by the Senate.

Prior to 1989, the FDIC insured deposits at member banks, while the Federal Savings and Loan Insurance Corporation (FSLIC) insured deposits at thrifts as a part of the Federal Home Loan Bank System. In 1989, Congress passed the Financial Institutions Reform, Recovery and Enforcement Act (FIRREA), which abolished the FSLIC and created in its stead the Savings Association Insurance Fund under the administration of the FDIC. At the same time, all banks which had been insured directly by the FDIC were placed in the new Bank Insurance Fund, also administered by the FDIC. These changes occurred as part of the Congressional "bailout" of the thrift industry, when it appeared that deposit losses of failed thrifts would exceed FSLIC funds by tens of billions (now hundreds of billions) of dollars.

Accounts of individual depositors are insured for up to $100,000. The limit is by account structure rather than by individual account. For insurance purposes, accounts in one name are aggregated and insured for no more than $100,000. Several accounts in the name of a spouse are together insured for up to $100,000, and the couple then would be insured for a maximum of $200,000. The two could have joint accounts which together would be insured for up to $100,000, so the couple now could be insured for up to $300,000. If there were two children, the maximum coverage could grow by $100,000 for each child for groups of accounts in each child's name. Then there could be joint accounts between the children, and between each child and each parent, and so on. The total deposit insurance coverage for the family of four could grow to over $1,000,000. And this coverage could be multiplied by having accounts in several different banks. The accounts that might be covered as a group by the $100,000 limit for one name include checking deposits, savings deposits, money market accounts whether checking or saving, and certificates of deposit. At the end of 1990, many proposed that Congress limit this available multiplicity of insured accounts because potential widespread commercial bank failures threaten the adequacy of funds in BIF just as thrift failures showed the FSLIC and its successor, SAIF, to be inadequate.

The two insurance funds are to be kept separate, and premiums paid into SAIF by thrifts were designed to be higher than those paid into BIF during the bailout period. If an insured bank or thrift fails, the FDIC meets the depositors' losses from the appropriate Fund up to the maximum coverage of $100,000. The full faith and credit of the U.S. Treasury stands behind each fund in guaranteeing the deposit insurance, a euphemism for the proposition that if the BIF or the SAIF runs out of money, the taxpayer pays.

It has been the policy of the FDIC that if a large bank in a major financial center failed, such as Continental Illinois, the FDIC also covered losses of deposits *over* $100,000 to avoid a possible disruption of financial markets. The message was, "the larger the bank that fails, the safer the depositor of large sums." It appeared that the policy would hold true for depositors in the Bank of New England, which failed at the beginning of 1991. The FDIC, of course, takes over the assets of a failed bank and disposes of them as partial repayment of the insurance claims.

Widespread anger over the huge size of the losses in savings institutions that must be covered by the general taxpayer, the possibility of many large commercial bank failures, and the unfairness of driving "jumbo CDs" out of small banks and into large ones all raise serious questions about the decision by regulators to cover uninsured deposits over $100,000.

In the 1989 legislation, Congress tried to strengthen the thrift industry for the future by shifting its deposit insurance program to SAIF from FSLIC, by abolishing the Home Loan Bank Board and dividing its responsibilities among other agencies, and by tightening regulations for thrift operation.

Some states permit state-chartered banks, thrifts, and credit unions to insure their deposits with private insurance companies. The number of such insured institutions usually is too small to spread the risks properly, so that one or a few bank failures will cause the insurance company to fail, leaving depositors in the other banking institutions uncovered. This problem arose in Maryland

and Ohio in the mid-1980s and in Rhode Island at the beginning of 1991. The matter is discussed under *Deposit Insurance*. See also *Bank Insurance Fund, Savings Association Insurance Fund, Federal Savings and Loan Insurance Corporation, Office of Thrift Supervision, Resolution Funding Corporation, Resolution Trust Corporation.*

FEDERAL FINANCING BANK   A federal credit agency which incurs debt to lend, in turn, to other federal agencies. It buys and sells obligations which are issued, sold, or guaranteed by other federal agencies. It helps hold down federal interest costs because it can borrow from the U.S. Treasury at low interest rates and can then lend to the other agencies at lower interest rates than they could find in the open market.

FEDERAL FUNDS   Excess reserves that banks may lend to one another for short periods of time, usually overnight, when some have excess reserves and others face a temporary decline of reserves below the legal minimum. All banks are required to keep reserves that are a proportion of the funds that are deposited with them. The overwhelming bulk of the reserves is kept on deposit in Federal Reserve Banks, while a minute fraction is kept in the banks as vault cash. See *Bank Reserves, Federal Funds Rate*.

FEDERAL FUNDS RATE   The interest rate at which some member banks borrow from others that have excess reserves on deposit in the Federal Reserve System (the Fed). The loans, usually for overnight, keep the borrowers' reserves from falling below the required legal minimum. The Fed can influence the Federal Funds Rate by buying or selling U.S. Treasury bills to the banking system, thereby increasing or decreasing excess reserves. Changes in the rate are considered an indicator of the state of the economy's monetary position and a signal of the Fed's intentions for monetary policy.

FEDERAL HOME LOAN BANK SYSTEM   A system of 12 regional banks created under authority of the Federal Home Loan Bank Act of 1932 to provide regulation and a source of credit for member savings and loan institutions, similar to the relationships of regional Federal Reserve Banks to their member commercial banks.

Prior to 1989, the system was coordinated by a three-member Federal Home Loan Bank Board (FHLBB) appointed by the President of the United States and confirmed by the Senate. It was located in Washington, D.C., and controlled chartering, credit, deposit insurance, supervisory regulation, and a secondary-market mortgage agency for federal savings and loan associations and other member thrifts.

In 1989, the Financial Institutions Reform, Recovery and Enforcement Act (FIRREA) made sweeping changes in the regulatory structure of the thrift industry. It had become clear that the federal government would have to provide tens of billions of dollars to depositors in failed thrifts after the funds of the Federal Savings and Loan Insurance Corporation (FSLIC) were exhausted. The FHLBB was abolished and its duties were redistributed as follows.

The Office of Thrift Supervision was created in the Treasury Department to charter federal savings and loan associations and federal savings banks and to perform supervisory functions. It is headed by a director and provides regulatory functions similar to those provided to commercial banks under the Office of the Comptroller of the Currency.

A new Federal Housing Finance Board (FHFB) was created to oversee the credit operations of the existing 12 regional Federal Home Loan Banks. It is headed by a three-member Board, each member appointed by the President and confirmed by the Senate for a 6-year term. The 12 regional banks are located in Boston, New York, Pittsburgh, Atlanta, Cincinnati, Indianapolis, Chicago, Des Moines, Little Rock, Topeka, San Francisco, and Seattle.

The FSLIC, under the control of the FHLB Board, was abolished. The Savings Association Insurance Fund (SAIF) was created in its stead and placed under the control of the Federal Deposit Insurance Corporation (FDIC). [Existing bank insurance operations which had been directly under the FDIC were placed in the new Bank Insurance Fund (BIF), also under the control of the FDIC.]

The Federal Home Loan Mortgage Corporation (Freddie Mac), which had been controlled by the FHLBB, was placed under a new 18-member board similar to that for the Federal National Mortgage Association (Fannie Mae). Both organizations participate in the secondary mortgage markets.

All federal savings and loan associations and federal savings banks are controlled and regulated by the new agency arrangement. The 1989 law also increased the amount of federal regulation of state-chartered thrifts. See *Bank Insurance Fund, Comptroller of the Currency, Federal Deposit Insurance Corporation, Federal Home Loan Mortgage Corporation, Federal Housing Finance Board, Federal Savings and Loan Insurance Corporation, Office of Thrift Supervision, Savings Association Insurance Fund.*

FEDERAL HOME LOAN MORTGAGE CORPORATION (FHLMC)

(FREDDIE MAC)   A federally sponsored agency created in 1970 as an arm of the Federal Home Loan Bank System to provide a secondary market, particularly for conventional home mortgages. Freddie Mac also has worked toward standardization of loan documentation which increases the efficiency of the whole secondary market.

A savings and loan association can originate mortgage loans to home buyers and then sell the loans at a discount to Freddie Mac, thereby freeing funds for further home loans by the thrift, while having earned fees and some interest on the loans sold. Freddie Mac packages loans of similar maturities and coupons into a pool and sells *pass-through* securities with the pool as collateral, similar to Federal National Mortgage Association (Fannie Mae) procedures. Both mortgage agencies finance their operations by the sale of their securities in the open market.

Prior to 1989, Freddie Mac had been controlled by the Federal Home Loan Bank Board which, with the District Banks, owned all its stock and treated it as a Bank member eligible to receive advances (loans) from the 12 Federal Home Loan District Banks. When the FHLBB was abolished in 1989, Freddie Mac was separated from the Federal Home Loan Bank System and placed under an 18-member governing board, subject to oversight by the Secretary of the Treasury and the Secretary of Housing and Urban Development. See *Federal National Mortgage Association (Fannie Mae), Collateralized Bond Obligations, Pass-Through Security.*

FEDERAL HOUSING ADMINISTRATION (FHA)   An agency of the

U.S. Department of Housing and Urban Development (HUD) which insures private lenders such as banks and thrifts against loss on loans that are secured by residential mortgages. See *Government National Mortgage Association.*

FEDERAL HOUSING FINANCE BOARD   Created by the Financial

Institutions Reform, Recovery and Enforcement Act of 1989 (FIRREA) to oversee the credit operations of the 12 regional Federal Home Loan Banks. The Federal Home Loan Bank System has authority to sell bonds which are U.S. Government agency bonds. The bonds raise funds that then are loaned as "advances" by the district Federal Home Loan Banks to the member savings and loan associations and savings banks. As U.S. agency bonds, these bonds carry a lower interest rate than private bonds, so that advances would be available to the thrifts at lower rates than they could arrange in the open market. In the mid–1970s, advances from the district Federal Home Loan Banks began to supplant savings deposits as a primary source of funds because of disintermediation.

The agency is directed by a three-member board of directors, each appointed by the President and confirmed by the Senate for a 6-year term. The law abolished the Federal Home Loan Bank Board (FHLBB) which had this oversight and divided the other responsibilities of the old FHLBB among several other agencies. See *Federal Home Loan Bank System, Disintermediation.*

FEDERAL NATIONAL MORTGAGE ASSOCIATION (FNMA) (FANNIE MAE) A private corporation sponsored by the federal government which was created to support the residential housing industry by providing a secondary market for mortgages. It originated in the National Housing Act of 1934 and is the oldest of the three organizations operating in the secondary home mortgage market (the others being the Government National Mortgage Association and the Federal Home Loan Mortgage Corporation).

Fannie Mae is a public corporation whose stock is traded on the New York Stock Exchange. It raises funds from the sale of capital stock and by selling short-term securities in the open market. Fannie Mae buys mortgages from the originators when funds are tight and sells mortgages when thrifts and banks have funds to invest. It also packages mortgages of similar characteristics into pools and sells mortgage-backed securities, known as *pass-through* securities, based on each pool. Until 1970 Fannie Mae was restricted to federally insured mortgages, but now it deals almost entirely in conventional mortgages. Fannie Mae is governed by an 18-member board and in 1989 was placed under the joint oversight of the Secretary of the Treasury and the Secretary of Housing and Urban Development. See *Federal Home Loan Mortgage Corporation, Collateralized Bond Obligations, Pass-Through Security.*

FEDERAL OPEN-MARKET COMMITTEE (FOMC) The group which makes U.S. monetary policy by trying to control the money supply and interest rates through open-market purchases and sales of U.S. Treasury securities. It is a committee of the Federal Reserve Bank System (the Fed), consisting of the 7 members of the Board of Governors of the Fed, the president of the New York Federal Reserve Bank, plus 4 additional members rotating from among the presidents of the other 11 District Federal Reserve Banks. The 7 District Bank presidents who are not Committee members usually sit with the FOMC but do not vote.

The FOMC may order the purchase or sale of U.S. Government securities on the open market. A Fed purchase will increase available reserves of member banks when the security sellers deposit the Fed checks in their checking accounts. A Fed sale will reduce member bank reserves as security buyers write checks to the Fed to pay for the purchases. The checks are cleared by increases or reductions in the reserve deposits that the affected member banks hold in regional Federal Reserve Banks. When reserves are increased, banks can lend more by creating checking accounts for the borrowers. This, in turn, increases the money supply, which includes checking accounts. When reserves fall below the required legal minimum, banks can lend less and the volume of checking accounts (money) decreases. See *Deposit Multiplier, Monetary Policy, Money Multiplier, Money Supply.*

FEDERAL RESERVE BANKING SYSTEM (THE FED) Created in 1913 by Congress to regulate money and credit and to serve as the bank for deposit and dispersal of funds for the United States Government. Fearing that a single central bank might be dominated by Wall Street interests, and recognizing different regional financial needs, 12 District Federal Reserve Banks were created. They are located in Atlanta, Boston, Chicago, Cleveland, Dallas, Kansas City, Minneapolis, New York, Philadelphia, Richmond, St. Louis, and San Francisco. Branch offices of the District Banks are located in a number of additional cities. All nationally chartered commercial banks must become member banks of the Federal Reserve System, while state-chartered banks may, but need not, join.

A seven-member Board of Governors located in Washington, D.C. coordinates the System. It makes monetary policy, controls the discount rate, fixes the margin requirement and, within limits provided by law, adjusts the member bank reserve requirements. It also performs regulatory functions such as deciding bank merger applications and enforcing the law regarding bank activities. The Board members are appointed for 14-year terms by the President of the United States with the advice and consent of the Senate. The Chairman of the Board is one of the Board members and is appointed for a 4-year term. The long terms for Board members were intended to provide independence from the administrative and legislative branches of the federal government, but few members serve their full term so that a one-term President may have the opportunity to appoint three or four Board of Governors members. Also, there is the implicit threat that what is created by legislation can be changed by legislation. Nevertheless, the Federal Reserve Board has operated in relative independence, sometimes pursuing monetary policy which is opposed by the White House and/or Congress.

An important monetary policy activity is the Fed's purchase and sale of government securities in the open market as the result of decisions of the Federal Open-Market Committee (FOMC). These activities have a quick impact on bank reserves and the money supply. See *Federal Open-Market Committee, Monetary Policy, Margin, Required Reserves.*

FEDERAL RESERVE NOTE   The predominant paper currency in the United States today. The notes are issued to the banks that ask for them and the banks' reserve accounts are then debited (reduced) by that amount. If the Fed wants to keep total bank reserves at the original level, it buys an equivalent amount of Treasury securities in the open market and the Fed's payments for the securities clear back through private deposits to the banks' reserve accounts. See *Currency, Fiat Money, Deposit Multiplier.*

FEDERAL SAVINGS AND LOAN INSURANCE CORPORATION (FSLIC)   A federal government agency which insured deposits in accounts at member thrifts for up to $100,000 against losses due to failure of a thrift. The FSLIC was abolished in 1989 by the Financial Institutions Reform, Recovery and Enforcement Act, which provided for the "bailout" of the thrift industry following widespread failure of savings and loan associations. The insurance function was shifted to the newly created Savings Association Insurance Fund (SAIF) under the control of the Federal Deposit Insurance Corporation (FDIC). See *Federal Deposit Insurance Corporation, Savings Association Insurance Fund.*

FEDERAL TRADE COMMISSION (FTC)   A U.S. antitrust agency created in 1914 by the Federal Trade Commission Act to protect competitors from unfair practices. The Act declared that unfair methods of competition are unlawful. Under the Wheeler–Lea Act of 1938, the FTC also protects consumers from unfair or deceptive practices such as false or misleading advertising or misrepresentation of goods and services. The FTC takes action by seeking court injunctions or by issuing cease-and-desist orders which are enforceable in federal courts. See *Antitrust.*

FIAT MONEY   Paper money not backed by some commodity such as gold, but rather, a medium of exchange that derives its acceptability from government decree (fiat) that it is legal tender for all debts, public and private. The government must restrict the issue of fiat money to the amount necessary to carry on the transactions of the country, or the money will lose purchasing power through price inflation.

The United States issued paper money without specific backing to help fund the Civil War. The money was known as *greenbacks* and is still in circulation through replacement as the paper wears out. See *Currency, Federal Reserve Note, Greenback, Gresham's Law.*

FINAL GOOD A product purchased by the final user. It is a concept used to calculate the gross national product, which is defined as the total value of all final goods and services produced in the economy during a specified period of time. The use of final goods avoids double counting when gathering the GNP figures.

FIRST IN-FIRST OUT (FIFO) A method for valuing inventory which prices all units in an inventory at the cost of the first unit purchased or produced, as though the first unit entering the inventory will be the first used or sold, whether or not it really is the first out. When costs are rising, FIFO will not reflect replacement costs, so that the firm will not allocate enough cost value to replace the inventory that goes out. Profit shown will be more than if the last in-first out (LIFO) method were used, and business income taxes will be higher.

When costs are falling, FIFO will show lower profit and will pay lower business income taxes than if the LIFO method were used. See *Last In-First Out.*

FISCAL POLICY Changes in federal government spending (G) and taxation in order to affect the general level of economic activity. Such policy was urged by John Maynard Keynes, the British economist, in the early 1930s when it appeared that monetary policy would not bring Great Britain or the United States out of deep depression. The U.S. Employment Act of 1946 adopted fiscal policy as a means of fighting unemployment. Particular acts involving spending or taxation are, of course, jointly determined by the President and Congress.

In a recession, the federal government can increase aggregate demand (AD) directly by an increase in spending for goods and services, which increases output (GNP) and employment. An increase in G substitutes for insufficient *private* spending by consumers and businesses. Or, the federal government can increase AD indirectly by lowering taxes, which would leave more money in the private sector and encourage private sector spending. Both policies would increase GNP and employment by a multiple amount according to the G multiplier or the tax multiplier, respectively.

Either policy involves some time between initiation and an actual increase in AD and GNP. Increased federal spending must be debated in Congress to determine what is important to do as well as whose constituents and financial supporters receive the benefits. Spending which can be implemented in just a few months often has the characteristics of make-work. Spending for capital improvements usually takes more months or even years from approval through design to commencement of construction.

For the alternative, tax reduction, to increase AD it must increase spending by consumers and businesses at a time when both groups are trying to conserve liquid assets in the face of declining sales and growing unemployment of labor and machinery.

Opposite policies would be instituted to ease labor shortages and reduce inflationary pressures. To slow an "overheated" economy, fiscal policy would reduce government spending and/or raise taxes. Congress and the President find either policy very hard to adopt. Either action is likely to lose votes and financial support for legislators and presidential candidates. Even when people agree generally that belt-tightening is required, each of us prefers that it be someone else's belt. See *Aggregate Demand, Deficit Spending, Deflationary Gap, Government Multiplier, Tax Multiplier, Monetary Policy.*

FISCAL YEAR Any 12-month period selected as the accounting period by a firm, government, or person. When a fiscal year deviates from the calendar year of January 1 through December 31, it usually is a response to the pattern of activities of the selector. For example, the fiscal year of a farmer might be chosen according to harvest time, say, August 1 through July 31; for a college, the fiscal year might run from September 1 through August 31, corresponding to the rhythm of semesters; some businesses choose July 1 through June 30; the U.S. federal government now uses October 1 through September 30 for its fiscal year.

FIXED COST Cost of production which does not vary with changes in output. It exists as a cost even when output is zero. When fixed cost is added to variable cost the sum is total cost. Fixed cost is a short-run concept representing some committed factors of production. In the long run, all inputs are variable so there is only variable cost and no fixed cost. See *Average Fixed Cost, Total Fixed Cost, Variable Cost, Total Cost.*

FIXED EXCHANGE RATES The most common form is the gold standard, in which a country fixes the value of its currency in terms of gold, say 1 ounce of gold equals $35. Others also equate their currency to an ounce of gold, e.g., France declares that F175 = 1 ounce of gold. Then $1 = F5. Suppose that the U.S. experiences a balance of payments deficit, which would tend to lower the value of its currency relative to others (others want to hold fewer dollars and want more dollars in exchange for francs). The U.S. government could buy dollars with any francs it had in its foreign exchange reserve, but the ultimate defense of the fixed rate is the flow of gold from the deficit country in exchange for some of its foreign-held currency (in our example, dollars).

Equilibrium in the balance of payments is supposed to be restored automatically by the outflow of gold from the deficit country and the inflow into the surplus country. The outflow of gold reduces the money base and pushes down prices. The inflow of gold increases the money base in the surplus country and tends to be inflationary. People in the deficit country buy more at home and less abroad because of the relative price changes. People in the balance-of-trade-surplus country buy more abroad and less at home because of the change in relative prices. Problems with this are discussed under *Gold Standard*. See also *Flexible Exchange Rates, Balance of Payments.*

FIXED-RATE MORTGAGE A note signed by a borrower, using real estate as collateral, which specifies the terms of repayment and a rate of interest that is fixed for the life of the note. Historically, savings and loan associations have originated 40–50% of the home mortgages in the U.S., commercial banks about 25%, mortgage bankers about 16% and, an expanding group which is relatively new in the primary mortgage market, builders, investment bankers, real estate brokers, etc., initiate the remainder. Fixed-rate mortgages had been the standard for home mortgages until the sharp increases in general market interest rates in the 1970s led to the introduction and expansion of adjustable-rate mortgages (ARMs), which periodically adjust the interest rate. See *Adjustable-Rate Mortgage.*

FLEXIBLE EXCHANGE RATES Sometimes called floating exchange rates. The value of a country's money in international transactions is established through the buying and selling of currency in international currency exchange markets. The value at any moment is expressed in terms of the money of other countries, e.g., the dollars required to buy a British pound, a Swiss mark, or a Japanese yen.

The value of a country's currency changes as the currency supply and demand change in the market rather than being fixed by government decree for indefinitely long periods of time, as with a gold standard. The exchange rates for dollars may shift because foreign people and businesses want to hold more dollars or fewer dollars than are provided by the purchase of foreign goods and services by people in the U.S., by gifts from the U.S., or by foreign investment by U.S. citizens. Or, government agencies may enter the market as buyers or sellers of currency to affect the exchange rates in pursuit of some economic policy, creating a dirty float. See *Balance of Payments, Exchange Rate, Fixed Exchange Rate, Gold Standard, Clean Float, Dirty Float.*

FLOATING EXCHANGE RATES   See *Flexible Exchange Rates.*

FOREIGN EXCHANGE RESERVES   Foreign currencies and gold held by a country's central bank or treasury department. These reserves may be used to buy and sell the country's currency on foreign exchange markets to affect the country's exchange rates. Sometimes, by agreement, several governments may enter exchange markets at the same time to influence a country's exchange rates. Such concerted action occurred near the end of the 1980s, when the central banks of several countries entered foreign exchange markets to sell dollars from their reserves to try to help the United States prevent the value of the dollar from rising. Under the post-World War II gold standard countries were called upon to maintain stabilization funds to maintain the international value of their currency short of transferring gold.

FORWARD MARKET   A designation used for some particular markets that are comparable to futures markets for securities and commodities. 1. A futures market for international currency exchange where contracts are traded for delivery of currency at some specified time in the future. 2. A market for agreements arranged in the over-the-counter market in which securities are purchased or sold for delivery after 5 business days from the date of transaction for Treasury securities or after 30 days for mortgage-backed federal agency issues. See *Futures Market, Hedging.*

FRACTIONAL RESERVE BANKING SYSTEM   Early in the history of banking it was found that all deposits placed in a bank need not be kept on hand because in normal times all depositors would not wish to withdraw their deposits at once. Banks could keep a portion of deposits on hand as reserves to meet a periodic excess of withdrawals over deposits, and they could lend the rest at interest.

The result, a fractional reserve banking system, today permits banks to make loans by creating new checking deposits for borrowers. It permits the money supply to expand or contract in accord with business needs within the limits set by reserve requirements. Without a 100% reserve requirement, checking deposits represent more than one-for-one substitutes for currency, so they are added to currency in circulation when determining the total money stock. Today, required reserves are important as the basis for monetary policy to control the money supply, but they tend to be set in the range of 10–20% of deposits rather than 100%.

During the nineteenth century, bank failures occurred in the United States because state banks were easy to form and many that followed unsound banking practices also kept too small a fraction of deposits in reserve. To protect depositors, laws were passed which set the minimum fraction of deposits that a bank must keep on reserve and the form in which reserves must be kept. However, abnormal times, or rumor, can cause a "run" on a bank as depositors scramble to withdraw their deposits (a scene that was common in historical Western movies and that occasionally occurs today). A legal minimum reserve short of 100% would be insufficient to pay off all depositors at once.

Other ways to safeguard depositors have been developed which include regulation of the type of asset which banks may accept in exchange for loans, deposit insurance such as that provided by the Federal Deposit Insurance Corporation (FDIC), and provision for a central bank to act as a lender of last resort by making loans to banks or purchasing assets of banks in trouble. Such safeguards have not always been enough, as runs on banks and bank failures in the 1980s so aptly demonstrate. Today, required reserves are most important for efforts to control the money supply, while deposit insurance provides the primary protection for depositors. See *Deposit Multiplier, Money Multiplier, Monetary Policy.*

FREDDIE MAC   See *Federal Home Loan Mortgage Corporation.*

FREE GOOD   Any good that is plentiful enough to be available to all comers without restriction. The air we breathe is an example, with the exceptions noted under *Economic Good.* Few goods are free goods. See *Economic Good.*

FREE ON BOARD (FOB)   A way of pricing goods that are to be transported from a seller's place of business to a buyer's location.

It places the costs of transportation, insurance, etc., directly on the receiving party rather than including them in the quoted price. For example, a price quoted FOB Chicago means that a buyer located in San Francisco will pay that price plus all shipping charges. It is used in foreign trade as well as domestic.

FREE-ENTERPRISE ECONOMY. An economy in which the means of production are controlled and directed by private individuals and private groups. Decisions are made in the context of a freely functioning price system. Private ownership prevails for land and capital goods. "Free enterprise economy" is a more accurate contrast to "socialist economy" than the designation "capitalist economy," because economies characterized by government control may make just as extensive use of capital goods as those characterized by private ownership.

FREE RESERVES Bank reserves that consist of excess reserves minus borrowings from the Federal Reserve. It is a measure sometimes used to predict how the money stock will change, rather than using the broader *monetary base* measure. It may be superior to the monetary base because it does not include currency, nor required reserves, and adjusts excess reserves for borrowings from the Fed; it focuses on those reserves which are most likely to result in a multiple increase in the money stock. Of course, banks may find it prudent to hold excess reserves in some circumstances, such as uncertainty surrounding a prospective recession, and neither free reserves nor excess reserves may be good predictors of what will happen to the money stock when these reserves increase. See *Excess Reserves, Required Reserves, Deposit Multiplier, Money Multiplier.*

FREE TRADE Open trade between countries, without any inhibitors such as tariffs, quotas, bureaucratic tangles, subsidies, etc. Most economists favor free trade because the benefits can accrue to all as total world output increases according to the principle of comparative advantage. Free trade is a relationship with a positive-sum result. Arguments against free trade and for protection generally are political and lack an economics basis, the primary exception being the infant industry argument. The General Agreement on Tariffs and Trade (GATT), an ongoing international organization despite its peculiar name, was created in 1947 to negotiate and regulate commercial policies. It is especially concerned with negotiating tariff reductions and eliminating import quotas. See *Comparative Advantage, Protectionism, General Agreement on Tariffs and Trade, Tariff, Quota, Subsidy, Infant Industry: Tariff Protection.*

FRICTIONAL UNEMPLOYMENT Unemployment that occurs because adjustments to change are not instantaneous. In changing jobs, a person typically quits his or her current job and then looks for another because firms' employment offices usually are open only during regular working hours. Or unemployment may occur because it takes time for firms to adapt to changed market conditions. Firms losing sales and building up unwanted inventories will lay off workers, while those with expanding sales may not immediately hire new workers or may be located in a distant section of town or in a distant city. Unemployed workers may not learn of the job openings immediately, or they may be reluctant to commute to work or to move to a new location.

Thus, frictional unemployment can be the result of freedom for workers to change jobs as well as adjustment to changing economic conditions that is not instantaneous. Public and private employment services may help to reduce the frictional impediments. Frictional unemployment contrasts with general unemployment caused by recession or depression in the economy, and with structural unemployment caused by obstacles to adaptation to change. See *Full Employment, Structural Unemployment, Technological Unemployment*.

FRIENDLY TAKEOVER See *Takeover*.

FULL EMPLOYMENT The full use of all available resources (factors of production) to produce goods and services for the economy.

Full employment in the labor market is achieved when there are enough jobs for all those who want to work. In the United States there is considered to be full employment when about 95 to 97% of the labor force is employed. The remainder is frictional and structural unemployment. The labor force consists of all people 16 years of age or older who are at work or are actively seeking work.

Economists consider manufacturing plants fully employed when operating at about 95% of rated capacity, allowing for down time for maintenance and repair. See *Frictional Unemployment, Technological Unemployment, Unemployment*.

FUTURES MARKET A market which provides for the sale and purchase of contracts for future delivery. Futures markets exist for commodities such as corn, wheat, cotton, oil, and pork bellies and for many financial assets such as shares of corporate stock, bonds, securities market indexes, and options to buy or sell commodities and securities. They are speculative markets which provide an opportunity for hedging by those who want to avoid risk. For example, futures markets permit processors to assure themselves of future supplies and to hedge against inventory value fluctuations during processing.

Financial futures trading in the U.S. is centered primarily in the Chicago Board of Trade and the Chicago Mercantile Exchange under the oversight of the Commodities Futures Trading Commission. Regulations differ from those of the Securities and Exchange Commission (SEC), which oversees the stock exchanges. The futures markets and the stock markets have become so interrelated through hedging and arbitrage that pressure has developed to give the SEC some authority in the financial futures markets.

Commodity futures markets are specialized by commodity and are concentrated in Chicago and New York. For example, the Chicago Board of Trade deals in grain futures, the Chicago Mercantile Exchange deals in livestock and meat futures, the Chicago Rice and Cotton Exchange deals in futures for those products, the New York Commodity Exchange deals in copper, gold, and silver futures, the New York Mercantile Exchange deals in petroleum products and natural gas futures, and the New York Cotton Exchange in cotton futures.

In contrast with futures markets, "spot" markets such as the New York Stock Exchange and the "wheat pit" at the Chicago Board of Trade develop spot prices in trading for *immediate* delivery.

Futures markets in foreign exchange are called forward markets. See *Forward Market, Hedging, Options Trading, Spot Markets, Stock-Index Futures.*

GENERAL AGREEMENT ON TARIFFS AND TRADE (GATT) Despite the designation "agreement" in its title, GATT is an international *organization* created in 1947 to provide a continuing basis for nations to negotiate and regulate commercial policies. The principal activity is multinational negotiation for tariff reductions. Its articles of agreement provide principles of behavior and a general set of rules governing the conduct of trade among nations. Negotiations toward more open trade have grown very intense in anticipation of 1992 when the nations of the European Communities become a single market for trade with the rest of the world. See *Tariff*.

GENERAL EQUILIBRIUM An analysis encompassing an entire economic system, that recognizes the interrelatedness of its many parts and involves the simultaneous determination of prices and quantities in all markets, where no variables are assumed constant. See *Partial Equilibrium*.

GENERAL OBLIGATION BONDS Certificates of indebtedness issued by state and local governments which are backed by the general taxing powers of the issuer. They differ from revenue bonds, which are issued against the revenues of a specific project. See *Municipals, Revenue Bonds, Government Bonds, Debenture Bond*.

GENERAL STRIKE A work stoppage in all (or most) firms in a city or in a country. Its purpose is to paralyze the city or nation to pressure the government to adopt a change supported by the striking workers. A general strike seeks a political solution to problems, while the more common strike of employees against an employer is used to create economic pressure on the employer to recognize the union as the representative of employees for collective bargaining or to change wages and/or working conditions in the plant. See *Strike*.

GINNIE MAE See *Government National Mortgage Association (GNMA)*.

GNMA See *Government National Mortgage Association*.

GNP See *Gross National Product*.

GNP DEFLATOR See *Gross National Product Deflator*.

GNP MULTIPLIER See *Gross National Product Multiplier*.

GOLDEN PARACHUTE An arrangement for the overgenerous provision of separation, retirement, and other benefits to principal officers of a company should control of the company change. It tends to entrench top management in control of the firm, and is one of the ways for incumbent management to try to protect itself when facing an unfriendly takeover. See *Takeover*.

GOLD EXCHANGE STANDARD A monetary system in which a country's money is equated to gold but is not freely exchanged for gold.

 Case A. A nation's government holds its monetary reserves in gold and buys gold at the rate (price) that it sets by law. It sells gold for international transactions but its money is not exchangeable for gold internally, except for small amounts made available for dental, medical, and jewelry uses. The United States was on this standard from 1933 to 1971. Its purpose was to prevent gold hoarding and keep domestic gold fully available as reserves for the money supply and for the settlement of international trade balances.

 Case B. A country holds little or no gold reserves for its money and therefore cannot freely exchange gold for its money at the treasury to settle international trade balances. Instead this country holds its reserves in the money of another country which is fully on the gold exchange standard or gold standard. Many small countries were indirectly on the gold exchange standard before 1971 by holding U.S. dollars as their monetary reserves. See *Fixed Exchange Rate, Flexible Exchange Rate, Gold Standard.*

GOLD STANDARD   A monetary system in which the monetary units are equated by law to ounces of gold at an official exchange rate, and currency is readily exchangeable for gold. When other countries also equate their money to gold, then gold becomes an international common denominator, establishing the legal exchange rate of each currency with all others in the system. For example, if 1 ounce of gold equals 19 British pounds and 1 ounce of gold equals 38 U.S. dollars, then 1 pound equals 2 dollars.

When a disequilibrium occurs in the international balance of payments, the exchange value of a deficit nation's currency will tend to fall. Countries are most reluctant to devalue their currency (by legally fixing a larger amount of currency equal to 1 ounce of gold) in recognition of this lower value. Instead, foreign exchange reserves may be used by the deficit country to buy up its currency held by foreigners and prevent the fall in exchange value. But the ultimate force for equilibrium under the gold standard is the flow of gold from the deficit country in exchange for its currency held by foreigners. See *Fixed Exchange Rate, Flexible Exchange Rate, Gold Exchange Standard.*

GOODWILL   In accounting, an intangible asset that is the value of a business over and above the tangible assets and other intangible assets such as patents. Often it represents the value of consumer loyalty to a firm. It may be based upon the recognition value of a firm's name or a product's name. Or it may be the value of the expected income from that proportion of clients or patients who are expected to continue to patronize a professional practice when it changes hands. The highest goodwill value seems to go to a brand name that has become the generic name for a class of products, for example, Coke, or Kleenex, or Xerox.

For an acquired company, goodwill is the total amount paid for the company minus the difference between the fair market value of its identifiable assets and its liabilities. As an asset claimed by a firm, it has special value to sellers of a firm and to buyers who hope that the "goodwill" value will carry over for the new owners.

Goodwill became a public issue when during the 1980s, the Federal Home Loan Bank Board persuaded solvent savings and loan institutions to buy insolvent ones in part by permitting the buyers to count an amount of goodwill associated with customers of the insolvent thrift as core capital for the capital/asset ratio requirement. The Financial Institutions Reform, Recovery and Enforcement Act of 1989 limits the counting of this supervisory goodwill as core capital to 5 years from date of the Act.

GOVERNMENT BONDS   Certificates of indebtedness issued by federal, state, or local governments. 1. At the federal level, government bonds may be considered narrowly as bonds issued by the U.S. Treasury with maturities of 10 years or more (today, 30-year maturities only), with shorter-term securities being called notes and bills. More broadly, the term may include federal bills and notes, federal agency securities such as those issued by the Export–Import Bank and the Federal Housing Administration, and also securities issued by federally *sponsored* agencies such as the Federal Home Loan Banks, the Federal Home Loan Mortgage Corporation, the Federal National Mortgage Association, and Farm Credit Banks.

The securities of federal agencies and federally sponsored agencies carry a slightly higher interest rate than U.S. Treasury securities because they are one step removed from the power of the Treasury. However, these agency interest rates are lower than market rates for state and local governments or private businesses because the full faith and credit of the U.S. stands behind them.

2. State and local government bonds, known as municipal bonds, may be issued against specified expected revenues, such as those from a state toll road or a community sewage disposal system. These are called revenue bonds. Or, the bonds may be general obligation bonds issued on the basis of the general taxing powers of the state or locality. Interest from state and local bonds usually is exempt from federal income taxation. States and localities usually provide an income tax exemption for the interest income from their own bonds which are held by their residents. The interest rates on tax-exempt state and local bonds are lower than on public and private taxable bonds as a reflection of these income tax advantages. See *General Obligation Bonds, Revenue Bonds, Treasury Bonds, Treasury Bills, Treasury Notes.*

GOVERNMENT MULTIPLIER   The number by which a change in government expenditure must be multiplied to measure the resulting final change in GNP after rounds of induced consumption expenditure occur. (It does *not* refer to the rate of growth in government bureaucracy.) For the multiplier process, see: *Gross National Product Multiplier.* Also see: *Tax Multiplier.*

GOVERNMENT NATIONAL MORTGAGE ASSOCIATION (GNMA OR GINNIE MAE) A federal corporation in the Department of Housing and Urban Development, created in 1968, which buys home mortgages guaranteed by the Federal Housing Administration (FHA) or the Department of Veterans Affairs (VA), puts mortgages with similar characteristics into groups, or pools, and then issues mortgage pass-through securities backed by those pools. The principal and interest payments from the mortgages are *passed through* to the holders of the GNMA securities.

Ginnie Mae also guarantees timely payment of principal and interest on securities backed by federally insured mortgages, which are issued by such holders of mortgages as thrifts and Fannie Mae. The Ginnie Mae guarantee means that the securities are backed by the full faith and credit of the U.S. government.

At the end of 1987 outstanding pass-through securities guaranteed by GNMA, the Federal Home Loan Mortgage Association, and the Federal National Mortgage Association totaled $718 billion, equal to nearly one-fourth of all residential mortgage debt outstanding. See *Collateralized Bond Obligations, Federal Home Loan Mortgage Corporation, Federal National Mortgage Association, Pass-Through Security.*

GOVERNMENT SECTOR OF GNP (G) Government is one of four sectors of the economy identified in analyzing gross national product, the other three being households, businesses, and foreign trade.
1. All government spending for goods and services (such as that for defense, highways, post offices, fire departments, judges, and legislators) is added into the total of GNP when we try to measure the total value created in the economy during a quarter or a year. Economists use the symbol G to stand for government spending.

2. Transfer payments by government, such as welfare payments, unemployment insurance claims, social security payments, and interest on the national debt, do not represent payments made in return for a current product or service and so are excluded from G, and thus from GNP. (GNP, remember, is a measure of the total value of all goods and services produced in the economy during a period of time.) However, transfer payments will show up later in GNP as consumer spending (C) or business investment spending (I) when the transfer payments are spent for goods and services by the recipients.

3. When government raises taxes (T) to pay for its spending, funds are taken away from consumers and businesses, so that the total of (C) and (I) entering into GNP may be smaller than without

taxes. When government borrows to pay for its spending it may crowd out consumers and businesses from access to available loanable funds by bidding up interest rates, thereby making it too costly for some consumers and businesses to borrow to spend. When government enters markets to buy goods and services, some consumers and businesses may be crowded out directly as government outbids them. See *Consumption Function, Crowding Out, Investment, Net Exports, Transfer Payments.*

GREENBACK A fiat paper money issued by the U.S. Treasury in 1862 to help finance the Civil War. The Treasury printed money without any thing of value designated as a reserve to "back" the currency. Backing consisted of the taxing powers of the U.S. Government, but the greenbacks were issued to avoid having to raise taxes by that amount. About $450,000,000 in greenbacks were issued during the war and about $300,000,000 continue in circulation today, as worn out greenbacks are called in and replaced in the hands of the public by the Treasury Department. See *Fiat Money.*

GREENMAIL Payment by a corporation to a shareholder to acquire the shareholder's stock when the same terms are not available to all shareholders. Often greenmail is associated with a possible unfriendly takeover attempt, as the outsider threatens to make a public tender offer for the company's stock and/or threatens a proxy fight for control of the firm. See *Takeover.*

GRESHAM'S LAW Bad money drives out good. When more than one kind of money is in circulation, e.g., gold and silver coins, the money which is overvalued at the official price will tend to remain in circulation because it is worth more as a medium of exchange than as bullion in the market. That money which is undervalued will disappear from circulation to be hoarded or to be melted down because it has higher value as metal than as legal tender. The undervalued coins also might disappear from domestic circulation by being used for foreign payments, where the higher market value (relative to the domestic legal tender value) would be effective.

Perhaps the "bad" money is paper money in which people have little confidence because of inflation when too much is issued. If it is legal tender, people will pay it out as they receive it, while hoarding coins of intrinsic value (good money) that they receive. Before the U.S. Civil War, private bank notes were not legal tender, but Gresham's Law applied as people kept the bank notes of highly reputable banks or specie and tried to spend the bank notes of more obscure banks. The law is named for Sir Thomas Gresham, master of the mint in England under Queen Elizabeth I in the sixteenth century. See *Bimetallism*.

GRIEVANCE   A complaint by an employee or group of employees that treatment by the employer is unfair or that the employer is not living up to the terms of the collective bargaining contract. Sometimes a contract will recognize grievances by employers against unions, such as complaints that the *union* is not living up to the terms of the collective bargaining contract. See *Grievance Procedure*.

GRIEVANCE PROCEDURE   An orderly process specified in working rules or in a collective bargaining contract for handling grievances as they arise, without recourse to cessation of production or other use of economic force. The procedure spells out the successive steps that a person with a grievance may take to resolve the problem, usually beginning with a discussion about the problem between the employee and his/her immediate supervisor and ending with arbitration as a last step. See *Arbitration*.

GROSS INVESTMENT   See *Gross Private Domestic Investment*.

GROSS NATIONAL PRODUCT (GNP)   The value of the total output of final goods and services in the economy for a particular time period, such as a year, plus the value of any net increase of goods-in-process (i.e., net changes in inventories). GNP is measured by adding up the value of all consumer goods and services sold (C), (I), or the value of all of the capital goods produced and sold plus net changes in inventories, the value of all government expenditures (G), and the value of net foreign trade known as net exports (NE). "Gross" refers to total production without accounting for depreciation (rather than to a teenage epithet). The term "final goods" means only those goods at the last set of transactions—the sale to the final user—omitting all intermediate production and distribution transactions. Its use is designed to avoid double counting which would occur if we were, for example, to count the value of automobile door handles when sold to the car company as well as the value of the car (which includes the value of the door handles) when it is sold to the consumer. See *Consumption Function, Government Sector of GNP, Investment, Net National Product, Net Exports*.

GROSS NATIONAL PRODUCT DEFLATOR   Sometimes known as the implicit price index. A price index which is the weighted average of more specialized price indexes, it is used to convert GNP current dollars into GNP constant dollars. It is a broader index than other available price indexes, such as the consumer price index or the producer price index. See *Price Index, Deflation.*

GROSS NATIONAL PRODUCT MULTIPLIER The amount by which one must multiply an autonomous change in one of the components of aggregate demand (AD) in order to determine the final change in gross national product (GNP), which is greater by the amount of induced consumption expenditure. For example, the investment multiplier is the amount by which one must multiply a given change in investment demand (I), say an increase of $1 billion a year in plant construction, in order to calculate the total effect of that change on GNP. Similarly, there is a government expenditure multiplier, a tax multiplier (negative), and a net foreign-investment multiplier.

The multipliers exist because the change in expenditure has induced effects on consumer demand (C). When GNP increases because of a $1 billion increase in I, consumer income will increase as people are put to work creating the new capital goods or new inventories and people earn new income not being paid before. There will be a consequent increase in C according to the marginal propensity to consume (MPC). If the MPC related to GNP is 0.8, consumers will spend 0.8 times the increase of $1 billion in GNP, so that AD and GNP will rise by $1 billion of I plus $0.8 billion of C.

But the effects do not end there, because production of more consumer goods also employs people and creates more household income. Consumers, given the MPC, will spend 0.8 times the $0.8 billion increase in C, or $0.64 billion. AD and GNP now will have risen by $1 billion of I, plus $0.8 billion of C, plus $0.64 billion of C, or a total of $2.44 billion. GNP will continue to increase until the long series of induced consumption expenditures has played out. Such a decreasing series of increases may be expressed algebraically as $1/(1 - \text{MPC})$. In the example, the multiplier is $1/(1 - 0.8) = 5$. If the MPC were 0.9, the multiplier would be $1/(1 - 0.9) = 1/0.1 = 10$.

The multiplier may work in reverse, as well. A fall in I may result in a decrease in GNP by a multiple of that initial drop in output because the reduction of investment expenditure induces a decrease in C as people are laid off and household incomes fall.

A change in government expenditure (G) will have a similar multiplier effect, as will an autonomous (nonincome) change in C, such as an anticipated increase in consumer goods prices. The latter is illustrated by a shift in the consumption function. A tax multiplier will have an inverse multiplied effect in that an increase in taxes may cause a multiplied *decrease* in GNP.

Some investment expenditure is induced by an increase in aggregate demand because larger inventories are required to service a higher volume of sales and, for firms near capacity, new equipment and factory space may be necessary. The relationship of a change in one of the components of AD to induced *investment* expenditure is called the accelerator. The total change in GNP following an autonomous change in investment, government expenditure, or consumer demand will be greater than that initial change because of the multiplier and the accelerator. See *Accelerator. Consumption Function, Marginal Propensity to Consume, Supermultiplier, Tax Multiplier.*

GROSS PRIVATE DOMESTIC INVESTMENT A component of gross national product (GNP) in national income accounting and analysis. It originates in the business sector of the economy and consists of all expenditures for plant, equipment, machines, buildings, and inventories in a country during a period of time. There is no adjustment for the wearing out of some capital goods in the process of production or for obsolescence due to the passage of time. Also known as gross investment. See *Autonomous Investment, Investment, Investment Demand, Net Private Domestic Investment.*

GROWTH STOCK The stock of companies with good earnings-growth histories that extend up to the present. Some examples are Coca Cola, McDonald's, and Proctor and Gamble.

GUILD An association of artisans in medieval and Renaissance times that was organized to control the quality and quantity of production of a commodity. It typically consisted of the self-employed or employers of journeymen, and so is similar to modern trade associations, and it is unlike modern labor unions of employees which are organized to bargain with employers over wages and working conditions. See *Union.*

HEAD TAX A tax of fixed amount levied on each person, man, woman, and child, in a group. Also known as a *poll tax*. A head tax is a regressive tax in the sense that those with low income pay a higher proportion of their incomes in tax than those with high incomes. Prime Minister Margaret Thatcher's government levied a head tax in Great Britain in 1989 and her popularity index plummeted. See *Regressive Tax*.

HEDGING Elimination of the effect of price fluctuations by participation on both sides of a market. Example: A miller who wishes to succeed as miller rather than as grain speculator buys wheat to process into flour during the next 30 days. Simultaneously he or she sells a futures contract on the commodity exchange for delivery of wheat in 30 days. If the price of wheat falls during the 30 days, the miller will experience an inventory loss which is offset by the gain when cheap wheat is bought to fulfill the futures contract that the miller sold for a higher price. If the price of wheat rises, the miller will experience an inventory value gain which is offset by the loss incurred when higher-priced wheat is bought to fulfill the futures contract. Either way, the miller has transferred the risk of grain price fluctuations to speculators whose activity creates the futures market. See *Futures Market, Stock-Index Futures, Options Trading*.

HIDDEN TAX A tax which is included in the purchase price of a good or service but not listed separately, so in a sense it is hidden from view. Hidden taxes usually are excise taxes levied on producers at some stage of production or distribution rather than levied on buyers at the time of the final sale. Examples are import duties, whiskey taxes, cigarette taxes, and gasoline taxes. Some sellers try to counter the hidden nature of federal and state taxes by publicizing them through advertising and listing them at the place of sale, as gasoline retailers do on their pumps. But buyers tend to lose awareness of the taxes when the tax is not separately calculated and added to the price at the time of the sale.

A retail sales tax usually is listed separately on a bill or cash register receipt rather than being hidden in a stated selling price. Income taxes and property taxes are other examples of "open" rather than hidden taxes.

HIDDEN INFLATION   Inflation that occurs through deterioration in the quality of goods and services sold at a constant price per unit rather than through rising prices for the same quality of goods. During World War II in the United States, price controls prohibited overt price increases, so manufacturing costs were reduced by shifting to lower-quality materials, lower-quality workmanship, and less varied choice. Men's shirts, for example, were made of poorer materials with poorer-quality tailoring, and high-quality shirts, colored shirts, and striped shirts were not available

Hidden inflation has occurred in recent years as, for example, distillers have reduced the "proof" of a bottle of whiskey from a typical 86 proof (43% alcohol) to 80 proof (40% alcohol) without any comparable reduction in price.

HIGH-POWERED MONEY   See *Monetary Base.*

HIRING HALL   A place, or a list of workers, usually maintained and controlled by a labor union, to bring together workers seeking work and employers seeking workers. A hiring hall is an employment exchange found in industries in which jobs are of short duration and workers may work for many different employers during the year, e.g., longshoring or carpentry and other building trades. It provides a way of sharing work as workers who complete a job sign in at the bottom of the list and employers hire from the top. The system requires that all on the list have acquired the necessary skills to perform the work. A hiring hall may serve to control entry into the labor pool. See *Closed Shop.*

HOARDING   The holding of something (e.g., money, gold, or wheat) from use.

Farmers in a command economy may hoard some of their crop to exchange it later in a black market rather than turn it over to the government at fixed low prices.

In wartime or times of scarcity the price system may not be effective in allocating goods in the manner desired, so prices are fixed by government. It is anticipated that some items will be scarce, such as sugar, and some people buy all they can get to hoard it in the basement, buying well beyond their normal current needs. When prices are not permitted to rise to allocate the scarce goods among those willing and able to pay, substitute allocating mechanisms are developed. One is the "first come-first served" principle, which results in lines of people and scrambles for position in line. Another may be a seller-imposed dictum of "one to a customer." Or, the government might ration goods by issuing ration coupons or stamps which must be used together with money to purchase the goods.

In national income analysis, savings are hoarded when not lent to others directly or through financial intermediaries. Hoarded savings may prevent the interest rate from equilibrating intended saving and intended investment, causing an excess of inventories followed by reduced production. See *Black Market, Rationing*.

HOLDING COMPANY A company created to hold controlling shares in other companies. Because control of a company is assured by holding just over 50% of the voting stock (and often much less), it is possible to control a very large amount of assets with a relatively small investment of money by pyramiding holding companies. Holding companies also provide a way of diversifying investment.

HOMOGENEOUS OLIGOPOLY Also known as undifferentiated oligopoly or pure oligopoly. A market composed of a few rival producers that make an undifferentiated product. Examples are the market for standardized structural shapes such as I-bars and T-bars in the steel industry or the market for aluminum ingots in the aluminum industry. There is a tendency for uniform pricing of products in a homogeneous oligopoly. See *Oligopoly, Differentiated Oligopoly*.

HOMOGENEOUS PRODUCT Each unit of the product is considered by buyers to be the same as any other unit, no matter who produced it. The market might recognize some different grades, but within a grade the product of one firm is indistinguishable from the product of others. Feed corn is an example. See *Differentiated Product*.

HORIZONTAL MERGER   A merger of firms which produce products or services competing in the same market. Examples are the merger of Crescent department stores with Frederick & Nelson department stores, each with stores in Spokane, Washington, or the merger of E.F. Hutton stock brokerage with Shearson Lehman. See *Merger, Conglomerate Merger, Vertical Merger.*

HOSTILE TAKEOVER   An attempt by a group outside a firm to take over the firm by stock acquisition despite opposition by the incumbent management. Even if the hostile takeover is unsuccessful, the instigators may make large profits as the price of the firm's stock is bid up beyond the prices paid for much of the stock purchased earlier by the hostile group. See *Takeover, Greenmail, Leveraged Buyout, Merger.*

HOT MONEY   In foreign exchange markets, money that shifts from one currency to others about as fast as a hot potato moves from one hand to another. The money, in the form of bank deposits, moves quickly to the country with the highest interest rates at the moment or to a currency which is expected to appreciate soon relative to others. Hot money moves at the bidding of speculators and also at the direction of money-management departments of large corporations that are heavily involved in international trade or finance. These firms develop large balances of foreign currency which, if passively held, could change quickly in value and wipe out any possible profit from their normal business.

HOUSEHOLD   In economics, the decision-making unit in which consumer spending and saving decisions, and factor-of-production selling decisions, are made. Usually it is a function of living and family arrangements. Examples: An individual living alone and supporting no one else; a person sharing a home with a parent; a family of mother, father, and children; a single-parent family; a woman or man living with a friend and sharing income and expenses.

HUMAN CAPITAL   Human assets in the form of ability, skill, and knowledge which contribute to the productivity of the economy through high output per labor-hour, high quality of output, or invention and innovation. Investment in human capital is made through education to produce scientists, inventors, and innovative managers and through training to produce skilled machine operators, tool makers, and computer programmers. See *Economic Growth.*

HYPERINFLATION   A very high rate of price inflation. Examples are the 1,500% annual rate of inflation experienced by Yugoslavia and the 3,000% annual rate in Peru in 1990, or the 12,000% inflation rate in Argentina in 1989. Sometimes run-away inflation develops, such as that in the Confederate states during the U. S. Civil War or in Germany between 1920 and 1923 where rapidly rising prices fed on themselves as people rushed to spend money that was rapidly losing its value. The velocity of circulation seems to increase exponentially. It often results in collapse of the monetary system and sometimes the entire economic and political order. See *Inflation*.

IMPERFECT COMPETITION 1. As a general concept, market structures other than pure competition. 2. In specific terms, it is a theoretical concept developed by Joan Robinson (1903–1983) in England in the early 1930s at approximately the same time that a similar concept, *monopolistic competition,* was developed by Edward Chamberlin (1889–1967) in the United States. The theories concern markets in which many firms vie with one another, producing differentiated products which buyers consider very similar. In numbers of rivals, there are too many to constitute oligopoly and too few (along with differentiation of products) to constitute pure competition. Differences among the products of the many firms may be real or imaginary, and producers attempt to emphasize differences through advertising. The two authors spent some time trying to differentiate their theories.

Edward Chamberlin gave more emphasis to the role of advertising and locational advantage in creating and maintaining product differentiation. He is credited with a more penetrating analysis of these peculiarities, which established the need for new theory rather than just a slight modification of the theory of monopoly. See *Monopolistic Competition.*

IMPLICIT COSTS Costs attributable to factors of production but which do not appear explicitly in a business income statement. Some examples, which often occur in single proprietorships, are (1) The wage or salary that is attributable to the owner–operator of a small business but is not paid, and thus is not separated out from gross returns as a cost. Instead it is recognized as part of net revenue. (2) Interest attributable to use of a business owner's own funds to finance a capital purchase but which is not included in the cost accounts because it is interest income foregone rather than an interest expense paid to someone else. (3) Rent attributable to land owned and used by a farmer or grocer but not appearing in cost accounts because it is rent foregone rather than paid out to another. The dollar value of implicit costs can be obtained by calculating them as opportunity costs.

Implicit costs are not included in business cost accounts because they are not expenses paid to or owed to others. Generally they do not affect taxes collected by the Internal Revenue Service from unincorporated enterprises. For tax purposes, the owner of the factor of production would receive the amount as personal income if it were received by the owner after being listed, for example, as salary, which is an explicit business cost, instead of being included in the net returns (profit) of the business after all other costs are deducted from business receipts. See *Implicit Factor Returns, Imputed Costs, Opportunity Cost.*

IMPLICIT FACTOR RETURNS Returns to factors of production which do not involve a market exchange and so may not appear in an accounting statement. The other side of implicit costs. Examples are rent from agricultural land farmed by the owner, interest on funds provided by a business proprietor for the purchase of inventory, or wages of an owner–manager. From an economic standpoint they must be recognized for there to be a continuing flow of those resources into production and an efficient allocation of resources in the economy. The dollar value of implicit factor returns may be obtained by calculating them as opportunity costs. See *Implicit Costs, Opportunity Cost.*

IMPUTED COSTS Costs which do not involve a money payment to others but which are necessary to maintain the flow of resources to the firm. A prime example is depreciation of capital goods, which is shown as an explicit cost in the accounts of both single proprietorships and corporations. Some other costs called implicit costs are imputed by economists but not by business firms. See *Implicit Costs.*

INCIDENCE OF A TAX See *Tax Incidence.*

INCOME: BUSINESS INCOME Business income may refer to gross receipts, or it may refer to net income, which equals gross receipts minus costs.

INCOME: DISPOSABLE PERSONAL INCOME In national income analysis, after-tax household income from all sources including transfer payments. It is what the household received during the period to either spend or save.

INCOME: FACTOR INCOME Income received by a factor of production from the sale of the productive factor's services. It consists of wages for the use of labor, rent for the use of land, interest for the use of capital goods, and profit for entrepreneurship.

INCOME EFFECT: NATIONAL INCOME ANALYSIS See *Gross National Product Multiplier*.

INCOME EFFECT: PRICE THEORY The effect of a product price change on the real income of a consumer. If price declines for a product which is consumed regularly, the fall in price is in effect an increase in income for the consumer. The consumer need not spend as much for the quantity of the product usually purchased and so has some income left over. That amount can be used in a variety of ways: the purchase of more of the product whose price fell, the purchase of more of other products and services, an increase in saving, or some combination of these.

When the price of a product falls, the quantity demanded also will tend to increase because of the substitution effect. Quantities of the good will be substituted in consumption for those goods which are close substitutes and whose prices are now relatively higher.

A price *increase* will produce an income effect and a substitution effect which are the opposite of those that follow a price decrease. See *Elasticity of Demand, Income Elasticity of Demand, Inferior Good, Substitution Effect*.

INCOME ELASTICITY OF DEMAND A measure of the sensitivity of the quantity of a product demanded to changes in a person's income. It is the percentage change in quantity of the good demanded divided by the percentage change in income. Point income elasticity of demand involves minute changes in income and in quantity demanded, while arc elasticity involves discrete changes of some magnitude so that it makes a difference whether one chooses the initial amount or the new amount to use in the denominator of the elasticity formula. The formulas for income elasticity of demand are as follows.

Point Income Elasticity of Demand

$$E_y = \frac{\dfrac{q_{x1} - q_{x2}}{q_x}}{\dfrac{y_1 - y_2}{y}} = \frac{(q_{x1} - q_{x2})\,y}{(y_1 - y_2)\,q_x}$$

Arc Income Elasticity of Demand

$$E_y = \frac{\dfrac{q_{x1} - q_{x2}}{q_{x1} + q_{x2}}}{\dfrac{y_1 - y_2}{y_1 + y_2}} = \frac{(q_{x1} - q_{x2})\,(y_1 + y_2)}{(q_{x1} + q_{x2})\,(y_1 - y_2)},$$

where E_y is the income elasticity coefficient, q_x is the quantity of product x demanded, and y is income. See *Elasticity*.

INCOMES POLICY Public policy designed to affect wages and prices directly in order to deal with the problem of an apparent trade-off between inflation and unemployment as described by the Phillips curve. In non-U.S. economies incomes policy often is synonymous with wage and price controls. In the U.S. incomes policy includes guideposts established by government for wage and price changes in the economy, wage and price controls for key economic sectors or for the entire economy, and structural changes such as government training of the untrained and reducing discrimination based on noneconomic characteristics. A tax-based incomes policy uses tax benefits to reward employees and employers who follow incomes guidelines and tax penalties to penalize those who do not.

During the 1970s, it seemed that any success in reducing unemployment through monetary and fiscal policy led to higher rates of inflation in the U.S., while reduction of inflation was accompanied by rising unemployment. The Nixon administration instituted the first peace-time wage–price controls in 1971 to try to deal with the problem. However, it did not take long for supply and demand conditions to change in some markets, so that relative prices in the controlled markets departed from free-market relative prices. That caused dislocations to occur despite some price and wage adjustments, and the program died. President Ford tried "jaw boning" to hold down prices and wages with his "WIN" motto (whip inflation now), to little avail. Toward the end of the decade inflation went on up into double digits. Monetary policy, pursued with vigor in the early 1980s to fight the double-digit inflation, caused substantial unemployment but broke the back of inflation. The recovery which followed lowered unemployment rates without being accompanied by rising rates of inflation.

Wage and price guidelines or controls undermine the important allocative role that is provided by flexible prices in markets, and they thereby reduce economic efficiency in the allocation of resources. Fiscal and monetary policies are alternatives to incomes policy to try to provide full employment without inflation. See *Phillips Curve, Monetary Policy, Fiscal Policy.*

INCOME VELOCITY OF THE CIRCULATION OF MONEY   The average number of times a dollar is used to buy final goods and services in the economy—the circle of income to expenditure to income. It is the ratio of gross national product to the money stock.

$$V_y = \frac{GNP}{M},$$

where V_y is the income velocity of money, *GNP* is gross national product, and *M* is the money stock. It is a concept used in quantity theories of money. See *Quantity Theory of Money, Transactions Velocity of the Circulation of Money.*

INCREASING COSTS   As the scale of output grows in a firm or industry the cost per unit of output (long-run average cost) rises. Change in scale refers to "the long run" in which there are no fixed costs because *all* factors of production are variable.

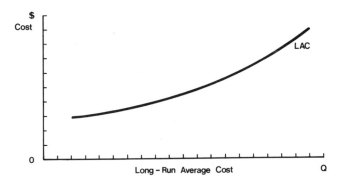

INCREASING COSTS CURVE

Long-run average costs might begin to rise as output expands because there are decreasing returns to scale. Management and communication problems may lead to growing inefficiency after some level of output is reached. Increasing costs also might occur because the firm has grown to be such a large buyer in some resource market that further expansion bids up resource prices. In the diagram (p. 147), the vertical axis measures dollars per unit and the horizontal axis measures level of output.

See *Decreasing Returns to Scale, Constant Costs, Decreasing Costs, Economies of Scale, Increasing Returns to Scale.*

INCREASING RETURNS TO SCALE   As all inputs are increased in the same proportion, output increases more than proportionally to the change in inputs. For example, if inputs double, output more than doubles.

Increasing returns result from the ability to combine factors of production more efficiently through specialization and division of labor and/or to use more efficient technologies where factors of production are somewhat specialized and not infinitely divisible. Hence increasing returns to scale lead to increased size of plant and firm, and thus large-scale output. Increasing returns to scale is a "long-run" concept and is a factor in explaining decreasing long-run average costs. If output expands more than in proportion to an expansion of inputs, then the input cost per unit of output will fall (assuming no external factors such as quantity discounts in the price of an input). If increasing returns to scale persist to very large outputs, oligopoly or monopoly may be the natural result. See *Decreasing Costs, Constant Costs, Decreasing Returns to Scale, Economies of Scale, Natural Monopoly.*

INCREASING RETURNS TO A VARIABLE FACTOR OF PRO- DUCTION   If successive units of a variable factor of production are added to a fixed amount of other factors, there may be a range of increasing returns before the beginning of the range of diminishing returns. Increasing returns may arise because there is a disproportionate amount of fixed factors relative to the small quantity of the variable factor, so that the effectiveness of each added unit of the variable factor increases relative to the previous unit; each added unit of the variable factor adds more to output than the preceding unit did. Here increasing returns is a matter of *varying the proportions among factors of production*, while increasing returns to scale occur with a *proportionate increase of all factors of production*. See *Diminishing Returns.*

INDEPENDENT UNION   A national or international union that is not affiliated with any federation of unions. Before the merger of the American Federation of Labor (AFL) and the Congress of Industrial Unions (CIO) in 1955, an independent union would have been independent of both. Some independent unions have been unaffilia-ted by their own choice, while others have been expelled from a federation in the past for being communist dominated or controlled by racketeers. The International Brotherhood of Teamsters, for example, was expelled from the CIO in 1957 on charges of corrup-tion and remained independent until joining the AFL–CIO in 1988. During that time, the Teamsters became a federation of sorts by organizing workers in a wide variety of jobs from clerks to public school teachers to truck drivers to university buildings and grounds employees. The United Auto Workers Union withdrew from the AFL–CIO in 1969 following disagreements between Walter Re-uther, president of the UAW, and George Meany, president of the AFL–CIO. The UAW and the Teamsters formed a short-lived federation named the Alliance for Labor Action. See *Union, Ameri-can Federation of Labor–Congress of Industrial Organizations.*

INDEPENDENT VARIABLE   See *Autonomous Variable.*

INDEX NUMBER   A number that summarizes a particular array of data for a time period and is expressed as a percentage of another summary number that is calculated for a base period. For example, the consumer price index number for all items in the "market basket" for all urban consumers in December of 1988 was 120.5 with 1982–84 = 100, which is to say that when the weighted average of consumer prices in the base period (1982–84) is placed equal to 100%, the weighted average of consumer prices at the end of 1988 was 20.5% higher. Index numbers are developed for such time series as GNP, agricultural output, and manufacturing output as well as for various price indexes. See *Price Index* for a discussion of constructing an index number and an index.

INDEX TRADING   Trading in futures and options markets on broad baskets of stocks, e.g., stock indexes such as Standard and Poor's 100 index, S & P 500 index, and the New York Stock Exchange Index. Index trading often is used as a hedge against trades in large blocks of stock by program traders. There is trading in options on an oil index, a gold/silver index, and a computer technology index, among others. See *Futures Market, Options Trading.*

INDIFFERENCE CURVE   A curve made up of a number of points, each of which represents a combination of goods, x and y, that a consumer finds equally satisfying to every other combination of x

and y on the curve. Hence the consumer is indifferent as to which of the combinations he or she receives.

On a graph, the curve tends to be convex to the origin, representing a particular trade-off of x for y as one moves from point to point, maintaining a constant level of satisfaction. When the consumer has but a small quantity of x and a large quantity of y, he or she will be willing to give up quite a large amount of y to get one more unit of x and still remain at the same level of satisfaction. As one continues to substitute x for y, the consumer will be willing to give up less and less y for additional units of x in order to maintain the same level of satisfaction. This expresses the Law of Diminishing Marginal Rate of Substitution. The slope at each point on the indifference curve represents the marginal rate of substitution of x for y (MRS_{xy}) for that combination of x and y. The marginal rate of substitution is the rate at which a consumer will substitute quantities of one good, x, for another good, y, while maintaining the same level of satisfaction.

More of both x and y would produce a higher level of satisfaction, shown as a shift to another indifference curve farther out from the origin. Conversely, less of both x and y would be shown as a shift to an indifference curve closer to the origin, representing a lower level of satisfaction for the consumer.

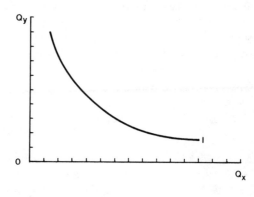

INDIFFERENCE CURVE

The indifference curve is an explanatory device used with a consumer budget line in the derivation of a consumer demand curve and in illustrating consumer equilibrium. It has the advantage of using an ordinal utility function rather than a cardinal one. That is, the desirability of another unit of a product is *ranked* in conjunction with less of another rather than being measured as precise *amounts* or quantities on some thermometer of desirability. See *Indifference Map, Equilibrium of the Consumer, Marginal Rate of Substitution.*

INDIFFERENCE MAP   A contour map representing three variables in the analysis of consumer demand. The x axis represents quantities of one consumer good, the y axis is quantities of another, and the height in this three-dimensional representation is the level of satisfaction. All points at the same height lie on a contour curve, called an indifference curve. The curve consists of various combinations of x and y, each of which provides a consumer with equal satisfaction to every other combination on that curve. Therefore, the consumer is indifferent as to which of the combinations to select.

Each successive indifference curve progressing out from the origin represents a higher level of satisfaction, because at least one point on the higher indifference curve represents *more of both goods* (and all other combinations on the higher curve provide equal satisfaction to that larger combination).

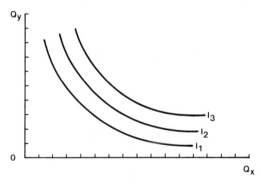

INDIFFERENCE CURVE MAP

See *Indifference Curve, Equilibrium of the Consumer.*

INDIRECT BUSINESS TAXES   A category used in national income accounting which is the principal item subtracted from *net national product* to arrive at the statistical measure of *national income.* It includes excise, sales, and real estate taxes—generally taxes other than those levied against income.

INDIVIDUAL PROPRIETORSHIP   See *Single Proprietorship.*

INDUCED CONSUMPTION In national income analysis, the volume of increased consumption expenditure that results from an increase in national income when there is an increase in one of the categories of aggregate demand (investment expenditure for capital goods, government expenditure, net exports, or an autonomous increase in consumption expenditure). Induced consumption expenditure will occur with an increase in national income according to the marginal propensity to consume. For example, if business firms increase their expenditure for capital goods, the capital goods manufacturers will increase their labor input (and payrolls) and buy more materials. More income is created for households and the income recipients will spend a portion of their increase on consumer goods. See *Marginal Propensity to Consume, Gross National Product Multiplier.*

INDUCED INVESTMENT Investment which is prompted by an increase in the level of GNP. If sales in the economy grow, firms that are close to capacity will need more capital goods to produce more output. A higher level of investment in inventories usually is required to service a higher level of sales. Even for "just-in-time" inventory management, the supplier's inventories and quantity of goods in transit would tend to grow.

Autonomous investment in capital goods and inventories, on the other hand, is independent of the level of economic activity and is the result of innovation or interest rate changes. See *Autonomous Investment, Investment.*

INDUSTRIAL RELATIONS Also known as labor relations. The whole gamut of relations between employers and employees. An area of study that includes such wide-ranging topics as slowdowns, strikes, and other manifestations of disputes between workers and employers; grievance procedures, arbitration, and mediation; hiring, promotion, layoff, and firing policies; sick leave, holiday, and vacation policies; job classification and pay scales; work rules including production quotas, rest periods, use of protective clothing, and clean-up around the work station; and collective bargaining.

INDUSTRIAL UNION A labor union composed of nonmanagement workers who are organized by plant, firm, and industry regardless of whether they are unskilled, semiskilled, or skilled workers. Some industrial unions are actually multiindustry unions. Industrial unionism spread rapidly in the mass-production industries of the U.S. during the Great Depression of the 1930s following the passage of the National Labor Relations Act (Wagner Act) in 1935, which provided for labor union organization and recognition by secret ballot. Until recent years, most industrial unions focused on production workers and did not try to organize white-collar and office workers.

Examples of industrial unions are the United Automobile Workers, the International Union of Electrical Workers, the United Steel Workers of America and, the most general of all, the International Brotherhood of Teamsters. An industrial union contrasts with a craft union, which is organized by occupation or skill regardless of plant, firm, or industry. Examples of craft unions are the United Brotherhood of Carpenters and Joiners, the Bricklayers, and the Plumbers Unions. See *Craft Union, American Federation of Labor–Congress of Industrial Organizations.*

INELASTIC DEMAND 1. The quantity demanded is rather insensitive to a change in price in a market for a product or service. More precisely, the percentage change in quantity demanded is less than the percentage change in price. Thus the price elasticity of demand coefficient is less than 1. It can be stated as $E < 1$ when the negative sign is ignored, that is, E is a positive fraction (or E is a negative fraction when the sign is recognized). When demand is inelastic an increase in price will result in an increase in total revenue because the price increase more than offsets the quantity decrease ($TR = P \times Q$). Similarly, a decrease in price will reduce total revenue.

An example of inelastic demand may be found in the demand for gasoline, which is derived from the demand for transportation and travel. In the short run, habit and necessary travel mean that even substantial price increases result in modest decreases in the quantity of gasoline demanded. This has been illustrated by public reaction in the U.S. to large increases in price as the result of OPEC's success in raising oil prices in 1973 and 1979, and by the effect of the embargo on oil from Iraq and Kuwait in 1990. It takes a considerable amount of time for any substantial decrease in quantity demanded to occur as habits reluctantly change, mass transportation is increased and accepted, fewer gas-guzzling vehicles are produced, and alternative energy sources are developed.

2. Inelastic demand also may apply to income elasticity of demand and cross elasticity of demand. In the first case, demand for a product is relatively insensitive to a change in income; the elasticity coefficient is less than 1 and positive because demand for the product and income move in the same direction (except for the rare case of an inferior good). In the second case, the demand for product *x* is relatively insensitive to a change in the price of *y*. The elasticity coefficient is a fraction that is positive when the goods

are substitutes and negative if they are complements. See *Elasticity, Elasticity of Demand, Income Elasticity of Demand, Cross Elasticity*.

INELASTIC SUPPLY   The quantity supplied is rather insensitive to a change in price in a market for goods and services. More precisely, the percentage change in quantity supplied is less than the percentage change in price. If price were to rise 10%, quantity supplied would rise less than 10%. If price were to fall 10%, the quantity supplied would fall less than 10%. Notice the positive relationship between *P* and *Q*, whereas the price elasticity of demand is negative, an increase in price results in a decrease in quantity demanded.

In the very short run, the supply of sweet corn in a local market is limited to that ripening daily in the surrounding countryside so that an increase in price will not cause much increase in quantity supplied. With a little more time, grocers can order corn to be trucked in from farther away and, in the long run, farmers can plant more sweet corn. Supply tends to be more inelastic the shorter the time period. See *Elasticity, Elasticity of Supply*.

INFANT INDUSTRY: TARIFF PROTECTION   Developing nations may have "infant industries" in which production is carried on by young, small firms which cannot compete immediately with rival mature industries in developed countries but might be competitive in the long run. The infant industries may face long-run increasing returns because of economies of scale. Also, the development of labor force attitudes and skills can lower costs, and the creation of social overhead capital in the developing country can contribute to the long-run increasing returns for infant industries, as well.

A tax, or tariff, imposed on importation of competing foreign products could provide time for the young firms to grow enough to achieve economies of scale and to develop collectively a skilled, production-oriented labor force. It would encourage the purchase of the products domestically by taxing imports. The tariff, of course, would have to be high enough to keep out the competing foreign goods by raising the total import price to equal or exceed the domestic price of the goods.

Economists generally agree that the infant-industry concept provides the only valid economic argument for tariff protection. (A tariff whose purpose is to produce *revenue* for government is a different matter because it must be low enough to permit a substantial flow of imports if it is to generate much revenue.) Problems do arise in pursuing a policy of protecting an infant industry, however. There are difficulties of assessing which infant industries really face long-run increasing returns and of determining how long an infant industry should be given to mature. Also there is the difficult political decision to remove the tariff once maturity is reached so that the benefits of international competition can be achieved. See *Protectionism, Tariff.*

INFERIOR GOOD   A good or service whose quantity demanded varies inversely with a change in real income: Consumption increases with a decrease of income, and consumption decreases when income rises. A good for which the income effect is negative. When the change in real income is due to a change in the price of the good itself, a price reduction (which increases real income) will cause less of the inferior good to be consumed. If the price of the good falls, the greater the increase in real income, the less of the good demanded. An example is a cheap good that nevertheless takes a high proportion of income as a principal source of food for poor people, such as potatoes. See *Income Effect: Price Theory.*

INFLATION   Rapidly rising prices for goods and services and for factors of production as reflected by sustained increases in price indexes for the economy. A classic case of extreme inflation is the hyperinflation in Germany after World War I, when prices rose so rapidly that printing presses couldn't keep up by printing new currency of larger denominations, so larger numbers were stamped on top of already issued currency. Money to buy everyday items literally required a wheelbarrow to carry it around. The entire monetary system collapsed.

In the United States, consumer price index increases of 5 or 6% are considered inflationary, while double-digit increases such as those in the late 1970s cause grave concern. In the 1980s, a number of countries experienced inflation rates of 50, 80, 100, and some more than 1000%, rates which were economically and politically destabilizing. Prices of consumer goods and services in an inflation usually outrun most prices of factors of production.

All people whose income does not rise at the same rate as rising consumer prices will suffer a loss of purchasing power, by definition. Creditors and those on fixed income, such as many retired persons, lose purchasing power during inflation. Debtors gain by paying back money of lesser purchasing power than when the money was borrowed. See *Cost-Push Inflation, Creeping Inflation, Demand-Pull Inflation, Hyperinflation.*

INFLATIONARY GAP   The gap that occurs when aggregate demand (AD) at full-employment exceeds full employment gross national product (GNP). The total of what people want to spend, i.e., consumer demand (C), plus business investment demand (I), plus government expenditure (G), plus net exports (NE), exceeds the total value of output (GNP), and output cannot expand because the economy is at full employment of resources. The result is inflation.

In the diagram below, the full employment level of GNP is at F on the horizontal axis. The aggregate demand (AD) and aggregate supply (AS) schedules at F show that the amount of intended spending, OC, is more than the full-employment GNP, OF. There is an excess of demand over the value of what is produced amounting to ab, which is the inflationary gap. Output cannot expand because the economy is at full employment, so the excess volume of spending will cause prices to increase.

See *Aggregate Demand, Aggregate Supply, Deflationary Gap.*

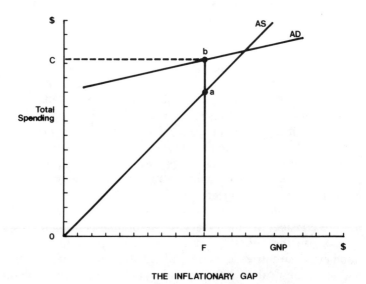

THE INFLATIONARY GAP

INJUNCTION   A court order prohibiting specified action because the harm that would be done by the action would be irreparable, i.e., the loss could not be recovered by later court suit. Examples often involve threats to personal safety, such as continued operation of a machine which threatens life or limb or mass picketing which threatens violence. Ignoring the injunction places one in contempt of court and subject to penalties imposed at the discretion of the judge. If an action appears to a judge to threaten irreparable harm, a temporary restraining order is issued to be in effect until a full hearing can be held with all affected parties having a chance to testify. A permanent injunction could then be issued, or the temporary restraining order could be lifted.

Injunctions have been used to control or prohibit picketing when picketing has exceeded free speech by blocking free access, by threatening violence, or when actual violence occurs.

In the 1920s and 1930s, prior to the passage of the Norris–La Guardia Act in 1932, which severely limited the use of injunctions by federal courts in labor disputes, injunctions were effective in preventing labor union organization when they were used to enforce "yellow dog" contracts. See *Yellow-Dog Contract*.

INNOVATION   Creative activity which introduces new methods of production or new goods or services and thereby causes change and growth in the economy. Innovation is the identification of the economic promise of something new and the marshaling of resources to introduce it. The innovator is not necessarily the inventor or the financier, but is the promoter. Once successfully introduced, imitators will flock in, attracted by the extraordinary profitability of the new method or product. The early development of railroads, the introduction of the automobile, and the establishment of assembly-line production were all key innovations in their day. Innovation plays a central role in *Business Cycles,* a theoretical and historical study by Joseph A. Schumpeter (1883–1950). See *Entrepreneur, Entrepreneurship, Technological Change.*

INPUT–OUTPUT RELATIONSHIP   1. The technological relationship between the quantity of input of all factors of production and the output of a particular product. Also known as the production function. The relationship assumes maximum engineering efficiency in the sense that the least quantity of each factor input will be used to produce a given amount of output. When one factor input may be substituted for another, determination of *economic* efficiency would require calculation of the amount of each alternative factor required per unit of output, and the price per unit of each of the alternative factor inputs.

2. "Input–output" also may refer to a framework of analysis developed by Wassily Leontief to establish production interrelationships and determine the production potential of an economy by tracing the complex web of factor inputs and product/service outputs which characterizes a modern economy. Such input–output analysis helps to identify where bottlenecks of materials or skills in short supply may arise as an economy approaches full employment. It is basic to economic planning. See *Isoquant Curve, Production Function.*

INSIDER TRADING   An illegal practice of trading on the stock market based on knowledge that is not available to the general public. By knowing, in advance of public notice, about merger plans, leveraged buyout plans, or an unexpected change in net income, it is possible to make millions of dollars buying stock that will appreciate or selling short stock that will decline in price. The inside trader might be an officer of the company or someone acting on his/her behalf, or a specialist in setting up mergers and buyouts, or even a friend of a relative of one of the above who acts on the basis of casually mentioned, but still private, information.

INSTITUTIONAL INVESTORS   Managers of large funds such as pension funds, insurance company funds collected as premiums, trust funds of various kinds, and university endowments led by Harvard's $5 billion. Institutional investors were the primary beneficiaries of the deregulation of the securities markets in 1975, which eliminated fixed brokerage fees. Their large transactions led to vigorous price bidding by brokerage firms seeking their business. Following 1975, broker commissions as a percentage of the value of orders fell by 50% for institutional investors. (Individual investors have benefited from deregulation by using discount brokers who soon appeared, but offer less service.)

INSURANCE   Protection from risk. Risk may be insurable when the existence of a large number of events will permit an average experience to be predicted and when the events are largely independent of one another so that extremes may be averaged out. The risks are spread, and the average cost represented by the premium for an insured is easier to bear than the possible high cost of an uninsured loss. A premium of $300 per year may represent the average cost of house fires for $75,000 houses among the tens of thousands of houses insured by a particular company. The annual premium is easier for the home owner to bear than the loss of a $75,000 house even though the chances of that particular house burning are slight. An event may be uninsurable where the outcome is unpredictable or *uncertain*. See *Risk, Uncertainty*.

INTANGIBLE ASSET   In accounting, an asset that has no physical existence and does not represent some material thing. Examples are copyrights, trademarks, franchises, patents, and goodwill.

INTEGRATION   See *Conglomerate Merger, Horizontal Merger, Vertical Integration*.

INTEREST   The price of money, usually expressed as a percentage per year of the principal amount that is loaned or borrowed. Money interest is the amount produced by the agreed-upon interest rate applied on the principal sum of a loan. A loan of $30,000 at 8% interest per year will produce $2,400 in interest per year. *Real* interest, on the other hand, takes into account changes in the purchasing power of money. In the case above, if price inflation is anticipated to be 10% per year, the lender would actually lose value even though paid the 8% ($2,400). The real interest rate is minus 2%, and the real interest is minus $600.

   Pure interest is the amount that must be paid for a perfectly safe loan or security which has no risk of loss from nonpayment.

   Lenders receive interest payments for giving up control over the use of their money. Lenders must be induced to (1) postpone the use of their money for goods and services and the immediate pleasure (or in the case of a firm, production) foregone, (2) accept the risk that the borrower will be unable or unwilling to pay back part or all of the principal, (3) accept the risk that the prices of goods and services, or the price of money, will rise between the time of lending and the time of repayment, and (4) accept the risk that an emergency may arise for which the lender would need the money but has given up control over it.

   Borrowers pay interest because they (1) prefer to spend future income for current purchases, (2) wish to buy resources for production which they anticipate will produce a total revenue to cover all costs, including the cost of money, and also provide a profit, or (3) anticipate that the price of money (interest rates) will rise. See *Profit, Uncertainty.*

INTEREST RATE   The rate of return paid by a borrower to a lender. If a borrower promises to pay $800 in interest on a 1-year loan of $10,000 the interest rate is 8% per year. The interest rate varies inversely with the price of a bond. Suppose that a 30-year negotiable bond is issued for $10,000 promising to pay interest each year at 8% of that face value, or $800. If the market rate of interest on new debt instruments of this quality were to rise to 8.7% the holder of the existing bond could only sell it for a price that would make $800 equal an 8.7% return, or $9,194.40 (that is, $800/.087). If the market interest rate were to fall to 7.4% the holder of the bond could sell it for $10,810.81 because 7.4% of that figure equals $800.

INTERLOCKING DIRECTORATE   An arrangement in which some persons hold membership on the boards of directors of several companies which are in competition with one another or do business with one another. If the firms are competitors, it may produce coordinated actions reducing competition and lead to the monopoly results of a cartel. If the firms do business with each other, it may exclude other potential suppliers or buyers than those represented in the interlocking directorate, and again reduce competition. Interlocking directorates are regulated in the U. S. under antitrust laws.

INTERMEDIATE GOODS Capital goods which are used to produce final goods for consumers, or inventories consisting of raw materials, semifinished goods, and finished goods not yet sold to the final consumer. The category includes all goods which enter into the production process, from extraction of raw materials to sale to consumers.

Intermediate goods are identified in part to avoid double counting when compiling data to measure gross national product (GNP). The price of an automobile produced and sold last year includes the value of coal, iron ore, steel, window glass, door handles, and all the component parts that ultimately were assembled into that automobile, as well as the value of plant and equipment used up in the production process. Many items were produced by independent firms and sold to the auto companies. But their value cannot be added into GNP because their value already is included in the price of the automobile. To add their values separately as well would constitute double counting.

INTERNAL RATE OF RETURN The rate of interest that will make the future flow of income from a proposed project equal to the cost of the project. If that rate of return is higher than the rate that could be earned on alternative investments of equal risk in the securities and money markets, it will be profitable to use available funds for the project or borrow the money for it.

INTERNATIONAL BANK FOR RECONSTRUCTION AND DEVELOPMENT Also known as the *World Bank*. An international bank formed in 1944 to make low-interest, long-term loans to people and governments for reconstruction (after World War II) and economic development when such loans are not available from private sources. Loanable funds are provided from subscriptions for capital stock from member nations according to their economic importance. It can also raise funds by selling bonds. The World Bank makes loans for economic development projects that are expected to produce a return to pay back the loan, such as cattle ranching in Spain. It also makes loans to governments for social overhead capital that increases the productivity of enterprise in a country, such as roads, schools, labor force training, etc. See *Agency for International Development, Export–Import Bank.*

INTERNATIONAL MONETARY FUND (IMF)   An international organization created in 1944 to eliminate foreign exchange restrictions, provide convertibility of currency, and encourage exchange-rate stability to promote trade.

The original IMF agreement was drawn to assist the functioning of an international gold standard system following the end of World War II. Each nation set an official par value for its currency in terms of gold or in terms of the U.S. dollar. The U.S. pledged to maintain the value of the dollar at $35 per fine ounce of gold by buying and selling gold at that price internationally. Some nations did not have enough gold for their currency to exchange freely for gold. Those nations set the par value of their money in terms of U.S. dollars, using dollars for their currency reserves. Thus they were indirectly on the gold standard. Market exchange rates were to be kept within 1% of par value by the use of each nation's stabilization fund. If a nation developed a chronic deficit in its balance of payments and a steady drain on its foreign exchange reserves, it could propose a change in its official par value. It happened that, in practice, countries would devalue their currency without prior approval by the IMF, to prevent speculator profits from the advance notice that an approval process would provide.

The IMF provided for a fixed exchange-rate system based on a gold exchange standard in the short run, while in the long run, some flexibility was provided through a mechanism for changes in official par values. The IMF also could lend to countries with balance-of-payments deficits with funds from the IMF holdings of gold and currency. The holdings arose from subscriptions of member nations determined by their quotas, which reflected each nation's economic importance in the world economy.

On January 1, 1970, the IMF was authorized to create Special Drawing Rights (SDRs) as a reserve asset that countries can use to settle international accounts. This potentially turned the IMF into a world central bank with the ability to create international reserves, but SDRs are allocated among participating countries according to their quotas, so they have been of limited help in coping with balance-of-payments problems.

In 1971, the U.S. stopped honoring its obligation to sell gold at $35 per ounce, which broke the dollar loose from its gold moorage. In 1973, European countries and Japan began to let their currencies float against the dollar, and the world was on a flexible exchange system.

With the end of fixed exchange rates, the International Monetary Fund has lost an important part of its purpose and its mechanism for achieving its goals. The IMF continues to pursue foreign exchange stability by being a source of short-term credit to acquire foreign exchange to pay for imports when exports and capital movements are insufficient to generate enough foreign exchange. The borrowing country is expected to take steps to correct the imbalance and, also, countries with persistent trade surpluses are encouraged to take steps to correct that imbalance. See *Fixed Exchange Rate, Flexible Exchange Rates, Gold Standard.*

INVENTORY   Goods or materials in stock. In a manufacturing firm, inventory would include raw materials and goods in process as well as finished goods in stock. In national income accounting, inventories are counted in the private *investment* category.

INVERTED YIELD CURVE   An inverted interest rate structure; occurs when short-term interest rates are higher than long-term rates. Normally, long-term rates are higher than short-term rates because of the longer period before the lender will be able to use the funds in other ways and the greater risk associated with the longer period before maturity. Sometimes these normal considerations are more than offset by a very strong short-term demand for funds, and short-term interest rates rise above long-term rates. See *Yield Curve* for an illustration.

INVESTMENT   1. To the economist, investment is expenditure for new structures, new producers' durable equipment, and net additions to inventories. In national income analysis, investment *always* means expenditure for *new* housing, plant, and equipment such as new factories, office buildings, apartments, turret lathes, looms, etc. (capital formation), plus additions to inventories. It is one of the categories of aggregate demand. Individually, we may speak of "investment" in a 20-year-old house when we buy it, but transfer of existing property involves "investment" by the buyer and "disinvestment" by the seller, with no change in the total volume of capital goods in the economy.

2. To the individual householder or business analyst, investment may mean not only the purchase of new real capital but also the purchase of existing capital goods and certificates of ownership or indebtedness such as stocks, bonds, mortgages, commercial

paper, etc. See *Autonomous Investment, Disinvestment, Gross Investment, Induced Investment, Investment Demand, Net Investment.*

INVESTMENT BANKING Dealing in large blocks of stocks and bonds for resale in smaller quantities and underwriting new issues of securities. Investment banks are not permitted to make commercial and personal loans nor take deposits as commercial banks and savings banks do. Consequently, they fail to meet the standard definition of a bank, but historical usage prevails. See *Bank.*

INVESTMENT DEMAND Investment demand, or intended investment, is that amount that business leaders wish to spend on new capital goods and additions to inventories. Actual investment may be greater or less than investment demand because of the piling up of unwanted inventories when sales start to fall off or the unwanted drawing down of inventories when sales are brisker than anticipated. See *Investment, Autonomous Investment, Gross Investment, Induced Investment, Net Investment.*

INVESTMENT MULTIPLIER See *Gross National Product Multiplier.*

INVISIBLE TRADE International payments for nonthings such as services, shipping, insurance, interest, and dividends. An interest payment by a U.S. bank to a French depositor has the same effect on the balance of payments as a merchandise import: it is an outpayment. Similarly, a Japanese visitor vacationing in the U.S. spends money in the U.S. with the same effect as a merchandise export: it is an in-payment, a receipt to the U.S.

Invisible trade is added to merchandise trade and unilateral transfers to arrive at the balance on current account. See *Balance of Payments, Balance on Current Account.*

INVOLUNTARY UNEMPLOYMENT A situation in which there is an insufficient number of jobs available in the economy for the number of qualified people seeking employment at prevailing wages. Prior to the 1930s, the overwhelming number of economists theorized that involuntary unemployment is temporary and would be corrected automatically in the long-run by market forces. The concept of automatically achieved equilibrium in the economy in the long run led John Maynard Keynes to comment that "in the long-run we are all dead." He argued in his 1936 book, *The General*

Theory of Employment, Interest, and Money, that involuntary unemployment might persist indefinitely, and he called for government fiscal policies to counteract it. The Great Depression of the 1930s bore out the proposition that widespread involuntary unemployment can continue for a long time. See *Deflationary Gap, Frictional Unemployment, Structural Unemployment, Unemployment, Voluntary Unemployment.*

IRON LAW OF WAGES   A proposition held by many economists in the early nineteenth century that wages would tend toward a bare subsistence minimum, because when wages rise above subsistence for a time, population would increase, the labor supply would increase, and the larger number of workers would drive wages back down. This is the conclusion of the theory of population propounded by Thomas Malthus, and it contributed to economics being called "the dismal science."

IRREVOCABLE TRUST   A "living trust" that cannot be revoked or amended by the person who creates it once it is set up. See *Trust, Revocable Trust.*

ISOCOST LINE   Sometimes known as "total outlay line." A line or curve in the theory of the firm which contains points that represent all of the combinations of inputs (in the example below, machinery and labor) that can be bought for a given outlay of funds. Isocost lines put together with isoquant curves can illustrate the economic choice of how to produce, i.e., what combination of resources to select for each possible level of total outlay and level of output. The isocost line is similar to the budget line in the indifference curve approach to consumer equilibrium; the level of outlay (isocost) constrains the level of output that can be attained, just as the consumer's budget level constrains the level of satisfaction that can be reached.

   In the figure below, the units of machinery are measured from zero on the vertical axis and the units of labor from zero on the horizontal axis. If all of the funds, say $150,000, are spent on machinery the firm could buy $0M_1$ units; if all were spent on labor it could buy $0L_1$ units. The straight line between M_1 and L_1 is an isocost line IC_1 which contains all of the combinations of machinery and labor that can be purchased with an outlay of $150,000. An outlay of $200,000 would produce an isocost curve IC_2 that lies farther out from the origin at M_2L_2. The point of tangency between an isocost curve and an isoquant curve identifies the most efficient combination of inputs for the maximum output attainable for that outlay of funds. See *Isoquant–Isocost Equilibrium.*

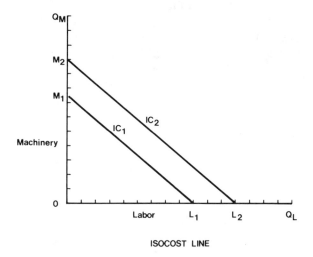

ISOCOST LINE

ISOQUANT CURVE   A curve in the theory of the firm which contains points that represent all of the combinations of inputs that will produce a particular total output with engineering efficiency (there is no unnecessary amount of any input). Isoquant curves put together with isocost lines can illustrate the economic choice of how to produce, i.e., what combination of resources to select for each possible level of output. Drawing on engineering information, the isoquant curve depicts the substitutability of factors of production in producing a given level of output.

The figure below illustrates a hypothetical example which treats two factors of production, labor and machinery, as partially substitutable for one another. Each isoquant curve consists of points which represent all of the combinations of labor and machinery that will produce a particular output. The curve is convex to the origin because the factors of production are not perfect substitutes for one another. As labor is substituted for machinery, more and more units of labor will be required to replace a unit of machinery. This expresses the *Law of Diminishing Marginal Rate of Technical Substitution.*

The isoquant curve is similar to the indifference curve in the theory of consumer equilibrium, but with this important difference: For isoquant curves labeled 1000 and 2000, the second curve represents twice as much output, while higher indifference curves merely represent greater utility ranking without anyone being able to specify *how much* greater the utility.

Combinations of labor and machinery that could produce a larger output are points which lie on an isoquant curve farther out from the origin. One would expect a larger output when both inputs are increased.

See *Isoquant–Isocost Equilibrium, Isocost Line, Marginal Rate of Technical Substitution.*

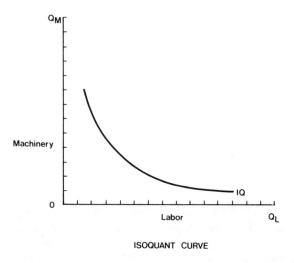

ISOQUANT CURVE

ISOQUANT–ISOCOST EQUILIBRIUM Combination of isoquant curves with isocost curves will provide an answer to the economic question of how to produce, that is, what combination of resources is best technically and economically for each possible level of output of the firm.

In the hypothetical example illustrated below, each isoquant curve contains engineering information about alternative combinations of machinery and labor that will produce that quantity of output (since machinery and labor are to some extent substitutable for one another). Isoquant curves that lie farther out from the origin represent larger quantities of *both* machinery and labor. Isoquant curve IQ_1 represents 1000 units of output; IQ_2 represents 2000 units of output; IQ_3 represents 3000 units of output.

Each isocost line contains points which represent all combinations of machinery and labor which can be bought for a particular outlay of funds, given the prices of machinery and labor. The intersection of the isocost line with the vertical axis shows the quantity of machinery that could be bought if all of the funds represented by that line were spent on machinery. The isocost line intersects the horizontal axis at the quantity of labor which could be bought if all available funds were spent on labor. Points on a straight line between these two extremes portray all combinations of machinery and labor that can be bought for that outlay of funds. Isocost line IC_1 represents an outlay of $150,000 for machinery and labor; isocost line IC_2 represents a total outlay of $200,000.

Combining an isocost line with isoquant curves will show the best combination of inputs (economically and technically) for the largest output attainable, given the amount of funds available to the firm and the prices of the inputs. The isoquant curve IQ_1 that is just tangent to the isocost line IC_1 identifies the largest output (10,000 units) that can be produced for an outlay of $150,000, and the point of tangency identifies the unique combination of labor and machinery (L_1 and M_1) that can produce that output and cost no more than the available funds. A larger outlay of $200,000 would produce an isocost line farther out from the origin (IC_2), which would permit a larger output of 16,000 units using a combination of L_2 units of labor and M_2 units of machinery.

See *Isoquant Curve, Isocost Line.*

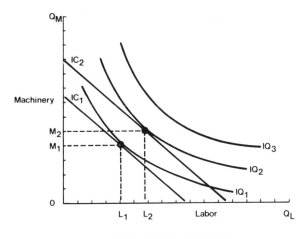

CHOICE OF HOW TO PRODUCE

J CURVE In international economics, a curve which illustrates the probable effect of devaluation or depreciation of the currency on the balance on current account. The initial effect of the decrease in the foreign exchange value of a currency is that imported goods and services cost more because it takes more dollars, for example, to buy the foreign currency to pay for the imports. Likewise, goods and services that are exported bring in less foreign currency, so the balance on current account deteriorates for both reasons. As people adjust to the lower value of the depreciated currency, imports decline in the face of higher costs and exports begin to increase in response to their lower cost abroad.

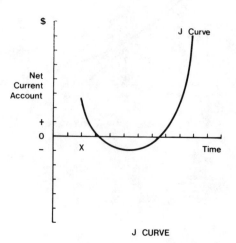

J CURVE

In the figure (p. 168), net balance on current account is measured on the vertical axis, and time is measured on the horizontal axis. X is the time at which devaluation or depreciation occurs.

The hook of the J is narrow or broad, flat or deep, depending upon the time it takes for importers and exporters to respond to the reduced value of their currency in foreign exchange markets. If importers accept lower profits by holding their prices steady despite having to pay more for foreign exchange to buy foreign goods, the volume of imports won't fall until importers are squeezed enough to increase prices. For a while exporters might accept the windfall profits which arise from receiving more of their own currency for each unit of foreign currency that sales bring in. Eventually, exporters may want to expand sales by shading prices if demand for the product is relatively elastic, or they may be forced to reduce prices, regardless of the elasticity of demand, if new competitors enter the market.

JOINT COST Cost that cannot be separated out by product when two or more products come from the same production process. Cost, then, is arbitrarily allocated among the joint products, often according to the demand for each product. Meat packers claim that they have developed uses and markets for every part of a slaughtered pig but the squeal. Hide, bristles, rind, pork, knuckles, and squeal are joint products from the slaughter of a pig. Slaughter costs for all but the squeal (apologies to the sensitivities of animal-rights activists) are allocated among the joint products in an arbitrary way, often related to market demand. See *Joint Products*.

JOINT DEMAND Occurs when two or more products are used together so that demand for one product accompanies demand for another. Examples are breakfast cereal and milk, waffles and syrup, or beer and pretzels. The cross elasticity of demand coefficient is negative, indicating that a price increase in x will cause a decrease in the quantity of y demanded as less of both x and y are consumed. See *Complementary Goods, Cross Elasticity*.

JOINT PRODUCTS Products that are produced jointly by necessity. For example, a meat-packing plant takes in hogs and produces pork, pig skin, bristles, and pork rind for processing, all as joint products from the same slaughtering process. Many of the slaughtering costs cannot be separated out by product, so they are allocated among the products arbitrarily, often in relation to the demand for each product. See *Joint Cost*.

JOINT SUPPLY   See *Joint Products*.

JUNK BONDS   High-risk, high-yield corporate bonds that are of varying credit quality below investment grade with, for example, Standard and Poor's ratings of BB+ and below as opposed to investment grade of AAA, AA, or A. Firms which are young and/or
unknown find it difficult to sell stock or borrow from financial
institutions, but they may be able to raise funds by selling bonds
that offer a high interest rate because of the high risk. Other junk
bonds started out as investment-grade bonds but were downgraded
to junk bonds when the firms issuing them ran into hard times.
Lower ratings push down market prices of the bonds and their
effective interest rate simultaneously rises.

Currently, the more common type of junk bond is issued against
the assets of companies involved in friendly or unfriendly highly
leveraged buyouts. Many of these firms are large and well known.
It has been possible to attract funds for the buyouts by issuing
bonds which have a high interest rate to offset their low rating and
high risk.

The junk-bond market boomed through the 1980s under the
leadership of the brokerage firm of Drexel Burnham Lambert. The
market began to slide at the end of the decade when some of the
giant mergers created by junk bonds fell into difficulty because of
too high a level of debt. The junk bond market was severely shaken
by the bankruptcy of Drexel Burnham Lambert at the beginning of
1990, under a cloud of charges of insider trading and other illegal
acts, and a very large fine was paid to the federal government. When
the economy experienced a "meaningful downturn in aggregate
output" during the last quarter of 1990 and faced, dare I say it,
recession in 1991, lower product sales created negative profits (a
euphemism for losses) and made it more difficult for many firms to
meet interest payments on high levels of debt. Bond ratings of many
firms were reduced from investment grade to junk status, including
bonds of a couple of U.S. automobile giants. See *Leveraged Buyout, Unfriendly Takeover*.

JURISDICTIONAL DISPUTE   A conflict between two or more labor
unions when they lay claim to the right to perform the same job or
the right to organize the same group of workers. It may lead to a
jurisdictional strike or picketing. The disputes have been prevalent
in such industries as construction where, for example, a carpenters'
union has always claimed the right to hang doors and a sheet metal
workers' union has always worked with metal and both claim the
right to hang metal doors. No matter which way the contractor

decides, the services of the other group of workers will be lost if the dispute turns into a strike, and the construction project is held up.

Jurisdictional disputes over jobs must be settled by arbitration under the Taft–Hartley Act of 1947. Jurisdictional strikes to organize tend to be prevented under the National Labor Relations Act of 1935 (the Wagner Act), which provides for worker selection of a particular union or no union by a secret ballot conducted by the National Labor Relations Board. The NLRB also determines which workers will vote, that is, be in the bargaining unit that a union represents. The Taft–Hartley Act made it an unfair labor practice for a union to interfere with these worker rights.

JURISDICTIONAL STRIKE   See *Jurisdictional Dispute.*

KEYNESIAN THEORY. Developed by the English economist, John Maynard Keynes (1883–1943), and presented in 1936 in his book, *The General Theory of Employment, Interest and Money,* it has had a profound effect on economic analysis and policy in the western world (Western Europe, Britain, Canada, the United States, etc.), most countries of which are characterized as predominantly market economies. The theory attempts to explain how the level of economic activity (i.e., the level of income, output, and employment in the economy) is determined. Keynes emphasized the role of aggregate demand in determining the level of national income and employment. He believed that monetary policy is ineffective relative to the more direct fiscal policy in efforts to bring an economy out of deep depression. Most economists today accept the broad framework of Keynes' analysis but have refined and revised the detail and emphases of the theory. Monetary policy has been restored to a position of importance for coping with the milder recessions that have been experienced since the 1930s. Keynes emphasized aggregate demand, but today some consider the supply side as important for economic policy. Many disagree with applying his particular policy recommendations to today's economic problems. See *Monetary Policy, Supply-side Economics.*

L 1. A money supply, or money stock, concept which equals M3 plus the nonbank public holdings of U.S. savings bonds, short-term Treasury securities, commercial paper, and bankers' acceptances, net of money market mutual fund holdings of these assets (*Federal Reserve Bulletin,* January 1991, **77,** A14). L provides the broadest definition of the money stock. See *M3.*

2. An abbreviation for ''labor'' in economics equations and diagrams.

LABOR A factor-of-production category which consists of human effort in production. It includes intellectual skills such as those developed by aeronautical engineers, computer programmers, teachers, and managers engaged in routine management functions, as well as the manual skills of skilled and semiskilled workers and work of the unskilled. Other general categories of factors of production are land and capital goods, and some would add- entrepreneurship.

LABOR BOYCOTT 1. A concerted refusal to work for a firm in an effort to pressure the firm to change some of its practices. A strike. 2. A labor boycott may occur because of picketing a firm at the employees' entrance or at the delivery-receiving door to persuade workers not to do business with the firm. Teamsters, for example, may boycott a firm by refusing to cross a picket line to deliver or pick up goods. See *Boycott, Consumer Boycott, Primary Boycott, Secondary Boycott.*

LABOR FORCE   The total number of people in the U.S. who are 16 years of age or older and who are at work or actively seeking work. *Civilian labor force* figures would exclude the armed forces. See *Full Employment, Unemployment.*

LABOR-INTENSIVE PRODUCTION   A high ratio of labor to capital and other resources used in a production process. See *Capital-Intensive Production.*

LABOR-MANAGEMENT REPORTING AND DISCLOSURE ACT OF 1959 (LANDRUM–GRIFFIN ACT)   An act to make labor unions more responsible to their members and the public. To prevent corruption, the law provides that labor unions and union officers must submit periodic and detailed financial reports to the Department of Labor, that embezzlement of funds is a federal offense, that ex-convicts and Communists cannot hold union office, that union officers cannot borrow more than $2000 from union funds, that employers cannot make payments to union officers other than wage-related payments, etc.

The law enhances union member rights by provisions that include regularly scheduled election of officers, the use of secret ballots, and provisions against summary discipline or expulsion of union members. In addition, the law restricts the use of secondary boycotts and picketing.

LABOR THEORY OF VALUE   A theory which holds that the value of all commodities is equal to the labor time used to produce them. Capital is considered merely indirect labor held by the laborer. All value, then, is created by labor. Daily prices of goods may differ from their value as determined by labor time, but over longer periods market prices are regulated by the necessary labor time in their production and are related by labor–time ratios. Uncultivated land has a price but does not have value because it embodies no labor. It is provided by nature, but its produce is harvested only by the application of labor.

The labor theory of value was used as an approximation by English classical economists Adam Smith (1723–1790) and David Ricardo (1772–1823). It was adopted and used by Karl Marx (1818–1883) to develop the theory of surplus value, in which the capitalist takes all of the value produced by labor beyond that amount needed for the laborer's subsistence.

LABOR UNION   A group of employees who organize to bargain collectively with an employer (or employers) over wages and working conditions. It may refer to a local, national, or international organization for collective bargaining. Union workers are members of a local union which represents workers in a plant or firm (or if a craft union, the local is defined by locality.) Local unions are affiliated with national unions, some of which have locals in Canada and use "international" in their names.

Collective bargaining may be carried on by a local union, though often with the help of an international representative. It may be carried on by the national union, especially when bargaining is multiemployer or industry-wide. Sometimes collective bargaining is carried on by an intermediate division which represents a number of locals that deal with a large employer with many plants, such as an automobile manufacturer. Power in the union structure has tended to center at the national level, particularly when the products are sold in a national market.

The term "union" is not used to refer to modern federations of unions, such as the American Federation of Labor–Congress of Industrial Organizations (AFL–CIO), because federations do not represent workers in collective bargaining with employers over wages and working conditions. Rather, federations engage in lobbying and public relations activities at the federal, state, and large-city levels. State and local AFL–CIO organizations also are loose affiliations engaged largely in political activities such as lobbying state legislators for bills in labor's interest.

Federations have tried to influence the behavior of their member national unions in order to win broad public support for the union movement. However, they have no power over members other than the extreme act of expulsion, and expelled unions have done rather well on their own. See *American Federation of Labor, Congress of Industrial Organizations, American Federation of Labor–Congress of Industrial Organizations.*

LAFFER CURVE A curve, named for economist Arthur Laffer, which illustrates a theory about the relationship between tax rates and total tax revenues. As the tax *rate* rises from zero toward 100%, tax *revenues* will rise, reach a maximum, and decline to zero. To increase tax rates beyond that which produces maximum tax revenues will only cause tax revenues to fall because of the adverse effect upon individual and business incentives. Some supply-siders argued in the early 1980s that the U.S. had gone beyond that maximum tax revenue on the curve, so that a reduction in taxes would actually increase tax revenues. President Ronald Reagan and a majority in Congress succeeded in reducing tax rates and the economy began to recover from recession. Whether the reduction in tax rates caused an increase in tax revenues is clouded by the myriad other changes that occurred simultaneously in the economy, including growing federal budget deficits, and the debate continues.

See *Supply-Side Economics, Tax Multiplier.*

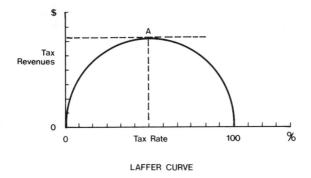

LAFFER CURVE

LAISSEZ FAIRE   A term used to identify an economy free from governmental regulation or interference. Government is restricted to provision of such things as legal tender, police, defense forces, and enforcement of contracts. From the French, "to let do," i.e., to let people do as they choose.

LAND   A factor-of-production category which represents all natural resources as found in their natural state, such as coal deposits, timber, or water, as well as agricultural land and urban land sites. Other categories are labor and capital goods, and some would add entrepreneurship.

LANDRUM–GRIFFIN ACT   See *Labor-Management Reporting and Disclosure Act of 1959.*

LAST IN–FIRST OUT (LIFO)   A method for valuing inventory which prices all units in an inventory at the cost of the last unit purchased or produced, as though the last unit added will be the first unit sold or used, whether or not it really is first out. When costs are rising, LIFO reflects replacement costs so that the firm would recover enough to replace the inventory that goes out. Profit shown by the firm will be less than if valuation were by the first in-first out (FIFO) method, and the business income tax will be less.

When costs are falling, LIFO will show a higher profit and will result in higher business income taxes than if the FIFO method were used. See *First In-First Out.*

LEADING ECONOMIC INDICATORS   An index of the U.S. Commerce Department designed to forecast economic activity 6 to 9 months in the future. When the index declines for 3 consecutive months, it is considered a sign that the economy is in a recession.

The index of leading economic indicators is made up of building permits, orders for consumer goods, orders for plant and equipment, the backlog of manufacturers' unfilled orders, business delivery times, the average manufacturing work week, weekly unemployment claims, the money supply, the price of raw materials, stock prices, and consumer confidence. Often, changes in some of the 11 indicators will foretell economic growth, while changes in others indicate economic decline ahead. An economic forecast based upon a change in the leading economic indicators index will depend upon the strength of change as well as the direction of change in each of the indicators.

There are other economic indicators economists sometimes include for their economic forecasting, such as personal disposable income adjusted for inflation, interest rates, net formation of new businesses, credit outstanding to consumers and businesses, and the percentage of the working-age population employed.

LEASEBACK   An arrangement for an owner to sell property (land, buildings, equipment, etc.) and then lease it back from the buyer for a period of years. The transaction provides immediate cash for the seller to use for other purposes and the ability to substitute a direct business expense for a depreciation charge in a business income statement.

LEGAL RESERVES   The reserves of banks and other depository institutions that qualify by law as reserves against deposits. Members of the Federal Reserve System hold their legal reserves as deposits in their district Federal Reserve Bank or, in small amounts, as currency in their vaults. Nonmember depository institutions hold their legal reserves in the same way, or may also count deposits in other approved institutions which in turn hold deposits in Federal Reserve Banks. Required reserves must be legal reserves, but there may be more legal reserves than required; these are excess reserves. See *Excess Reserves, Required Reserves.*

LEGAL TENDER   Currency and coins designated by a government as legal payment for transactions and the repayment of debt. If legal tender is proffered in repayment of debt it must be accepted, because if it is not the debt nevertheless will be considered paid.

LESS DEVELOPED COUNTRIES (LDCs)   An economic designation for countries that have not reached some selected level of per-capita output and income. The benchmark level differs among students of economic development. These countries formerly were called undeveloped or underdeveloped countries, but those appellations carried a stigma of general inferiority to which the countries objected. (Some had complex civilizations thousands of years before the inhabitants of some "developed" countries.)

LEVERAGED BUYOUT   The purchase of a firm from its owners by raising the necessary funds through the sale of bonds which are secured by the cash flow and assets of the firm being acquired. In the process, ownership shares are converted to debt. A highly leveraged transaction is one in which the buyers cover only a very small portion of the purchase price with their own funds, and a very large portion by bonds secured by the assets being purchased. Often some assets of the firm (perhaps a division in a conglomerate company) have to be sold to reduce the debt burden and pay the costs of the takeover. Low-rated, high-yield "junk bonds" are the usual type issued in a leveraged buyout. Takeover specialists lick their lips over a firm whose net worth exceeds the market value of its stock. Sometimes corporate raiders spin off all of the assets acquired in the buyout and the purchased firm disappears. Diamond International, a timber and wood products company, was bought out by financier Sir James Goldsmith and sold off bit by bit until nothing was left but a profit for Goldsmith.

Sometimes the leveraged buyout is initiated by incumbent management fearful of an unfriendly takeover. At other times the technique will be used by a corporate raider. See *Junk Bonds, Takeover.*

LEVERAGED BUYOUT FUND   A fund created through the sale of shares by an investment firm to finance the usually small equity base for leveraged buyouts. Often as much as 90% of the purchase price of a takeover is financed with junk bonds and the buyout fund provides the rest. Institutional investors such as pension-funds managers are primary buyers of shares in these funds. See *Leveraged Buyout.*

LIABILITIES   What is owed to others, such as accounts payable for goods and services purchased from others but not yet paid for, or notes payable for amounts borrowed from others, or bonds and mortgages which are longer-term forms of indebtedness to others.

Items on the right-hand side of an accounting balance sheet which, together with net worth (ownership items), exactly equal total assets listed on the left-hand side. The balance is always there because, by definition, assets minus liabilities equal net worth. Net worth thus may be negative, as some unfortunate firms that face bankruptcy have found.

LIMITED LIABILITY A grant of protection by the state to owners of corporations and some partnerships. It limits the liability of the owners for the debts of the business or professional practice to no more than their proportionate ownership share of the assets of the business. Owners don't have to come up with additional cash from their personal assets to pay off creditors. Single proprietors and many partnerships, on the other hand, are liable for business debts to the full extent of their personal assets (with some exceptions such as one's home, as defined in bankruptcy law). Occasionally, a state will grant charters to some kinds of business, such as banks, in which each shareholder is liable for an additional amount equivalent to the face value of the shares he or she owns, as well as being liable for the share of assets of the business that the stock represents.

LIMITED PARTNERSHIP A form of partnership which is designed to raise capital funds more easily by providing that inactive, or "passive," partners are liable for the debts of the partnership only to the extent of their investment in the partnership. Active partners are liable to the full extent of their personal wealth (except for exemptions provided by bankruptcy laws, perhaps one's home). Sometimes a limited partner is called a "silent partner." See *Partnership*.

LINEAR PROGRAMMING A mathematical technique which involves maximizing or minimizing some linear function subject to linear constraints. It is used to help business managers reach decisions about such things as input mix, plant expansion, or advertising plans which involve maximizing profits or sales or minimizing costs. The calculations involve certain given constraints such as size of plant, size of budget, or prices of inputs.

LIQUIDITY In economics, the ease with which one asset can be exchanged for other assets without losing money value. Cash (legal tender) is the most liquid asset because it can be exchanged readily for all other economic assets in the country (except in some cases of hyperinflation when it is more advantageous to hold on to "real" assets). Other assets have a degree of liquidity related to how fast you can convert them to cash. Checks written against bank deposits are not quite as liquid as cash because they are not universally accepted, may require identification of the writer, etc. Other kinds of bank deposits are less liquid, with the degree of liquidity declining as one moves through various kinds of bonds and shares of stock and on to varieties of real property. The degree of liquidity of these assets that are not cash is a function of the cost of finding buyers and inducing them to exchange cash for the asset.

Businesses and households may seek greater or less liquidity in the array of assets they hold, depending upon their expectations about the future course of prices, wages and salaries, interest, profits, the volume of sales, the rate of obsolescence, etc. See *Negotiable Instrument, Liquidity Preference,* and the definitions of money stock, *M1, M2, M3.*

LIQUIDITY PREFERENCE   A basic concept in the interest theory of John Maynard Keynes (1883–1943) in which the interest rate is determined by the supply and demand for money to *hold.* Liquidity preference expresses the demand for money to hold which consists of three categories: (1) the transactions demand which arises because the timing of receipts does not coincide perfectly with the flow of expenditures, (2) the precautionary demand which arises from the need to respond to possible future contingencies, and (3) the speculative demand, which depends upon anticipations about the future course of asset prices, particularly bonds, and the opportunity cost of holding money (the additional interest that money might have earned if instead it had been invested in an earning asset other than a checking account). The speculative demand for money to hold plays the key role in Keynesian interest theory. (The supply of money is determined by the central banking authority—in the U. S. that is the Federal Reserve Banking System.) A different theory of the interest rate is the loanable funds theory below. See *Demand for Money* for more detail, also *Supply of Money.*

LOANABLE FUNDS THEORY OF INTEREST   A theory in which the quantity of money in financial markets and its price, the interest rate, are determined by the supply of and demand for loanable funds. The higher the interest rate, the more money that is supplied by lenders. The supply curve for loanable funds slopes up to the right in the diagram below.

The higher the interest rate, the lower the quantity of money that is demanded by consumers to buy houses, automobiles, etc., or by businesses to buy new plant and equipment or to increase inventories. The demand curve for loanable funds slopes down to the right.

The vertical axis measures the interest rate in percentages and the horizontal axis measures the quantity of loanable funds in dollars. The equilibrium interest rate and quantity of loanable funds are determined by the intersection of the supply and demand curves at point A.

See *Demand for Money, Supply of Money.*

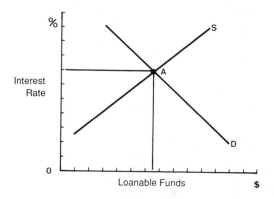

MARKET FOR LOANABLE FUNDS

LOCKOUT An action by an employer to close down the plant to put pressure on employees in connection with a labor dispute. Comparable to a strike by employees to close the plant to put economic pressure on the employer. In the spring of 1990, the baseball team owners locked out the baseball players to win concessions from the players' union. Here the pressure was intended to be both economic and psychological. The players would not receive salaries, the spring training locales would lose large sums of money, and irate baseball fans would press for a settlement. Very high salaries and very high profits from television rights made it unclear which side would suffer more economically and sustain the most fan anger.

LONG RUN A period of time in which *all* costs are variable; none are fixed. Sometimes it is used to refer to an intermediate length of time which is long enough to permit some, but not all, capital inputs in a firm's production process to change in quantity. For a market, the long run may be a period long enough to permit entry and exit of firms as well as expansion or contraction in the size of existing firms. For the economy, it may be a period long enough to achieve a new equilibrium following, for example, a change in monetary policy which provides more reserves and encourages growth in the money supply according to the deposit multiplier. See *Short Run, Equilibrium of the Firm, Equilibrium of the Market.*

LONG-RUN AVERAGE COST   In the theory of the firm, the cost per unit of output as it varies over ranges of output when all factor-of-production inputs are variable; there are no fixed costs. Long-run average cost data is used to create a long-run planning curve to project optimum size of firm in terms of lowest unit costs. It must be combined with long-run demand and revenue projections to determine optimum size of firm in terms of maximum profitability.

LONG-RUN AVERAGE COST CURVE   The long-run average cost curve is considered to be U-shaped. It consists of an envelope of projected short-run average cost curves, each representing a plant size, so it often is called a planning curve. Economies of scale may occur as output grows from low levels with small quantities of inputs, including small plant size, to larger levels of output and larger plant size. The economies arise because some technologies are efficient only at large outputs. This will cause the long-run average cost curve to fall as output expands. Eventually economies of scale may be exhausted and further expansion of output causes diseconomies of scale. Management coordination and communications problems tend to lead to growing inefficiency after some large level of output is reached, so that long-run average costs begin to rise.

In the illustration below, each short-run average cost curve (SAC) represents a plant size from smaller to larger, reading from left to right. The long-run average cost curve (LAC) is tangent to each of the plant curves and is drawn as a continuous line on the supposition of an almost infinite number of plant sizes as we move from small plants to very large ones. The LAC curve is tangent to SAC curves at the lowest average cost *only* for that SAC curve which represents the plant size where economies of scale are at a maximum, and any higher output will lead to diseconomies. In the illustration, that tangency at lowest short-run average cost occurs at output X_3. Outputs X_1 and X_2 identify minimum short-run average costs that do *not* lie on the long-run average cost curve. If the firm can sustain sales of the output shown at X_1, for example, it would be profitable to enlarge and move to a short-run average cost curve to the right that *is* tangent to the LAC curve. Similarly, if at output X_4, it would be lower unit cost to reduce the firm's size, but

determination of the most profitable size requires revenue information as well as cost data.

See *Economies of Scale, Decreasing Returns to Scale, Increasing Returns to Scale.*

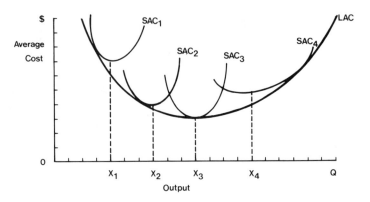

LONG-RUN AVERAGE COST CURVE

LORENZ CURVE   A curve illustrating the degree of inequality in the
distribution of a society's income. It relates percentages of total
income distributed to various percentages of the population. The
Lorenz curve illustrates one aspect of the basic economic question
facing societies: For whom to produce? That is, how equally is
income to be distributed?

In the illustration below, the percentage of income distributed
is shown on the vertical axis from 0 to 100%. The horizontal axis
measures the percentage of people ranked from lowest income to
highest. A straight line from the origin at 45% represents a perfectly
equal distribution of income, i.e., everyone receives the same income. The 10% of the people receiving the lowest income are paid
10% of the total income distributed. The 10% of the people receiving
the highest income also receive 10% of the total. Lowest and highest
are equal.

The bowed curve shows an income distribution for a country
in which the poorest 10% of the people receive 2% of the income,
while the richest 10% of the people receive 30% of the income. The
more that the curve is bowed to the right, the more unequal is the
income distribution.

Absolute *inequality* is illustrated by moving out on the horizontal line from zero to the hundredth percentile and thence up to
100% of the income, showing one person with all of the income.

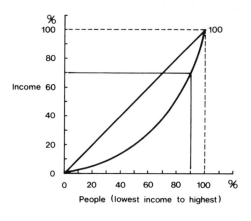

LORENZ CURVE

LUMP-OF-LABOR CONCEPT   A view that there is only so much work to be done in the short run so that the more workers there are, the less work each will have. Belief in the concept supports exclusionary policies of labor unions whose members are employed in short-term jobs and then move on to another employer, as in the construction and maritime industries. If there is only so much work, self-interest leads to excluding newcomers. The lump-of-labor concept also is a view that may underlie arguments for restrictions on immigration. The lump-of-labor concept is similar to the view that the economy is a fixed-size pie, so that if some gain others must lose. Both views tend to ignore dynamic elements that even in the short run (if that is not a mere instant) can cause variations in the demand for labor or in the size of the GNP.

M The total money stock, or money supply, without distinguishing which particular definition of money (M1, M2, etc.) applies. Sometimes it refers to the narrowest definition of money—as legal tender, that is, coins and paper currency. See *Money Supply, M1, M2, M3.*

MI A money stock concept which consists of coins and currency, traveler's checks, and checkable deposits at banks excluding those held by the Treasury and the Federal Reserve Banks. Next to legal tender (coins and currency), it is the most liquid of the money stock concepts, which means that it is easiest to exchange for some other asset.

M1 has been used by the Federal Reserve Open-Market Committee (FOMC) as one measure of the rate of economic expansion or contraction. When, for example, M1 is growing rapidly the FOMC may see it as a precursor of growth in the rate of inflation and so take steps to reduce growth in M1. Monetary theorists debate whether M1 or M2 is the better barometer on which to base monetary policy. Today, the Fed concentrates on M2 and M3 in setting targets for rate of growth in the money supply. Each of the money supply categories is tracked regularly.

M1 is defined more precisely by the Federal Reserve Board as a part of the money stock consisting of "(1) currency outside the Treasury, Federal Reserve Banks, and the vaults of depository institutions; (2) travelers checks of non-bank issuers; (3) demand deposits at all commercial banks other than those due to depository institutions, the United States government, and foreign banks and official institutions less cash items in the process of collection and Federal Reserve float; and (4) other checkable deposits (OCD) consisting of negotiable orders of withdrawal (NOW) and automatic transfer service (ATS) accounts at depository institutions, credit union share draft accounts, and demand deposits at thrift institutions" (*Federal Reserve Bulletin,* January 1991, **77,** A14). See *M, Money Supply, M2, M3, M1A, M1B.*

M1A A temporary money supply concept which consisted of currency and coins in circulation and demand deposits of commercial banks excluding those held by the Treasury and Federal Reserve Banks. It was used for a few years following passage of the Depository Institutions Deregulation and Monetary Control Act of 1980. M1A is identical to the definition of M1 prior to 1980 and was created to provide statistical continuity with historical M1 data collected before 1980.

   The DIDMC Act, for the first time, permitted the general offering of other checkable deposits (OCDs) by other financial institutions: NOW accounts by savings banks and savings and loan institutions, and share-draft accounts by credit unions. These were equal in liquidity and in direct competition with demand deposits of commercial banks, so M1B was created to include OCDs for monetary policy purposes. M1A disappeared after a few years, when a sufficiently long data record of M1B had accumulated for monetary policy purposes. M1B then became the new M1. See *M1B, M1, Bank Transaction Accounts, Demand Deposits, Negotiable Orders of Withdrawal, Share-Draft Accounts.*

M1B A temporary money supply concept which is identical to M1 (the new M1), as defined above. It was used for a few years after passage of the Depository Institutions Deregulation and Monetary Control Act of 1980, which for the first time permitted checkable accounts known as "other checkable deposits" (OCDs) in savings banks, savings and loan institutions, and credit unions. For monetary policy it was necessary to take into account the new checkable deposits because they are of equal liquidity and used the same way as demand deposits in commercial banks. M1B became M1 when a sufficiently long data record of the new concept had accumulated for monetary policy purposes to be able to dispense with M1A (the old M1). See *M1A, M1.*

M2 A money supply concept which consists of M1 plus savings deposits, time deposits (certificates of deposit, or CDs) of less than $100,000, money market deposit accounts (MMDAs), and money market mutual funds. M2 is a broader money stock concept than M1, including slightly less liquid accounts, but the overall liquidity is still very high. Liquidity represents the ease with which an asset may be exchanged for another asset. The Federal Reserve Board (the Fed) at the beginning of the 1990s concentrates more on M2 and M3 than on M1 in pursuit of monetary policy.

M2 is precisely defined by the Fed as a component of the money stock consisting of "M1 plus overnight (and continuing contract) repurchase agreements (RPs) issued by all depository institutions, and overnight Eurodollars issued to U.S. residents by foreign branches of U.S. banks worldwide, money market deposit accounts (MMDAs), savings and small denomination time deposits (time deposits, including retail RPs in amounts less than $100,000), and balances in both taxable and tax-exempt general purpose and broker-dealer money market mutual funds. Excludes individual retirement accounts (IRA) and Keogh balances at depository institutions and money market funds. Also excludes all balances held by U.S. commercial banks, money market funds (general purpose and broker-dealer), foreign governments and commercial banks, and the U.S. government" (*Federal Reserve Bulletin*, January 1991, **77,** A14). See *Money Supply, M, M1, M3*.

M3 A money supply concept which consists of M2 plus time deposits (CDs) and repurchase agreements (RPs) of $100,000 or more, term Eurodollars held by U.S. residents at foreign branches of U.S. banks and all United Kingdom and Canadian banks, and balances in institution-only money market mutual funds.

It is precisely defined by the Federal Reserve Board as "M2 plus large denomination time deposits and term RP liabilities (in amounts of $100,000 or more) issued by all depository institutions, term Eurodollars held by U.S. residents at foreign branches of U.S. banks worldwide and at all banking offices in the United Kingdom and Canada, and balances in both taxable and tax-exempt institution-only money market mutual funds. Excludes amounts held by depository institutions, the U.S. Government, money market funds, and foreign banks and official institutions. Also subtracted is the estimated amount of overnight RPs and Eurodollars held by institution-only money market mutual funds" (*Federal Reserve Bulletin*, January 1991, **77,** A14). See *M, M1, M2, Money Supply*.

MACROECONOMICS The study of what causes the general level of economic activity in a country's economy to be what it is. It is the study of such aggregates as gross national product (GNP), employment, and price levels to understand why there are periods of inflation, of prosperity and depression, of full employment and unemployment, and what may be done by public policy to affect these aggregates.

Macroeconomics compares with the study of the forest, while microeconomics compares with the study of the trees, individually and in thickets. See *Microeconomics*.

MALTHUSIAN POPULATION THEORY   A theory developed by English economist and parson Thomas Malthus (1776–1834) which holds that population tends to grow at a geometric rate (2, 4, 8, 16, 32 . . . .), while sustenance (the food supply) tends to grow at an arithmetic rate (1, 2, 3, 4, 5 . . . .). Population growth tends to occur by unrestricted reproduction charged by passion between the sexes, while growth in agricultural output is restricted by the law of diminishing returns, i.e., the growing labor supply applied to a fixed amount of land will reach the point of diminishing returns. Each unit of labor may add more to output, but the additional product will be less than that added by the previous unit of labor. The interaction of these two growth ratios will result in a tendency toward poverty and misery for the masses.

This unfortunate tendency can be prevented by late marriages, celibacy, and moral restraint, and Malthus was not sanguine about these. Otherwise the positive restraints on population growth would take over, restraints such as famine, disease, and war. Malthus wrote before the development of birth control devices and pills and before seemingly miraculous improvements in agricultural productivity based not only on application of capital inventions but also on such things as genetic experiments on plants and animals. Even so, some today point to areas of the world such as Bangladesh and India as proof of the theory, and many worry about the rate of growth in the world's population relative to the arable land available to feed the population of the future.

MARGIN   1. A percentage of the purchase price of securities, including futures contracts in the commodities markets, that is paid down by a buyer who buys on credit. A down payment. A person buys on margin in the expectation that the price of the securities will go up enough that a future sale of the securities will produce a profit after paying off the margin loan and interest. Margin requirements are set by the Federal Reserve System. Margin buying is the opposite of a short sale which is made with borrowed shares in the hope of a price decline and profit from replacing the shares borrowed at a lower price. See *Short Sale*.

2. Margin also is a widely used concept in economic theory in marginal analysis. Economists are concerned with changes "at the margin." For example, the change in cost associated with the last added unit of output (marginal cost) is compared with the change in revenue associated with one more unit of output (marginal revenue). The comparison of marginal cost with marginal revenue leads to definitions of equilibrium conditions for a firm. The list of "marginal" concepts used in economics is a long one, not exhausted by the entries below.

MARGINAL COST (MC) The change in total cost resulting from a change of one unit of product output.

$$MC = \frac{TC_n - TC_{n-1}}{Q_n - Q_{n-1}} = \frac{dTC}{dQ}$$

See *Marginal Cost Curve*.

MARGINAL COST CURVE A curve illustrating marginal cost (MC), i.e., how total cost of a firm changes as output varies (or, for a factor of production, how total cost changes as input of the factor varies). If the change in total cost (MC) is less than the average cost for the previously produced unit (lies below it on the curve), the new MC will pull the average down; if MC is greater than the previous AC (lies above it), MC will pull the average up; if MC remains the same, the average will not change. Therefore, as shown in the following figure, the marginal cost curve cuts the average cost curve from below at the lowest point on the average cost curve.

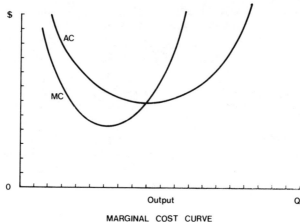

MARGINAL COST CURVE

MC is compared with marginal revenue to determine the level of output (or input) which will provide the greatest total profit. See *Equilibrium of the Firm*.

MARGINAL COST PRICING   Pricing products and services at their marginal cost when all opportunity costs have been included, so that MC reflects the social cost of producing the last added unit. If these costs equal price, the flow of resources to this production will continue indefinitely. If price is above marginal cost, output should expand because people are willing to pay more than the added cost of producing another unit. If price is below marginal cost, people are not willing to pay the cost of producing the last added unit and it should not be produced. When each product in society is produced at the point where price equals marginal cost, output will be at a social optimum. If market power interferes with this outcome by holding price above marginal cost to maximize profits, too little is produced and society would benefit by expansion of output to the point where marginal cost does equal price. Some public utility commissions now set prices at marginal cost for the industries they regulate in an effort to simulate this beneficial outcome of pure competition. See *Equilibrium of the Firm: Pure Competition, Equilibrium of the Firm: Monopoly*.

MARGINAL EFFICIENCY OF CAPITAL (MEC)   Also known as the Marginal Efficiency of Investment (MEI). The MEC is the rate of discount which would make the present value of the expected returns for a potential capital asset over its life equal to the supply price (replacement cost) of that capital asset. Put another way, it is the expected rate of return over cost, excluding interest cost, for a prospective real investment expenditure. The MEC is compared with the interest rate (the explicit or implicit cost of using funds for new capital goods) to determine if a capital good will produce a net economic profit.

MEC is an element in the investment expenditure theory of the English economist John Maynard Keynes (1883–1946), which in turn is a part of his theory explaining the general level of economic activity in his path-breaking 1936 book, *The General Theory of Employment, Interest, and Money*.

MARGINAL EFFICIENCY OF INVESTMENT   See *Marginal Efficiency of Capital*.

MARGINAL FACTOR COST (MFC)   For a factor of production such as labor, the change in total cost of labor associated with a change of one unit of labor. $MFC = dTC_L/dQ_L$. See *Equilibrium of the Firm: Factor Market, Marginal Factor Cost Curve.*

MARGINAL FACTOR COST CURVE   Depicts the change in the total cost of a factor of production, such as labor, as the quantity of the factor changes.

The curve shown below illustrates an MFC curve in a labor

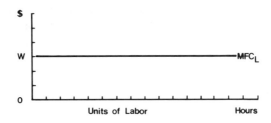

MARGINAL FACTOR COST CURVE: PURE COMPETITION

market of pure competition. The firm can hire more hours of labor at the going hourly wage.

When competition is imperfect and the firm is large enough that its hiring affects the market wage rate, the wage curve (average cost of labor curve) will slope upward. The MFC_L curve also will slope upward and lie above the AC_L (wage rate) curve. As the firm hires more labor it typically must pay a higher wage and pay it to all workers of that grade, not just those newly hired. Such a curve is shown below.

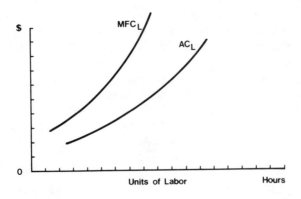

MARGINAL FACTOR COST CURVE: A NONCOMPETITIVE MARKET

MARGINAL LAND   Land which produces zero rent, i.e., the unit cost of production for the produce grown on marginal land is just covered by the market price of the products and there is nothing left over to pay to the land owner. Potential users will bid for the more fertile land with the winner willing to pay rent for the land just short of the amount by which the market value of its produce exceeds production costs. More fertile land will be put in use first because of its greater productivity. Less and less fertile land will be put to use until that unit of land is reached that no one will bid for—it produces no net value (rent) and is marginal land. As population grows over time and agricultural products increase in price, the market value of the produce may begin to exceed the cost of production on the least fertile land in use. What had been marginal land begins to produce a rent; less fertile land is brought into production and the new marginal land becomes that which in use produces no net value, no rent. See *Rent*.

MARGINAL OUTPUT   1. The last added unit of output. 2. The output attributable to the last added unit of a variable factor of production. See *Marginal Physical Product*.

MARGINAL PHYSICAL PRODUCT (MPP)   The change in total product (output) resulting from a change of one unit of a variable factor of production, *ceteris paribus*. $MPP = dTP/dF$.

$$MPP_F = \frac{TP_n - TP_{n-1}}{F_n - F_{n-1}} = \frac{dTP}{dF}$$

See *Diminishing Returns, Total Product Curve, Marginal Revenue Product*.

MARGINAL PHYSICAL PRODUCT CURVE   A curve depicting changes in output as a variable factor input changes, *ceteris paribus*. Suppose that the variable factor input is labor. At low levels of labor input, there is too much of the other factors, such as machinery and equipment, relative to the quantity of labor. The combination cannot be utilized efficiently, so output per labor unit input is low. Each added unit of labor will make the ratio of labor to the fixed factors more productive and will add more to output than the previously added labor unit. Eventually however, the ratio of labor to capital will change enough to cause the amount of *added* output (MPP) to decrease as labor units are added. At that point the MPP curve begins to slope down, an illustration of diminishing (though still positive) returns. Eventually as labor units are added, there will be so much labor that adding another unit of labor will *reduce* *total output* so that MPP becomes negative. See *Diminishing Returns*.

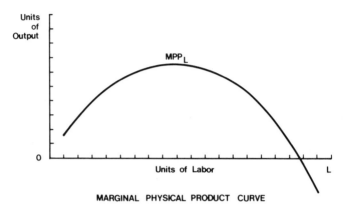

MARGINAL PHYSICAL PRODUCT CURVE

MARGINAL PRODUCTIVITY THEORY OF INCOME DISTRIBUTION
A theory that each factor of production will tend to be paid according to its marginal revenue product. Firms will continue to buy units of a factor of production up to the point where its marginal cost (MFC) equals its marginal revenue product (MRP), i.e., the point where the revenue from the output of the last added unit of a factor just equals the cost of that factor unit. Short of that point, each additional unit of a factor adds more to revenue than to cost. Beyond that point each additional unit of a factor adds more to cost than to revenue.

In a factor market of pure competition, the factor price is the marginal cost of the factor. There are enough units of the factor offered for sale that the firm can buy all that it wants at the going price; it will not have to pay a higher price to buy more. In these circumstances justice prevails in that each factor (for example, labor) gets paid the value of what it contributes to production.

In a factor market where there is market power, the firm will have to pay a higher price per unit to get more units. MFC exceeds factor price P_f. The firm will, as usual, find it most profitable to produce where MFC = MRP. However, $MFC > P_f$, so $MRP > P_f$, too. The factors will be paid an amount less than the value of their contribution to production (their MRP). See *Equilibrium of the Firm: Factor Market, Marginal Factor Cost Curve, Marginal Revenue Product, Marginal Revenue Product Curve*.

MARGINAL PROPENSITY TO CONSUME (MPC)
The change in consumption (dC) divided by the change in income (dY). $MPC = dC/dY$. The consumption function is defined as $C = f(Y)$,

and the MPC is the slope of the consumption function curve. In the national income analysis of J.M. Keynes (1883–1946), consumption expenditure is considered to be dependent upon the level of income, other determinants of consumption remaining constant in the short run. That relationship also is known as the *absolute income hypothesis*.

Other hypotheses about the relation between consumption and income are the *relative income hypothesis* and the *permanent income hypothesis*. Post-Keynesian analysis also has given some weight to such considerations as expectations about future prices and income, especially as they affect the demand for durable goods, and the effect of savings plans on consumption, which can affect consumption expenditure even though there is no independent change in the level of income. In such cases, C is an independent variable, and changes in C may cause changes in Y, as well as the other way around.

The MPC may be used to analyze a household or an economy. In the latter, C is most dependably related to the national income concept *disposable personal income* (DPY), which households either spend for consumption or save. It is less dependably related to gross national product (GNP), which contains amounts that do not directly find their way into householders' hands because of taxes, retained earnings of corporations, etc. See *Absolute Income Hypothesis, Relative Income Hypothesis, Permanent Income Hypothesis, Average Propensity to Consume, Consumption Function, Marginal Propensity to Save.*

MARGINAL PROPENSITY TO IMPORT　The ratio of the change in imports to a change in national income. The ratio is positive in all countries and has tended to grow in recent years as markets have become more international. Smaller countries tend to have a higher marginal propensity to import because of a smaller variety of domestic resources (but Japan is evidence that a small country geographically may also *export* huge quantities, producing a large trade surplus).

MARGINAL PROPENSITY TO SAVE (MPS)　The change in saving (dS) divided by the change in income (dY). $MPS = dS/dY$. In the national income analysis of J. M. Keynes (1883–1946), changes in saving in the economy are considered to be largely dependent upon change in income, because saving is looked upon as a residual after decisions to spend for consumption have been made. For disposable personal income (DPY), $MPS = 1 - MPC$, where MPS is the marginal propensity to save and MPC is the marginal propensity to consume. Post-Keynesian analysis considers saving to be less of a residual in societies where large numbers of people have discretionary income beyond the income required for basic necessities. Decisions to save because of price expectations, fear of income loss, or anticipation of college expenses or old age often compete directly with decisions to spend for consumption. See *Marginal Propensity to Consume, Saving*.

MARGINAL RATE OF SUBSTITUTION (MRS)   The rate at which a consumer will substitute a unit of one good (x) for units of another good (y) and yet maintain the same level of satisfaction with the new combination as with the old. The marginal rate of substitution of x for y is the slope of an indifference curve for an individual. The curve illustrates all of the combinations of x and y that provide the individual with the same level of satisfaction. $MRS_{xy} = dQ_y/dQ_x$

Generally, as x is substituted for y in successive combinations of the two goods, the consumer will be willing to give up less and less y for each additional unit of x, to achieve a new combination of x and y that will provide the same level of satisfaction as the previous combination. The indifference curve is convex to the origin. This is the *Law of Diminishing Marginal Rate of Substitution*.

MRS is a concept used in economic theory to derive consumer demand. See *Equilibrium of the Consumer, Consumer Demand, Diminishing Marginal Rate of Substitution, Indifference Curve*.

MARGINAL RATE OF TECHNICAL SUBSTITUTION (MRTS)   The rate at which a firm can substitute a unit of one factor of production, say labor (l), for units of another factor of production, machinery (m), and maintain the same level of total output with the new combination as with the old. The marginal rate of technical substitution of l for m is the slope of an isoquant curve for a firm. An isoquant curve illustrates all of the combinations of two factors of production (l and m) that provide the firm with the same level of total output.

$MRTS_{lm} = MPP_l/MPP_m$ where MPP_l is the marginal physical product of one factor, labor, and MPP_m is the marginal physical product of another factor, machinery.

Generally, as l is substituted for m in successive combinations of the two factors of production, the firm will be required to give up less and less m for each additional unit of l in a new combination of l and m that will provide the same level of total output as the previous combination. The isoquant curve is convex. This is the *Law of Diminishing Marginal Rate of Technical Substitution*. See *Isoquant Curve, Isoquant–Isocost Equilibrium*.

MARGINAL RETURN 1. The change in physical output of a firm resulting from a change of one unit of a factor of production (MPP). 2. The change in revenue of a firm resulting from a change in one unit of a factor of production. 3. The change in revenue of a firm resulting in the change of one unit of output. See *Marginal Output, Marginal Physical Product, Marginal Revenue, Marginal Revenue Product, Diminishing Returns.*

MARGINAL REVENUE (MR) The change in total revenue (dTR) associated with a change in one unit of output (dQ). MR = dTR/dQ. In pure competition marginal revenue is the same as price because each firm can sell all that it can produce at the market price; the demand curve facing the firm is horizontal. If the firm does not have to reduce price in order to sell more, the sale of one more unit will increase total revenue by the amount of the price per unit. MR = P.

In markets characterized by some degree of sellers' market power, marginal revenue is *less* than price because, in a continuing operation where price discrimination cannot occur, the seller must reduce price on all units in order to sell more; the demand curve facing the firm is downward sloping. Thus, marginal revenue equals price minus the loss of receipts from the reduction of the price on all of the units of output prior to this one. MR = $P_n - [(P_{n-1} - P_n) \times Q_{n-1}]$.

As long as increases in output add more to revenue than to cost (MR > MC), total profit (which is TR − TC) will increase, so output should be expanded. When MR < MC, profits will be increased by reducing output until MR = MC. See *Equilibrium of the Firm, Marginal Revenue Curve.*

MARGINAL REVENUE CURVE A curve illustrating changes in a firm's total revenue as output varies.

1. In pure competition a firm's output is such a small part of the total market that it can sell any additional amount it can produce at the going market price. (The wheat market is an example.) Therefore, each time the firm adds a unit of output, it adds to total revenue the price of the unit. MR = P. The demand curve is a P–Q relationship and the MR curve is an MR–Q relationship, so that when MR = P, the demand curve and the MR curve are the same.

2. In monopoly or monopolistic competition the firm faces a downward sloping demand curve. In order to sell more, the firm must reduce price. In a continuing operation without price discrimination, the firm must reduce price on all of its output, not just the additional unit. The change in total revenue (MR), then, is the price

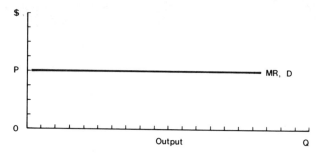

MARGINAL REVENUE CURVE: PURE COMPETITION

of the added unit *minus* the loss from reducing the price on all of the units that could have been sold before this unit was added. MR is less than P, and the MR curve lies below the demand curve for each level of output. See *Marginal Revenue*.

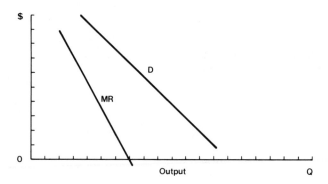

MARGINAL REVENUE CURVE: SELLER MARKET POWER

MARGINAL REVENUE PRODUCT (MRP)   The MRP is the change in total revenue (TR) associated with a change of one unit of a variable factor of production (F), *cet. par*. It is the marginal revenue of a unit of *input*.

$$\text{MRP}_F = \frac{\text{TR}_n - \text{TR}_{n-1}}{\text{F}_n - \text{F}_{n-1}} = \frac{d\text{TR}}{d\text{F}}$$

The term "marginal revenue product" identifies a discussion involving a factor market rather than a product market. The "product" of one more unit of a factor of production may be more or less than one unit of the firm's output. The marginal revenue product is found by converting marginal physical product to its dollar value, i.e., marginal physical product times marginal revenue.

In microeconomic analysis, the MRP of a factor of production is compared to the marginal cost of the factor (MFC) to determine whether it is profitable to employ it. The firm will tend to employ that quantity of a factor of production where $MRP_F = MFC_F$. See *Equilibrium of the Firm: Factor Market.*

MARGINAL REVENUE PRODUCT CURVE A curve which depicts the change in revenue to the firm as the quantity of a factor of production changes, *ceteris paribus*. It is the slope of the total revenue product (TRP) curve. Only the downward sloping section of the MRP curve is relevant. The firm can continue to add to revenue relative to cost (hence add to profit or reduce loss) right up to point b in the illustration below.

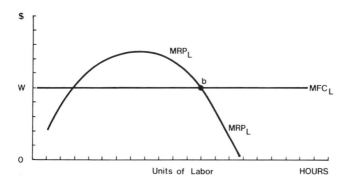

MARGINAL REVENUE PRODUCT CURVE

MARGINAL UTILITY (MU) The additional satisfaction for the consumer from an increase in consumption of one additional unit of a good in a given period of time. The concept is used in the theory of consumer demand. Amounts of satisfaction are not measurable so, in an effort to achieve empirical results, economists have developed indifference theory using the marginal rate of substitution concept. Indifference theory also has shortcomings for empirical research. See *Equilibrium of the Consumer.*

MARGIN CALL A call to a securities buyer for additional cash or securities when the market price of securities bought on margin falls. When the market price falls the lower value of the securities held may no longer meet the margin-to-loan requirement. It also is used in futures markets for both long and short sales. See *Margin.*

MARGIN REQUIREMENT   The percentage of the purchase price of a block of marketable securities that must be paid down when buying on credit. The Federal Reserve Board of Governors is given the power to regulate the purchase of securities on margin. When the Fed wishes to slow down securities market transactions it raises the margin requirement, thereby reducing the amount that may be borrowed to purchase securities. Margin requirements are applied to futures markets on commodity exchanges as well as to stock and bond markets. See *Margin*.

MARKET   The sum of contacts between buyers and sellers of a product or service. A market is a collection of individual decision-making units, some of whom desire to buy (demand) a particular good or service and are in touch with those who desire to sell (supply). Price is established in these contacts. A market need not have a specific physical location.

MARKET DEMAND CURVE   A curve showing the aggregate amounts demanded (Q) by all buyers in a competitive market at each possible market price (P). (In monopoly, the firm's demand curve *is* the market demand curve, while in monopolistic competition differentiated products prevent simple summation.) The market demand curve is the horizontal addition of the demand curves of all buyers in the market as illustrated in the curves below, assuming just two buyers for simplicity. The quantity demanded by Buyer 1 at $4 (0a) is added to the quantity demanded by Buyer 2 at $4 (0b) to produce the total quantity demanded in the market [0 (a+b)] at $4 per unit. The same horizontal addition for higher and lower prices will produce the market demand curve D_M.

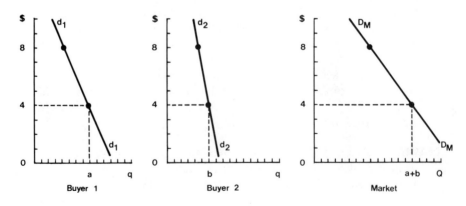

DERIVATION OF A MARKET DEMAND CURVE

MARKET ECONOMY   An economy characterized by decentralized decision making by private individuals and groups working through markets in which sellers typically produce for unknown and unseen potential buyers. The interaction of buyers and sellers in markets provides the answers to the basic economic questions of what to produce, how, and for whom.

The market economy often is contrasted with centrally planned economies in which public authorities make the basic economic decisions. See *Price System*.

MARKET EQUILIBRIUM   The price that clears the market; the price at which the quantity that buyers want to buy equals the quantity sellers want to sell. See *Equilibrium of the Market: Monopolistic Competition, Equilibrium of the Market: Pure Competition*.

MARKET POWER   The power of one seller or a group of sellers to affect the quantity offered in a market, and therefore the price. Or, the power of one *buyer or group of buyers* to affect the quantity demanded in a market, and therefore the price.

Sometimes the best way to illustrate a concept is by reference to its opposite, in this case, pure competition. A market of pure competition has so many buyers and sellers of a homogeneous product that no one participant, or viable group, can affect price by withholding demand or supply of the product. Buyers and sellers can enter and leave the market without serious restriction. The absence of any of these conditions will mean that some degree of market power exists.

A monopolist firm exercises seller control because it is the only producer of a product with no close substitutes, and entry of other firms is restricted. Sometimes a group of sellers will get together to attempt to control output and exercise market power as a monopolist would.

The Organization of Petroleum Exporting Countries (OPEC) is an example of such a group, known as a cartel. The market power of a cartel is a function of how much of the market it controls and how effectively the group controls itself. These circumstances have changed for OPEC in the decade of the 1980s as new, nonaligned production of oil has appeared in the North Sea, Alaska, and Latin America, as some nations have pursued energy conservation, and as some OPEC members have been unwilling to restrict themselves to assigned production quotas.

In the U.S., government intervenes in markets with its antitrust policies to prevent monopoly, cartels, and market control behavior. In the case of natural monopoly, such as local telephone service, government acknowledges the productive efficiency of monopoly by permitting it, but government regulates the monopoly in order to redirect the market outcome to something more closely resembling pure competition.

There may be market power even where there is rivalry, such as in a market of monopolistic competition, where a firm produces a product which has close, but not perfect, substitutes made by others. To the extent that the firm can differentiate its product from others, it can raise its price without losing all of its customers; it has some market power. New firms can enter the market rather easily, which limits but does not eliminate the market power of individual firms.

On the buyers' side of a market, a monopsonist exercises market power by being the sole buyer and can affect price by controlling demand. A firm in a small group of buyers (oligopsony) may exercise substantial market power, even though it is limited by the existence of the other buyers. An automobile company has substantial market power in dealing with small firms supplying parts. But automobile companies buying tires have market power that is limited not only by competition among themselves, but also by the concentration of only a few firms on the *sellers'* side of the market (a situation of bilateral oligopoly).

Even the great market power of a monopolist or monopsonist is restricted because the firm does not control the other side of the market. A monopolist is limited in its price increases by the affect a price increase has on quantity demanded. If quantity demanded is very sensitive to price changes (elastic demand), a price increase will reduce total revenue; the seller's market power is limited. If quantity demanded is insensitive to price changes (inelastic demand), the seller may raise price very high without much effect on quantity sold; market power is very great. On the other side of the market, buyers are limited in their ability to press down prices because of the effect lower prices may have on quantity supplied (i.e., the elasticity of supply), which depends upon cost of production. Such limitations on market power may be limited. See *Cartel, Monopoly, Monopolistic Competition, Monopsony.*

MARKET PRICE 1. The price charged in the market at an instant in time. 2. Equilibrium market price is that price which clears the market; the price of homogeneous products at which the quantity sellers wish to sell equals the quantity buyers wish to buy. In pure competition, it is the equilibrium price where the market supply curve intersects the market demand curve. In imperfect competition there is no *market* price. Price is each firm's price associated with the output where marginal cost equals marginal revenue. Each firm has some market power and price may differ from firm to firm. See *Equilibrium of the Market: Pure Competition, Market Equilibrium.*

MARKET SUPPLY CURVE   A curve showing the aggregate amounts (Q) supplied by all firms in the purely competitive market at each possible market price (P). (In monopoly, the firm *is* the market, while firms in monopolistic competition supply differentiated products so simple summation will not do.) It is derived by the horizontal addition of the supply curves (marginal cost curves) of all firms in the market. In the simplified example below, the quantity supplied by Firm 1 (0a) at a particular price ($5) is added to the quantity supplied by Firm 2 (0b) at that price ($5) to make up the market quantity supplied [0 (a + b)] at that price ($5). Horizontal addition of quantity is made for every other possible market price to produce the market supply curve SM.

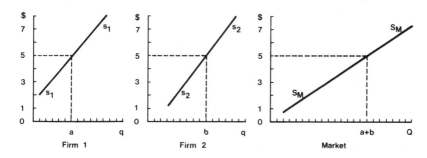

DERIVATION OF A MARKET SUPPLY CURVE

In like manner, the market supply curve for a *factor of production* is produced by the horizontal addition of the supply curves of individual factor suppliers. See *Marginal Cost Curve, Marginal Factor Cost Curve, Equilibrium of the Market: Pure Competition.*

MARKET SYSTEM See *Market Economy, Price System*

MARXISM   A theory of economic and social development by Karl Marx, German economist–social philosopher (1818–1883), which holds that capitalism, although an improvement over prior economic and social organization, will inevitably fail and give rise to socialism as the ownership of capital concentrates in fewer and fewer hands while the workers, the proletariat, become more and more numerous and fall ever deeper into poverty and misery.

In 1989 and 1990, most of the socialist regimes of eastern Europe collapsed in a domino-like chain as their economies failed. The new leadership rallied around the call for democratic government and "free markets." They turned to the West for help and guidance to shift to market-directed economies. The politburo of the USSR voted on September 24, 1990 to adopt free markets in the Soviet Union, but little progress had been made toward that goal as economic and political disintegration continued into 1991.

MASS PRODUCTION   The production of standardized goods in large quantities for sale in large, impersonal markets. The opposite of special-order production. Mass production usually is associated with mechanized production in large factories involving a high capital-to-labor ratio.

MEDIATION   A process for dealing with disputes between two parties such as a labor union and an employer. A third, neutral, party enters the negotiations and meets with the disputing parties separately to try to find some common ground for agreement. It is especially useful where positions of the disputants have become frozen because of an attempt to call a supposed bluff or to save face. Often, in such cases, each opponent in fact would be willing to settle for less than their last stated position. Mediators are facilitators who help disputants to find a solution, while arbitrators are judges who impose a decision. Mediation may be requested by the parties, or in some cases mediation may be initiated by government.

MERCANTILISM   A descriptive term invented in later years to describe writers of the sixteenth and seventeenth centuries who advocated similar policies, such as an emphasis on manufacture rather than on the production of agricultural raw materials, and protectionist foreign trade measures, both of which would produce an excess of exports over imports, i.e., a "favorable balance of trade." Net exports would enrich the state when other countries paid off the balance in precious metals. Some writers confused money, in the form of precious metals, with wealth. Many were more sophisticated and looked on the flow of precious metals as a source of purchasing power for such things as navies and standing armies for emerging nation states.

Adam Smith, in *The Wealth of Nations,* showed that imports bring in useful goods and services while exports send out the nation's goods in return for sterile metals. In this view exports are a necessary evil to finance imports. See *Protectionism.*

MERGER   The joining together of two or more existing firms to form a single larger one. Horizontal mergers join firms which produce competing products. Competition tends to be reduced directly. Vertical mergers join firms in successive stages of a production process, such as a bauxite mining company, an aluminum ingot producer, and an aluminum can fabricator. Competition is reduced in a horizontal merger by definition, but it may not be a significant reduction. Competition may be reduced in a vertical merger if it reduces the availability of supplies to outsiders or reduces the number of buyers for products of firms not included in the merger. Conglomerate mergers join together firms that do not have any market relations with each other, such as a steel company and a savings and loan institution. See *Conglomerate Merger, Horizontal Merger, Leveraged Buyout, Takeover, Vertical Merger.*

MICROECONOMICS   The study of the individual parts of the economy and how they relate to one another. It is the study of individual household demand or market demand for a product and household or market supply of factors of production. It is the study of a business firm's demand for resources and organization of production to meet demand for the firm's output. It is the study of the system of markets that interrelates decisions of households and business firms, establishing prices and determining output. It is the study of such matters as monopoly, mobility of labor, distribution of income, agricultural instability, and production of public goods such as safety, public health, or transportation facilities. Microeconomics compares to the study of individual trees and groves of trees, while macroeconomics compares to the study of the forest.

MINIMUM WAGE   A wage "floor" established by law, raising the lowest wage that can be paid to a level above the market rate. No employer subject to the legislation can legally pay a wage below the established minimum.

Analysis of the demand for a factor of production shows that if the price of a factor goes up, *cet. par.*, the quantity demanded goes down. In the labor market, an increase in wages will lead to a reduction in employment, *cet. par.* Those who remain employed will benefit; those affected by the loss of jobs will lose.

The employment effect of an increase in the legal minimum wage often is denied by politicians because the relationship may be disguised when other labor-demand determinants than the price of labor, for example, the demand for the product, *do not* remain the same. Or, there may be a time lag in the adjustment of employment by many firms because it takes time to replace labor with machines.

Such circumstances make statistical measurement of cause and effect difficult. When the problem is acknowledged, there may be an effort to counteract the employment effects of the wage increase by making other political decisions to protect those adversely affected by the wage increase. See *Demand*.

MIXED ECONOMY   An economic system in which there is some private ownership and management of natural resources and capital goods, together with some public (government) ownership and management of natural resources and capital goods. It is a mixture of capitalism and socialism. See *Capitalism, Socialism, Free-Enterprise Economy*.

MONETARISM   The belief that control of the quantity of money is sufficient for the attainment of price stability, full employment, and general economic stability, at least in the longer run. Monetarists applauded when, in 1979, the Federal Reserve shifted from interest rate targets to money supply targets to try to control inflation and the level of economic activity. Keynesians, on the other hand, emphasize fiscal policy for control of the economy, while acknowledging in recent years that money matters, somewhat.

Monetarists differ in their policy recommendations for control of the money supply. Some support the Federal Reserve Board policy of setting money stock targets, which increase or decrease the rate of growth in the money supply to combat inflation and the business cycle. Many, including Professor Milton Friedman, who is probably the most famous contemporary monetarist, hold that the Federal Reserve should follow a rule of increasing total bank reserves (high-powered money) by a constant percentage per year, a percentage increase just sufficient to accommodate the long-run average rate of economic growth. This, in turn, would control the other money supply aggregates. Business leaders, labor union leaders, and others, understanding the relation between money stock, inflation, and levels of economic activity, would accommodate their actions to the anticipated economic effect of the Fed persistently following this rule. See *Money Supply*.

MONETARY BASE   (Or Money Base.) The sum of reserve deposits that banks hold with the Federal Reserve System, plus currency held by the public. The money base, then, consists of the monetary liabilities of the Federal Reserve System and of the Treasury that are held by the public. The money stock (M1, or M2, etc.) is a multiple of the monetary base, so the monetary base often is called high-powered money; changes have a multiplied effect. See *Deposit Multiplier, Money Multiplier, Money Stock.*

MONETARY POLICY Policy to influence the general level of economic activity by trying to regulate the quantity of money and its price. An alternative to fiscal policy. Monetary policy is carried out by a *central bank.* In the U.S., that is the Federal Reserve System (the Fed), and its chief policy arm, the Federal Open Market Committee (FOMC).

1. The Fed has authority to *change reserve requirements* within a range established by law. By raising or lowering the reserves required for checking account deposits, the Fed can decrease or increase excess reserves. When reserve requirements are *raised*, the amount of excess reserves will shrink. Excess reserves in the banking system can be reduced sufficiently that the reserves of many banks will fall below the legal requirement. That will cause a multiplied reduction of the money supply (checking accounts), primarily by banks taking action to increase the ratio of loan repayments to new loans. *Lowering* the reserve requirements will create excess reserves and encourage an expansion of the money supply in the form of new loans and checking accounts. The expansion of the money supply will be a multiple of the increase in excess reserves. See *Deposit Multiplier.*

2. In a second, more commonly used policy known as *open-market operations,* the Fed can affect bank reserves through the purchase or sale of Treasury securities in the open market by the FOMC. If the FOMC *buys* Treasury securities, total privately held checking deposits will increase when sellers of the securities deposit the checks they receive from the Fed into their checking accounts. As checks clear, the total deposits held by banks at the Fed also will increase by an equal amount. These are legal reserves. The banking system had to meet its reserve requirements before these transactions occurred, so these new *excess reserves* may encourage expansion throughout the banking system.

If the FOMC *sells* Treasury securities, people will pay with checks drawn on their bank deposits. Total bank deposits at the Fed (bank reserves) will decrease as checks clear and the Fed is paid. If there are insufficient excess reserves to cover this decrease, banks' reserves will fall below the amount required, and banks will have to contract their deposit obligations by a multiple of the shortfall. See *Deposit Multiplier.*

3. The Fed's *discount rate* provides a third tool of monetary policy. The Fed may raise or lower the discount rate in order to affect borrowing of reserves by the financial institutions that are

required to keep reserves with the Fed. Credit is extended by the Fed to depository institutions with temporary liquidity problems or other special problems. The Fed, unlike the Federal Home Loan Bank System, has controlled its credit to prevent banks from borrowing for profit, treating borrowing from the Fed as a privilege, not a right. The Fed discount rate seldom is used to affect the general level of excess reserves directly. However, a change in the rate is taken by the financial and business communities as a signal that the Fed believes that the economy is expanding too fast or too slowly. Consequently, a change in the discount rate may bring about changes in business decisions which can move the economy in the desired direction.

In the 1980s, the FOMC tried to change the quantity of M2 to respond to changes in economic activity as represented, for example, by leading economic indicators. The overriding concern was to control inflation, although at the end of the decade there was a growing concern to prevent recession. As described in the *Monetarism* entry, some economists advocate an alternative policy of holding the rate of increase steady at the long-run average rate of economic growth. See *Deposit Multiplier, Money Multiplier, Excess Reserves, Monetarism, Fiscal Policy.*

MONETIZING THE DEBT Turning federal debt into money when the Federal Reserve System buys bonds from the Treasury. When Congress has authorized and appropriated more funds for government spending than taxes will support, the Treasury must borrow by selling bills, notes, and bonds. If the Fed buys the new Treasury debt instruments directly from the Treasury, the Treasury deposit at the Fed will increase by the amount of its securities sale. There will be no offsetting *decrease* in deposits at the Fed, as would occur in the reserve deposits of banks if the general public bought the bonds and paid from their bank checking accounts. As the Treasury spends from its new deposits to buy goods and services, the checks are deposited in the bank accounts of businesses and households. These are net new deposits and are an increase in the money supply—the same result as when the Fed buys Treasury bonds from the public in the open market. When the banks send the Treasury checks to the Fed for collection, the banks' free reserves at the Fed increase by an equal amount. Banks now can expand their loans and deposits, and the money supply can expand by a multiple of the Treasury spending. The Fed returns interest that it receives to the Treasury, so the borrowing is essentially costless to the government, but it is inflationary. See *Deposit Multiplier, Money Multiplier.*

MONEY   Anything in general use as a means of payment. 1. In functional terms, money is a medium of exchange, i.e., it is accepted in exchange for a good or service because the seller knows that he or she can, in turn, exchange the money for other goods and services. To be generally accepted money must be recognized as a common denominator, a standard of value, and a unit of account in which the value of everything else is expressed. For something to serve well as money it should be a good store of value, not fluctuating much in value over time, so that a seller may accept it and hold it for a while without it losing value. Money should be a good standard of deferred value, i.e., a unit in which debts are expressed; stable value over time returns to the lender the same purchasing power as the sum that was lent. Money should be convenient in form, i.e., easily divisible or enlarged in amount without great change in bulk.

   2. Empirical definitions of money focus on those items that are counted in the money supply or money stock. See *Currency, Fiat Money, Federal Reserve Note, Money Stock, M, M1, M2, M3.*

MONEY BASE   See *Monetary Base*

MONEY ILLUSION   A hypothesis that people respond to changes in their money income even though their real income doesn't change. If a householder's income rises by 10% and consumer prices rise by 10%, the household's real income is constant, but its members will tend to increase consumption based upon the money wage increase, according to this theory.

MONEY INCOME   The actual amount of money received by a factor of production. It differs from *real income,* which is money income corrected for inflation or deflation to reflect its relative purchasing power for goods and services. Converting money income to real income permits it to be compared with income of other time periods in terms of what the income will buy. See *Real Income, Real versus Money Data.*

MONEY MARKET   The market for short-term financial instruments such as negotiable certificates of deposit (CDs), banker's acceptances, commercial paper, and U.S. Treasury bills.

MONEY MARKET DEPOSIT ACCOUNTS   Deposit accounts in banks which yield a rate of interest related to the money market rate. There are minimum balance requirements and limits on the number of transactions per month. Unlike ordinary certificates of deposit, there are no minimum time requirements on deposits, and rates are adjusted periodically to changes in market rates. Unlike money market mutual funds, the deposits in banks are insured by the FDIC. See *Money Market, Money Market Mutual Funds.*

MONEY MARKET MUTUAL FUNDS Investment funds, offered to the public by investment companies, whose rates of return are related to money market rates. The funds consist of such short-term instruments as jumbo certificates of deposit and U.S. Treasury bills. The funds are managed so that relatively rapid turnover of holdings will keep the rate of return close to the short-term money market rate. Most are open-end funds, meaning that shares may be freely bought from and sold to the issuing mutual fund company in minimum amounts. Closed-end funds, on the other hand, consist of a specific total of shares which then trade on the open market. During the 1980s, money market mutual funds offered rates of return closer to the money market rate of return than did the money market deposit accounts of banks, especially when market rates were rising. The mutual funds, however, are not insured by the FDIC, while the bank deposit accounts are so insured. See *Mutual Association.*

MONEY MULTIPLIER The money stock is a multiple of the monetary base, which is the sum of reserves held with the Federal Reserve System plus currency held by the public. To find, for example, the multiplier of the money base in order to calculate M1, one must modify the simple *deposit multiplier, $1/r$,* to account for currency in the base as well as currency leakage from checking deposits. The deposit multiplier may vary depending upon a variety of other leakages. For example, financial intermediaries, such as brokerage houses with money market mutual funds, act as substitutes for banks with checkable deposits so that all checks don't immediately find their way back into checking deposits. Other potential leakages occur because of an increase in voluntary excess reserves which are affected by the willingness of banks to loan and of businesses to borrow, a change in public holdings of time deposits which have their own required reserves, a change in expectations about price changes, and a change in decisions by households and businesses about how much money to keep in their portfolio balances relative to other assets. See *Deposit Multiplier, M1, M2, M3, Money Base.*

MONEY PRICES The prices at which transactions occur. Sometimes called current prices, or nominal prices. Money prices are corrected by an appropriate price index to arrive at *real prices,* i.e., the real value of transactions with inflation or deflation removed. The adjusted data then can be used for value comparisons with other periods of time. See *Real Versus Money Data.*

MONEY STOCK   Money supply. The quantity of money in circulation outside the accounts of the federal government and outside the Federal Reserve Banks. See *M, M1, M2, M3,* for various definitions of money in measuring the money stock. The money *base,* or high-powered money, is the total monetary liabilities of the Federal Reserve System and the Treasury, i.e., reserve deposits with the Fed plus currency in the hands of the public. The monetary base times the appropriate money multiplier produces M1, M2, etc.. See *Deposit Multiplier, Money Base, Money Multiplier.*

MONEY SUPPLY   See *Money Stock.*

MONOPOLISTIC COMPETITION   A market structure character-ized by a large number of firms (similar to pure competition) but with each firm producing its own, unique commodity (similar to monopoly). Although unique, the product of one firm is highly substitutable for the similar products of other firms in the industry. New firms or other firms not in this market find it relatively easy to enter the market with a similar product. A firm in monopolistic competition attempts to differentiate its product from others and acquire consumer loyalty for its particular product in order to gain market power and higher profit. Advertising plays a large role in these efforts, and locational advantage can make a difference. The large number of firms means there is not the degree of interdepen-dence that exists among oligopolists.

Monopolistic competition is a market structure concept that was developed in the U.S. by Edward H. Chamberlin (1889–1967) for his doctoral dissertation at Harvard in 1933. At about the same time, a similar concept was developed in England by Joan Robinson (1903–1983), who gave her concept the differentiated name "imper-fect competition." (As a generic term, imperfect competition is used to describe *all* markets that are not characterized by perfect competition, including not only monopolistic competition, but such market forms as monopoly, duopoly, and oligopoly, as well.) Cham-berlin is credited with more a penetrating analysis of advertising and location as well as establishing the need for new theory rather than just a slight modification of the theory of monopoly. See *Competition, Differentiated Product, Equilibrium of the Firm: Monopolistic Competition, Equilibrium of the Market: Monopolis-tic Competition, Imperfect Competition, Monopoly, Nonprice Competition, Oligopoly.*

MONOPOLY   A market condition in which a single seller controls the supply of a product for which there are no close substitutes, and there are restrictions which prevent new firms from entering the market. The single seller is a single decision-making unit, e.g., an individual, a firm, a cartel, etc. The monopolist may set any price, but the quantity sold at any price will be determined by the buyers' willingness to buy. A *natural* monopoly is one which exists because two or more firms operating in the market would be grossly inefficient, since a single firm faces a decreasing long-run average cost curve over the relevant range of output. Utilities distributing electric power or telephone service in a local market are examples of natural monopoly. The holder of a patent is an example of legislated monopoly. (In the game *Monopoly* each player aspires to control the entire economy of the game, not just one market.) See *Bilateral Monopoly, Equilibrium of the Firm, Monopsony, Natural Monopoly, Patent.*

MONOPSONY   A market condition in which a single buyer controls the demand side of the market for a product or factor of production. The monopsonist may state any price for purchases, but the quantity supplied at any price will be determined by the sellers' willingness to sell. See *Monopoly, Oligopsony.*

MOST-FAVORED-NATION CLAUSE   An agreement in international trade which provides that a tariff reduction negotiated with one country will apply to all other countries with most-favored-nation status.

MULTIPLIER: Applied to GNP   See *Gross National Product Multiplier.*

MULTIPLIER: Applied to Bank Deposits   See *Deposit Multiplier.*

MULTIPLIER: Applied to Money   See *Money Multiplier.*

MUNICIPALS   Marketable bonds issued by state and local governments and their agencies, i.e., states, counties, cities, water districts, sewer districts, school boards, etc. The interest income from municipals usually is exempt from federal income taxes and usually is exempt also from state and local income taxes on residents in the issuer's locale. See *Government Bonds.*

MUTUAL ASSOCIATION   An organization whose members (depositors or fund investors) share the expenses of managing the association and share in the profits. For many years, federal savings and loan associations were all mutual associations. In recent years, many have chosen to become stock corporations. Many savings banks are mutual associations and use the word *mutual* in their names. See *Mutual Fund, Money Market Mutual Funds*.

MUTUAL FUND   A fund of securities represented by shares which are sold by the financial institution which manages it. The fund, for example a mutual fund for growth stock, buys stock shares in a variety of companies which the mutual fund managers identify as having substantial growth potential, so that the value of the stock shares is expected to grow at an above-average rate over time. An investor can then buy shares in the mutual fund and spread risk, as opposed to buying an equivalent value in the shares of just one or two companies. There are mutual funds for virtually every type of security, including corporate stocks, corporate bonds, money market securities, municipal bonds, U.S. Treasury securities, Government National Mortgage Association-backed mortgages, etc.

NATIONAL ASSOCIATION OF SECURITIES DEALERS AUTO-MATED QUOTATIONS (NASDAQ) The electronic trading system in the U.S. for over-the-counter securities, which do not have to meet the more stringent listing requirements of securities listed on such organized exchanges as the New York Stock Exchange (NYSE) or the American Stock Exchange (AMEX). The computerized system provides virtually instantaneous price quotations and electronic execution of trades for thousands of dealers throughout the U.S. See *Over-the-Counter Securities.*

NATIONAL BANK A commercial bank chartered by the Comptroller of the Currency, an agency of the U.S. Treasury Department. Being federally chartered, national banks are federally regulated. All national banks must be members of the Federal Reserve Banking System and must participate in the deposit insurance program of the Bank Insurance Fund of the Federal Deposit Insurance Corporation. State-chartered commercial banks may apply to become members of the Bank Insurance Fund and of the Fed System and, when accepted, they come under more general federal regulation. National banks constitute less than one-third of all commercial banks (the rest are state chartered) but hold over half of all demand deposits. See *Commercial Bank, Federal Reserve Banking System, Bank Insurance Fund, Federal Deposit Insurance Corporation, State Banks.*

NATIONAL CREDIT UNION ADMINISTRATION An independent agency, directed by a board of three members who are appointed by the President and confirmed by the Senate, which charters, regulates, examines, and insures federal credit unions. The National Credit Union Share Insurance Fund insures the accounts of all federal credit unions and those state-chartered credit unions which apply and qualify. See *Credit Union*.

NATIONAL DEBT The total value of the interest-bearing obligations issued by the U.S. Treasury. It is the current net sum of all federal budget deficits over the years, counting those occasional surpluses as negative deficits (in good economics jargon). The U.S. Treasury has run a budget deficit through prosperity and recession, and thereby increased the national debt, in all but 5 years between 1949 and 1990. The most recent surplus (reducing the debt) was $0.3 billion in 1960.

Most economists have not considered the U.S. national debt a major problem until recent years. It was internally held so that, as a nation, we owed it to ourselves. To pay off the debt to ourselves we would tax ourselves, so that it would be ''out of one pocket and into the other'' for the nation as a whole. At time of repayment there might be a redistribution of income if different people were taxed than held the debt instruments, but there was no ''generation'' problem of having future *generations* pay for our current public expenditures. The sacrifice is current, it was argued; it is not passed on. At the time of the deficit people give up private goods for public goods if there is full employment. If there is not, there is no *current generation* sacrifice either.

The national debt, and perennial budget deficits adding to it, are considered a problem now for several reasons. The national debt was $3233 billion at the end of the 1990 fiscal year. Interest payments on the federal debt for fiscal 1990 were 14.7% of federal outlays of $1252 billion, up from 14.2% in 1988. When interest payments are large, the internal redistribution of income can be substantial, especially when the interest payments are funded by taxation rather than by more Treasury borrowing. While there is no generational cost, or net cost considering the total population, the income redistribution that occurs is unintended rather than the result of explicit social and political decisions.

Foreign holdings of U.S. Treasury debt do create a cost to U.S. citizens as interest and principal payments flow out of the country. Foreign holdings grew to $393.4 billion dollars by the end of 1989, or 13.3% of the federal debt, so that interest and future principal repayments *are* noticeable sacrifices for present and future generations of U.S. citizens.

Another problem arises when interest on the debt is large as a percentage of the annual budget: It becomes much more difficult to reduce the budget deficit because the interest comes off the top and cannot be reduced by simple legislative action to reduce the appropriation, as is a possibility for highways and national defense. Furthermore, if the deficit is large going into a recession, as it was in 1991, fiscal policy is stymied as politicians fear to pass spending legislation that would increase output and employment but also would make the deficit even larger. (Taxation to pay for increased spending in a recession will tend to dampen the expansionary effect of the increased government spending by reducing the disposable personal income of those taxed.) See *Budget Deficit, Deficit Spending, Crowding Out, Federal Open-Market Committee.*

NATIONAL INCOME 1. As a generic term, "national income" is used in such phrases as "national income analysis" or "national income accounting" to refer to the whole system of total income or total product categories in the economy.

2. "National income" (NY) also may be a specific category in national income accounting. In this meaning, one subtracts capital consumption allowance from gross national product (GNP) to obtain net national product (NNP). Then NNP is adjusted by subtracting indirect business taxes and business transfer payments while adding in subsidies minus the current surplus of government enterprises to arrive at "national income" (NY, or NI). See *Gross National Product, Capital Consumption Allowance.*

NATURAL MONOPOLY Identified by Adam Smith as a kind of production which by its very nature must be provided by only one seller, so that the market regulation provided by competition cannot come into play. There is room for only one producer because in the relevant range of output the producer experiences economies of scale (decreasing long-run average costs). To produce at lowest average cost, there is room for only one producer in the market.

The number of natural monopolies probably has increased over time because of technological developments. Adam Smith pointed to national defense as an example. In the modern world some common examples are telephone service to a community, a municipal water service, or a community's sewer system. For a time, railroads held a monopoly in interurban transportation service to small communities.

Some monopolies are not natural, but rather are created by government for defense purposes or to encourage invention. A notable example of the latter was the Aluminum Company of America, which held a patent for the only low-cost method for processing bauxite ore. The monopoly existed for decades until demands for aluminum during World War II led to expanded production in government plants that were sold later to Kaiser and Reynolds aluminum companies.

Government regulation of natural monopolies is common. If it is most efficient to have but one producer it does not make economic sense to try to force the development of competitors in order to achieve regulation by market forces. Usually a governmental unit such as a city will grant the exclusive right to serve a given area to one producer. A public commission then regulates prices and service to protect buyers. If the law provides for fixing prices to achieve a normal rate of return, it also becomes necessary to regulate cost decisions and accounting practices to prevent the development of uncompetitive costs in high salaries, executive fringe benefits, and other corporate forms of featherbedding.

Over the long run, competitive forces might contribute to market regulation of natural monopolies as entrepreneurs develop new industries which displace the old, a process described by Joseph Schumpeter (1883–1950) in his *Theory of Economic Development*. A well-used example is the competition in interurban transportation felt by railroads when the internal combustion engine put automobiles and trucks on the road. Many small and moderate-sized communities were freed from the monopoly power that a single railroad had held in transporting their goods to market.

The concept of countervailing power, developed by John Kenneth Galbraith, provides another kind of potential market pressure on natural monopolies. When economic power develops, a countervailing power sometimes develops on the other side of the market. Most examples of countervailing power are found in oligopolies of giant concerns where long-run average costs decline up to very large outputs and result in a few large producers. It is natural market power but not natural *monopoly* power. The automobile industry grew into a few powerful firms that, as buyers, challenge the market power of giant firms in the steel industry. In turn, the United Auto Workers union grew to be a powerful counter to the power of the automobile companies. Sometimes countervailing power protects the consumer from market power, but at other times it merely produces a sharing of monopoly profits. See *Monopoly, Patent, Public Utility*.

NATURAL RESOURCES   Resources in their natural state before any labor or capital goods have been applied to their use. Examples are beds of iron ore or coal, rivers that are not dammed or dredged, and land before clearing or cultivating. The term "land" often is used to stand for "natural resources" when dealing with categories of the factors of production, as in "land, labor, and capital."

NEGATIVE AMORTIZATION   The build-up of debt (the principal) during the term of a mortgage. It can occur with a fixed-rate graduated-payment mortgage or with an adjustable-rate mortgage. Negative amortization may be specifically written into a mortgage as a way to permit a borrower to make payments based upon an artificially low interest rate. The process creates deferred payments which are added to the principal of the loan so that the principal grows over time. The deferred payments are the difference between what the payments would be at the going market rate of interest and the smaller payments at the actual adopted interest rate. The mortgage then will call for payments to increase at some future date, to move to normal amortization with gradually decreasing principal.

Adjustments in an adjustable-rate mortgage (ARM) also may cause the principal owed to increase. The interest rate of an ARM adjusts periodically so that the proportion of each mortgage payment going to interest and the proportion going to principal varies, but the size of the payment adjusts only every 6 or 12 months. Negative amortization may be built in, or it may occur inadvertently when the interest rate rises sharply and the new amount of interest owed exceeds the scheduled principal payment. This will cause an addition to the principal of the mortgage rather than the usual reduction, until the size of the payment is adjusted.

Negative amortization mortgages are popular in times of rising real estate prices, when both the borrower and the lender bet that real estate inflation will keep pace with or exceed the scheduled increases in the principal of the mortgage. By 1990 it was clear that some borrowers and lenders had lost the bets they had placed during the expansion of the 1980s. See *Adjustable-Rate Mortgage, Amortization.*

NEGATIVE INCOME TAX   A procedure for meeting welfare needs through the income tax system. A poverty level of income is defined according to family needs and prevailing price levels. Above the poverty income level, the traditional income tax structure is in effect. Below that income level, the family receives a grant, graduated according to the level of earnings. As earnings rise toward the poverty-level benchmark, the grant declines at a rate that is designed to maintain the incentive to earn more income through work when that is possible.

Both conservative and liberal economists believe that this system is superior to traditional welfare programs which may create a disincentive for work. Welfare programs frequently cut off high proportions of aid when a job is found, even though earnings may be well below the poverty benchmark. The administrative costs of the negative income tax system are estimated to be far less costly than traditional welfare systems.

The earned income credit in the federal income tax system is an example of a negative income tax which provides aid for low-income wage earners and tries to maintain the incentive to seek more work. It applies only to a worker with a child, not to the unemployed or childless, and is a modest supplement rather than a substitute for the welfare system. The earned income credit is a refundable credit that is paid to those who qualify even though they never paid any income tax or had any tax withheld from their wages. To qualify, the taxpayer must have some earned income in the form of wages, salary, tips, etc.; have earned income and adjusted gross income below a specified amount ($20,264 for 1990); file as head of household, married filing jointly, or qualifying widow(er); and have a qualifying child living with him or her. The credit is small at very low levels of income, rises with income to a peak ($953 for incomes between $6,800 and $10,750 in 1990), and then gradually falls as income continues to rise beyond poverty-level income to $20,264.

NEGOTIABLE INSTRUMENT   A document of obligation or owner-ship which can be transferred legally from one person to another by delivery or by endorsement. Currency is the most common negotiable instrument. Other examples are checks written on check-ing accounts, shares of stock issued by corporations, and most bonds. Series E and EE bonds issued by the U.S. Treasury are not negotiable, nor are savings accounts and time deposits in banks. Each of these latter must be cashed in with the issuer for the holder to receive money (usually a check), which is negotiable. See *Liquidity, Negotiable Order of Withdrawal.*

NEGOTIABLE ORDER OF WITHDRAWAL (NOW)   A check writ-ten on an interest-bearing checking account (NOW account) which is offered by savings and loan institutions and savings banks under authority of the Depository Institutions Deregulation and Monetary Control Act of 1980. NOW accounts were introduced experimen-tally in thrifts in New England beginning in 1974. The experience seemed successful so the Federal Reserve Board authorized com-mercial banks to pay interest on demand deposits (their checking accounts) in 1978. Commercial banks had not been permitted to offer interest-bearing checking accounts since the 1930s, and thrifts had not been permitted to offer any kind of checking account. NOW accounts are included in the Other Checkable Deposits (OCDs) category in the Fed's definition of the money stock, M1. See *Other Checkable Deposits, Transaction Accounts.*

NET EXPORTS (NE)   Net foreign trade. The total value of exported goods and services minus the total value of imported goods and services. In national income accounting, the value of net exports of goods and services is a category of aggregate demand or GNP, together with consumption expenditure, investment expenditure, and government expenditure. See *Balance of Trade, Favorable Balance of Trade, Gross National Product.*

NET INVESTMENT   See *Net Private Domestic Investment.*

NET NATIONAL PRODUCT (NNP)   Gross national product (GNP) minus capital consumption allowance equals net national product (NNP). It is net in that the amount of capital goods used up in the production process is subtracted from the gross investment expenditure category of GNP leaving just the net addition to the capital stock of the country. NNP may be measured by the market-price approach, that is, by adding together consumption expenditure, *net* private domestic investment expenditure, government expenditure, and net exports. Or it may be calculated by adding factor costs, i.e., NNP = wages + interest + rent + profit + indirect business taxes. These factor costs make up the value of consumer goods, net producer goods (depreciation is deducted in calculating "profit"), government expenditure, and exports. Imports do not have to be removed because they have not been entered in the factor-cost approach; imports *are* included when calculating NNP by the market-price method of adding the market value of all final goods purchased, so they must be removed. See *Capital Consumption Allowance, Net Private Domestic Investment.*

NET PRIVATE DOMESTIC INVESTMENT (NPDI)   The value of all of the capital goods produced in the private sector of the economy during a period of time, plus net changes in inventories, minus capital consumption allowance (depreciation). NPDI represents the net addition to the capital stock of the country. It is one of the components of Net National Product. See *Capital Consumption Allowance, Depreciation, Gross Private Domestic Investment.*

NET WORTH   The difference between the total assets of a person or corporation and the total liabilities. Also known as equity, the owners' claim against assets. In accounting, net worth is an entry on the right-hand side of a balance sheet reflecting the net ownership value after total liabilities are subtracted from total assets. The addition of net worth to liabilities produces a sum which equals total assets on the left-hand side of a balance sheet, it is the balancing residual. When net worth is negative it foretells bankruptcy. See *Balance Sheet, Bankruptcy.*

NO-LOAD MUTUAL FUND A mutual fund which does not charge a broker's fee for purchase and redemption of shares in the fund. The expenses of such transactions are included in the management fee which is deducted from fund income, thereby affecting the shareholders' return. When the rate of return of a no-load fund equals the rate of return of one charging purchase and/or redemption fees, the no-load fund is a better buy, other things being equal.

NOMINAL YIELD The rate of return specified on the face value or par value of a negotiable security. The specified (nominal) rate might be 7% on a $10,000 (face value) security, providing a return of $700 per year. The *market value* of the security might be $9,000, in which case the $700 produces a *market yield* of 7.78%.

NON-PRICE COMPETITION Efforts by sellers to win customers from rival firms in a market by means other than price reduction. It commonly occurs in markets characterized by oligopoly and monopolistic competition. Firms try to differentiate their products or services from the products and services of others in the market.

Prior to deregulation, airline prices were fixed by the Civil Aeronautics Board. Airlines serving the same route would compete in the convenience of their schedules, the quality of their food, and in other services. Coca-Cola has competed with other cola drinks by the patented shape of its bottle, the created image of its customers as portrayed in song and picture, as well as by offering a distinguishable flavor.

Some forms of nonprice competition are of benefit to consumers when they are offered services that they really want and would be willing to pay for or when the nonprice competition becomes the stimulus to technological change to improve the product, offer real variety, or reduce costs.

There also are forms of nonprice competition that are questionable in their use of the country's resources, often including large advertising outlays which only neutralize the advertising of rivals. Some firms try to create differences which add nothing to quality, but through advertising the firm hopes to attach customers to its product. Others try to create the illusion of difference (where none really exists in the product itself) by design of the container, slogans, and user testimonials. Also, there are efforts to identify a generic product with the brand name of one's own firm. Some are very successful. "Gimme a Bud Light." "It's Miller time." "Bayer aspirin, please." "A box of Kleenex, please." "I'll Xerox it." See *Differentiated Product*.

NONRECOURSE LOAN   A loan based upon a particular property or commodity as collateral, with the lender having no recourse for repayment of the loan other than the collateral. Most home mortgages are nonrecourse loans. Nonrecourse loans also have been a part of the U.S. agricultural price-support programs to provide a price floor for some crops. For example, the government makes a loan on the corn crop of a farmer at the established support price for corn. If the market price falls below the support price, the farmer keeps the funds loaned, and the government takes ownership of the corn but has no other recourse to recover the value of the loan. If the market price rises above the support price, the farmer sells the crop and repays the loan. In past years, the U.S. has taken ownership of vast stocks of agricultural commodities under this program as market prices stayed below support prices. The government stocks destabilized markets as there was a constant threat of their being thrown on the market. See *Commodity Credit Corporation*.

NOTES PAYABLE   Promissory notes that are certificates of indebtedness to others and state the terms for payment on the face. Some are negotiable. They are liabilities entered on the right side of a balance sheet. "Notes payable" applies to notes of any maturity, unlike Treasury notes, which mature in 2 to 10 years from date of issue. See *Bills Payable, Bonds, Treasury Notes*

NOTES RECEIVABLE   Promissory notes which are certificates of indebtedness to the firm from others and include the terms of payment on the face. They are assets entered on the left side of a balance sheet. The term applies to notes of any maturity, unlike Treasury notes, which mature in 2 to 10 years from date of issue. See *Bills Receivable*.

OBSOLESCENCE   The reduction in the value of capital goods as the result of technological change or a shift of demand away from the product. It is a part of depreciation which also includes reduction in the value of capital goods because of wearing out from use and age. See *Depreciation*.

OCCUPATION TAX   A tax levied by government on people engaged in specified occupations. In some instances it is levied to pay for the costs of regulating the occupation; in others it is an important source of general revenue. In the state of Washington, for example, there is a *business and occupation tax* which is the bane of businesses because it is levied against gross revenue rather than profits, so the tax revenue rolls into state coffers in times of loss as well as times of profit. "Occupation" is specified, as well as "business," so that gross revenue from the sale of services is taxed along with that from the sale of goods. (The state has a constitutional ban on income taxes so it can't levy a *net* revenue, or profits, tax on business.) The business and occupation tax tends to discourage new firms and new professionals whose start-up costs may prohibit profitable operations for some time, even though they would be viable in the long run.

OFFICE OF THRIFT SUPERVISION (OTS)   A federal agency under the administration of the Secretary of the Treasury whose duties are to charter and supervise federal savings and loan associations and federal savings banks, to supervise state-chartered thrifts, and to supervise thrift holding companies. The Office of Thrift Supervision regulates capital standards for thrifts within limits set by law. The head of the Office is appointed by the President and subject to Senate confirmation.

The Financial Institution Reform, Recovery and Enforcement Act of 1989 (the savings and loan bailout and restructuring law known by the acronym FIRREA) set a transition period for thrifts to meet capital standards similar to those for national banks. The OTS is comparable to the Office of the Comptroller of the Currency, which has similar responsibilities relating to national banks and also is under the administration of the Secretary of the Treasury.

Prior to 1989, the duties of the Office of Thrift Supervision were carried on by the Federal Home Loan Bank Board (abolished by FIRREA), which also had other responsibilities that now are assigned to the Federal Housing Finance Board and the Federal Deposit Insurance Corporation. See *Federal Home Loan Bank System, Federal Housing Finance Board, Federal Deposit Insurance Corporation, Savings Association Insurance Fund.*

OLIGOPOLY   A market in which there are so few sellers that they are highly interdependent; each must take into account the reactions of the other sellers in arriving at a decision to make a change. For example, if Firm *X* considers a price reduction, it must take into account that other firms in the market will be sufficiently affected that they might reduce their prices as much or more, rather than hold their prices the same. Or, if Firm *Y* considers a new major advertising blitz, it must estimate the effects of a response (perhaps in kind) by its rivals, who will lose if they sit idly by.

Homogeneous, or pure, oligopoly involves rivalry among a few producers of products which are identical with one another. Differentiated oligopoly involves rivalry among a few producers of similar (in the eyes of the purchasers) but not identical products. Monopolistic competition is another kind of market which also comprises rivalry among producers of differentiated products, but the market contains a large number of producers rather than just a few.

Oligopoly is considered a common market condition. A localized example of interdependence among a few is the location of three gas stations on three corners of a rural intersection. If one lowers the price per gallon the others will follow or lose most of their business. Examples in national markets include the automobile industry, the tire industry, the steel industry, and the beer industry. Some small firms may operate at the periphery in national markets dominated by a few, with their actions failing to elicit any reactions, but a giant firm must anticipate reactions from its fellows when it introduces a change. See *Homogeneous Oligopoly, Differentiated Oligopoly, Parallel Pricing, Oligopsony.*

OLIGOPSONY   A market in which there are so few buyers that they are highly interdependent; each must take into account the reactions of the other buyers when contemplating a change. For example, if one firm offers to purchase at a higher price, it must recognize that the other purchasers will be affected so significantly that they may offer more rather than hold their purchase-price offers constant. See *Oligopoly.*

OPEN-END MUTUAL FUND   A mutual fund with no limit on the number of shares it will sell. The value of each share (net asset value) is calculated daily by dividing the total value of the fund's investments at the end of the day by the number of fund shares outstanding. Closed-end mutual funds have specific limits on the number of shares that can be issued and the shares are traded on the open market. See *Mutual Fund, Closed-End Mutual Fund.*

OPEN-MARKET COMMITTEE   See *Federal Open-Market Committee.*

OPEN-MARKET OPERATIONS   The activity of the Federal Open-Market Committee (FOMC) of the Federal Reserve System to affect the rate of growth in the money supply and the level of interest rates by selling or buying Treasury securities on the open market. Historically, it has been the most commonly used tool of monetary policy. See *Monetary Policy, Monetizing the Debt.*

OPEN SHOP   Ostensibly an employment arrangement in a firm in which persons are employed whether or not they are affiliated with a union. However, historically it has been embraced by employers who have not wanted to deal with a union, and so open shop has come to mean that only nonunion workers would be employed. Since the passage of the National Labor Relations Act (Wagner Act) in 1935, it has been unlawful to discriminate against a union member in hiring. See *Closed Shop, Agency Shop, Union Shop, Right-to-Work Laws, Yellow Dog Contract.*

OPPORTUNITY COST   The value of the next most desired alternative to the one selected. Where choice is possible, indeed necessary, opportunity cost is the sacrifice of what is foregone when a particular choice is made. Consumers experience opportunity costs when they choose to spend their incomes one way rather than another. Students face an opportunity cost amounting to the income lost from work foregone when they devote full time to their studies. A society encounters opportunity cost when it is near full employment and chooses to use resources for sophisticated defense weapons rather than highways or child-care programs.

The opportunity cost principle may be used to estimate cost when a market transaction does not provide it. For example, the value of management activity in a single proprietorship may be estimated by determining the salary paid by employers to managers with similar responsibilities, on the assumption that such employment is the next best alternative for the owner–manager.

OPTIONS TRADING   Trading of an option agreement which gives the holder of the option the right to buy or sell specified securities or specified commodities at a fixed price prior to a fixed expiration date. Options trading is similar to futures trading in securities and commodities and is based upon diferent views on the part of buyers and sellers concerning what will happen to the spot price during the period of the contract. "Futures trading" involves trade in agreements that contain the *firm obligation* to carry out the trade *on the specified date,* rather than the *option* to carry it out *during* the specified time period or to let it lapse. Options trading takes place on such exchanges as the Chicago Board of Trade or the Chicago Mercantile Exchange.

A financial *call* option permits the holder to buy (call for delivery of) the specified securities, at the specified price from the writer (seller) of the call option, during the specified term of the contract. The option buyer pays a fee for the right to buy under the contract. Purchase is at the discretion of the option buyer (holder), and the option need not be exercised; it expires on the expiration date of the contract.

A financial *put* option permits the option holder to sell ("put," or deliver) the specified securities at the specified price to the writer (seller) of the put, at the holder's option, during the period of the contract. The option buyer pays a fee for the contract containing the right to sell, a fee the option writer receives for the obligation to buy should the option be exercised. Exercise of the put is at the discretion of the option buyer (holder), and the option need not be exercised.

In each case, the option buyer is in a "long" position, while the option writer, or seller, is in a "short" position. See *Futures Market, Hedging, Spot Price.*

ORGANIZATION OF PETROLEUM EXPORTING COUNTRIES (OPEC)   An international organization whose purpose is to restrict the supply of crude oil by allotting output among its members in order to hold the price of crude oil above its free market price. An oil cartel.

The success of OPEC has been sporadic because of forces which tend to undermine international cartels. It prospered in the 1970s and early 1980s when a number of conditions converged: World demand for oil had grown rapidly, the U.S. had come to depend upon imports for a high percentage of its oil consumption, OPEC membership encompassed most of the major oil producers, and all members could see the immediate benefit of abiding by quotas. OPEC was a major force in causing the price of crude oil to rise from $4 per barrel in 1973 to over $24 by 1980. However, the high prices attracted new production in areas outside of the cartel, such as Alaska and the North Sea, and they made drilling and pumping profitable in some old producing areas outside OPEC. The additional production outside of the OPEC countries undercut the cartel's output controls. New supplies combined with a slowed growth in demand because of energy conservation to press down prices. Lower revenues led some OPEC producers to ignore their output quotas, which further depressed prices. See *Cartel.*

ORIGINAL-ISSUE DISCOUNT SECURITY (OID)   A debt instrument such as a bond or a note which is issued at a price below its stated redemption price at maturity. The interest accumulates as increases in the value of the instrument. Some OIDs provide for some periodic interest payments while some interest accumulates. A zero-coupon bond provides no interest payment until maturity, so its issue value tends to be the present discounted value of its maturity value at the stated rate of interest.

When OIDs were developed, they were intended to produce income as a capital gain through accumulation in value over time. The capital gains tax rate on income was lower than the top brackets of ordinary income, providing a tax break. The tax loophole has been closed so that the increase in value generally is treated as an ordinary income tax liability that must be paid annually as it accumulates. It is considered interest income. Exceptions are (1) U.S. Savings Bonds whose increased value is treated by the IRS as ordinary interest income at maturity, or when the bond is cashed in, if before maturity, (2) short-term debt instruments with fixed maturity dates of a year or less from the date of issue, and (3) debt instruments issued by an individual before 1984 (*IRS Publication*

17 for 1990 tax returns, pp. 53–54). See *Deep-Discount Bond, Zero-Coupon Bond,* and your tax consultant for more information.

OTHER CHECKABLE DEPOSITS (OCDs)   A money stock category that "consists of negotiable orders of withdrawal (NOW) accounts and automatic transfer service (ATS) balances at all depository institutions, credit union share draft balances, and demand deposits at thrift institutions" (*Federal Reserve Bulletin,* January 1991, **77,** A14). It is a category of the money stock, M1. OCDs are "other" than, or separate from, demand deposits at commercial banks. See *Checking Account, Negotiable Order of Withdrawal, Automatic Transfer Service Accounts, Share-Draft Account, M1.*

OUTPUT   The amount of product or service produced by a production process per unit of time.

OUTPUT PER LABOR HOUR   Total output for a period of time divided by the number of labor hours put into the production process during that time. A measure of labor productivity which sometimes is used to represent changes in productivity in general. Productivity, of course, is a function of the input of *all* resources, not just labor, but labor-hour output is widely used because it is more easily and quickly collected than output data per unit of capital or per unit of natural resource. Sometimes called worker-hour output; in earlier published data it is called man-hour output. See *Productivity.*

OUTSIDE DIRECTOR   A director of a corporation who is not employed by the corporation and whose stock holdings in the company, if any, are minimal. Typically, an outside director is an officer of another business who thereby has "proven" business acumen.

OVER-THE-COUNTER MARKET   A market for over-the-counter securities of companies that often are small and/or new, in contrast to a market exchange of quite limited membership such as the New York Stock Exchange (NYSE) and the American Stock Exchange (AMEX), which are organized to carefully screen securities according to strict standards before listing. See *Over-the-Counter Securities, National Association of Securities Dealers Automated Quotations.*

OVER-THE-COUNTER SECURITIES   Securities of generally newer and smaller companies that may be somewhat riskier than those that meet the more stringent requirements for listing on the New York Stock Exchange (NYSE) or the American Stock Exchange (AMEX). Exceptions to this characterization include Intel, an innovative leader in the microchip industry that is more than 20 years old.

PARADOX OF AGGREGATION   See *Fallacy of Composition.*

PARADOX OF THRIFT   How can it be that if many people in an economy try to save more, they may altogether succeed only in saving less? The answer is that a widespread effort to save more will result in a widespread reduction in consumption expenditure, which in turn will reduce output of consumer goods, and hence GNP. Some investment expenditure is dependent upon the level of GNP, so that a fall in GNP will induce a reduction in investment expenditure and another fall in GNP. When national income (the other side of GNP) falls, there is less income flowing to people to divide between consumption and saving, and people will reduce both consumption (C) and saving (S). The reduction in total saving may come earlier than proportional reductions in C and S would indicate because people are more likely to try to maintain their spending habits than their saving when faced with reduced income.

In the diagram below, Y stands for national income, I for investment, and S for saving in the economy. The I curve slopes upward to the right, indicating that some investment expenditure is induced by rising national income. When the S curve shifts up as people try to save more at each level of Y, the equilibrium of saving and investment occurs at a lower level of national income *and* a lower level of saving.

An increase in thrift could be helpful in an economy near full employment, or facing an inflationary gap where aggregate demand exceeds aggregate supply at full employment, because it would

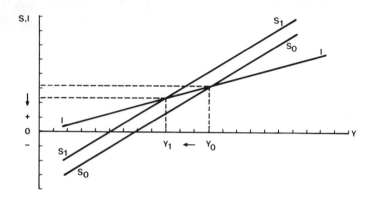

PARADOX OF THRIFT

release resources from consumer goods production and make them available for capital formation. But in a depressed economy, private virtue (thrift) can be a public evil (falling national income and rising unemployment) when there are unemployed resources, and changes in consumption expenditure and investment expenditure are complementary rather than substitutes in their effect upon the economy. See *Loanable Funds Theory of Interest, Demand for Money, Supply of Money*.

PARADOX OF VALUE Why does a necessity, such as drinking water, have a lower value (price) than a luxury, such as diamonds? The answer lies in considering *marginal* utility and *marginal* cost. The alternative that people face is not some water or none (a total utility view). Water often is abundant and can be "produced" at low marginal cost. The last cubic foot bought has a low use-value when one already has a lot of water. A consumer would not pay much for this marginal unit and, because one cubic foot of water is the same as another cubic foot, the price is low as determined by the utility of the marginal unit and its marginal cost of production.

On the other hand, diamonds are scarce, so the marginal utility of a 1-carat diamond is high. The marginal cost of "producing" one more 1-carat diamond also is high. Therefore, the price of a 1-carat diamond is high.

PARALLEL PRICING Prices charged by two or more firms move up or down together. It applies to an oligopoly situation in which the firms are so interrelated that a price change by one firm is followed immediately by price changes by other firms in the market. A price cut by one substantially and adversely affects sales of the others, so the others follow with price cuts of their own.

A price increase often is followed immediately when market demand appears to be inelastic. To follow a price increase under those circumstances will provide higher total revenues (and higher profits if costs do not rise as fast or faster); not to follow would provide the laggard with only a temporary benefit in larger sales because the price-leader firm would be so adversely affected it would have to nullify the increase. Several gasoline stations on a busy intersection provide a clear picture of parallel pricing, of the perils of not following a price cut, and of the often-rapid general rise in the price of a gallon of gas following an increase by one station.

Perfect parallel pricing, in which prices of firms change simultaneously, suggests collusion, either by shared information or by outright agreement. Parallel pricing with a time lag may indicate tacit collusion in which followers change price with no overt agreement, or it may simply be intelligent reaction by rivals to the oligopoly situation. Identical prices are charged by different firms in perfect competition because each firm responds to an impersonally determined market price. No one *can* sell at a higher price, and a seller does not *need* to lower price to sell more. See *Price Leadership, Oligopoly, Tacit Collusion.*

PARITY PRICE: AGRICULTURE   A price received by farmers for their crop that is in the same ratio to current prices paid out by farmers as the ratio of prices received to prices paid out in a base period (historically in the U.S., 1910–1914).

Except for wartime, farm prices have not kept pace with non-farm prices, in large part because productivity increases on the farm have outrun productivity increases off the farm. Farm prices have fallen relatively, with adverse effects on relative farm income. A fall in absolute prices because of increased world supply will reduce total revenue to farmers because of inelastic demand for most agricultural goods. Many farmers argue that the historic ratio of prices is ''fair'' and that the government should support agricultural product prices above the current market prices whenever the ratio falls below 100%, or parity. However, when farm price supports have been adopted through government purchase or loan programs, with price goals even 10% or more *below* parity, serious problems have arisen in the form of growing government-held surpluses which overhang the market and increase the gap between the support price and the free-market price. In recent years, the government has held the support price very low and the market price has been well above it, even at the market's worst, so the problem of growing government-held surpluses has not occurred. Support for farmers has taken the form of subsidies rather than price support.

As an alternative to price support, price subsidies in the U.S. take the form of deficiency payments based upon target prices that are deemed to be "fair." Subsidies avoid the problems of storage costs and market effects that are created when government owns the surplus produce under a price support program. But subsidies can be costly when the market price falls well below the target price as has been true in 1990 and 1991. Both price supports and price subsidies distort a farmer's decisions about what crop to produce and how much to produce from decisions that are purely market driven. See *Price Support, Deficiency Payment, Target Price.*

PARITY PRICE: INTERNATIONAL EXCHANGE See *Purchasing-Power Parity.*

PARTIAL EQUILIBRIUM An equilibrium in a subunit of the total economy such as a household, a firm, or a market, considered in isolation from the rest of the economy. Partial equilibrium analysis holds some but not all variables constant. In the theory of the firm, an economist may assume, for example, that the cost and revenue conditions facing the firm at a moment in time are given in particular cost and revenue curves and combine them to determine the most profitable input and output (and, in imperfect competition, price). This is the equilibrium position for the firm under the given conditions. A change in one of the cost or revenue conditions can be traced through the partial equilibrium system to determine a new equilibrium position for the firm. When studying market equilibrium, an additional variable is added—the entry and exit of firms to and from the market. Other conditions, such as the relationships with other markets and the entire economy, continue as given, so the study of a market also is one of partial equilibrium. See *Equilibrium of the Consumer, Equilibrium of the Firm, Equilibrium of the Market, General Equilibrium, Microeconomics.*

PARTNERSHIP A business or professional organization consisting of two or more partners who are responsible for the affairs and obligations of the firm to the full extent of their personal wealth. A limited partnership limits the personal liability of inactive partners to the amount that they invested in the partnership. See *Corporation, Limited Partnership, Silent Partner, Single Proprietorship.*

PAR VALUE   1. The value of a security that is stated on the document. It is a nominal value that may be unrelated to market value of the security or earning power of the firm.

2. On a gold standard in international exchange, the officially stated value of a nation's currency in terms of gold. Or, as under the Bretton Woods agreement (1944) for the international gold standard, another nation's currency value could be stated in terms of the dollar (and the dollar was fixed in terms of gold). See *Gold Exchange Standard.*

PASS-THROUGH SECURITY   A security that uses a pool of assets, such as home mortgages with similar interest rates and maturities, as collateral and passes through the principal and interest payments (less servicing costs) received from the mortgages to the security holders in proportion to their share of the pool. A *straight pass-through security* provides for payments to the security holder only if they are received by the issuer from the mortgagees. A *modified pass-through security* provides for payment to the security holder whether or not the principal and interest payments have been collected by the issuer, a valuable guarantee for the investor. See *Collateralized Bond Obligations, Federal National Mortgage Association, Federal Home Loan Mortgage Corporation, Government National Mortgage Association.*

PATENT   A government grant of exclusive right to an invention for a limited time, usually 17 years. Patents are designed to encourage invention by granting the inventor a temporary monopoly so that he or she may profit from an invention before copiers can compete. Patent holders may license others to produce under a patent. Scientists working in corporate or governmental laboratories usually are required to turn over patent rights for their inventions to their employer in return for some specified compensation.

Because of the limited time period of a patent, some inventors prefer to produce with "secret designs" or "secret ingredients" which may, however, give rise to industrial espionage. Sometimes a firm will try to extend the duration of a patent by periodically patenting design changes and "improvements" to the initial invention. See *Monopoly.*

PAY-AS-YOU-GO   1. The policy of paying for capital goods or durable goods from current and accumulated income, rather than borrowing the needed money. A policy that may be followed by households, businesses, or governments.

2. The policy of requiring payment of taxes as income is earned, by having employers withhold employees' estimated taxes from

salary and wage payments and then transfer the funds to the government. Self-employed persons periodically remit payment of estimated taxes under this system. The total tax liability is calculated annually with deficits paid and surpluses returned. U.S. federal income taxes have been on a pay-as-you-go basis since 1943, and most state and local income tax systems have adopted the policy since.

PAYROLL TAX   A tax based on wages and salaries that often is levied against both employer and employee but is collected for the government by employers. The U.S. social security tax is a payroll tax levied against employer and employee in equal proportion on wages and salaries up to a maximum level of pay and is collected by the employer. (A comparable self-employment tax for social security benefits is paid directly by the self-employed.) Unemployment insurance is an example of a payroll tax levied only on the employer. In many states the percentage varies according to an "experience rating" of an employer, i.e., how much unemployment occurs in the firm; the system implies that a firm "causes" the unemployment, which may be true in prosperity but may not be true in a general recession.

PER CAPITA   A Latin phrase that designates data that is adjusted to a "per head" or per individual basis. Per capita GNP is the total GNP divided by the number of people in the country's population. When a cost is involved, such as the estimated cost of bailing out failed savings and loan associations, the per capita cost often is dramatized by stating it as "a charge of $2500 against every man, woman, and child in the United States."

PERCENTILE   A scale for classification of data into 100 parts. The first percentile is the lowest 1%, with 99% of the data ranking above it. The first percentile of students ranked by grade-point average consists of the poorest students, with 99% of the students having higher grades. The seventy-fifth percentile of income receivers are in an income range that is relatively high, with 75% of income receivers having lower income and only 25% having more income. A person at the one-hundredth percentile would have all of the other people below; if also at the 100% of income point in the income example, one person would receive 100% of the income. See *Decile, Quartile, Lorenz Curve*.

PERFECT COMPETITION   A hypothetical market of pure competition to which is added perfect knowledge about conditions in the market and instantaneous adjustment to any change of conditions.

The latter requires that resources be perfectly mobile. *Pure competition* requires a large enough number of buyers and sellers that no one can affect price, firms' products are identical, and there is unrestricted entry into and exit from the industry. Perfect competition is a concept used by economists to study market relationships in some aspects of microeconomic theory. See *Pure Competition.*

PERFECTLY ELASTIC DEMAND   Infinite elasticity. The sensitivity of quantity demanded to a price change is such that the smallest increase in price will result in zero quantity demanded, while a decrease in price will not increase the amount that can be sold. It is illustrated by a straight, horizontal demand curve facing a firm at the market price in pure competition. The opposite extreme from perfectly inelastic demand.
　　See *Elasticity, Equilibrium of the Firm: Pure Competition.*

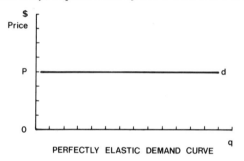

PERFECTLY ELASTIC DEMAND CURVE

PERFECTLY ELASTIC SUPPLY   Infinitely elastic supply. The quantity supplied is perfectly sensitive to a price change. The supplier will supply all that it can at the going market price. When price declines even slightly, quantity supplied falls to zero, while a slight price increase will not increase quantity supplied since that is already at the maximum. It is illustrated by a perfectly horizontal supply curve. The opposite extreme from perfectly inelastic supply.
　　See *Elasticity.*

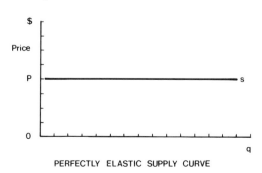

PERFECTLY ELASTIC SUPPLY CURVE

PERFECTLY INELASTIC DEMAND   Zero elasticity of demand. Quantity demanded is perfectly insensitive to changes in the market price. No matter what the price, the same quantity will be demanded. It is illustrated by a demand curve that is a vertical straight line at the fixed quantity demanded. The opposite extreme from perfectly elastic demand.

   See *Elasticity*.

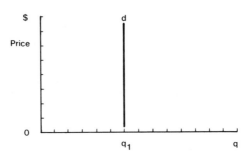

PERFECTLY INELASTIC DEMAND CURVE

PERFECTLY INELASTIC SUPPLY   Zero elasticity of supply. Quantity supplied is completely insensitive to changes in the price. No matter what the price, the quantity supplied is fixed. An example is the quantity of fresh produce at a farmers' market on a particular morning. It is illustrated by a demand curve that is a vertical straight line at the fixed quantity supplied. The opposite extreme from perfectly elastic supply.

   See *Elasticity*.

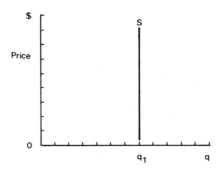

PERFECTLY INELASTIC SUPPLY CURVE

PERIL-POINT TARIFF   A tariff system which maintains low import duties on the products of an industry so long as the domestic industry remains healthy. If imports rise enough to threaten the existence of the domestic industry (or sometimes just threaten its degree of profitability), the tariff rates rise to assure its survival. This system is a type of protective tariff and violates the principal of comparative advantage. See *Comparative Advantage, Tariff.*

PERMANENT INCOME HYPOTHESIS   A theory of the consumption function which holds that household expenditure is proportional to an average of expected long-run (permanent) income rather than to the current (absolute) level of disposable income. American economist Milton Friedman has used this hypothesis in his analysis of national income. See *Absolute Income Hypothesis, Relative Income Hypothesis.*

PERSONAL INCOME (PY)   A national income accounting concept equal to National Income (NY) minus corporate profits, minus employee and employer social security taxes, minus corporate income taxes, plus transfer payments, plus corporate dividends, plus interest on the national debt. Disposable Personal Income (DPY) equals Personal Income (PY) minus personal income taxes. See *National Income, Disposable Personal Income.*

PHILLIPS CURVE   Illustration of a "trade-off" relationship between the rate of inflation and the rate of unemployment, presented in 1958 by A. W. H. Phillips (1914–1975). The curve refers to the apparent incompatibility of price stability and full employment. Reduction of the rate unemployment is accompanied by an increase in the rate of inflation, while reduction in the rate of inflation is accompanied by an increase in the rate of unemployment.

Causes of the trade-off seemed to be that, in recession, when there is high unemployment of workers, they do not press for wage increases and employers try to cut costs and prices (hence low rates of inflation). In prosperity, unemployment is low and demand for goods and services is high. As employers compete for workers there is pressure for wage increases, strikes are costly in lost output, and higher costs can be more than passed on in higher prices (inflation). The relationship suggests that public policy decisions to reduce the rate of unemployment must rest on a calculated cost in higher rates of inflation. Unfortunately, a specific trade-off relationship appeared to be temporary. As rates of inflation and rates of unemployment rose together during the 1970s in the U.S. and in Great Britain, the trade-off point was ratcheted upward, a situation that has been named "stagflation."

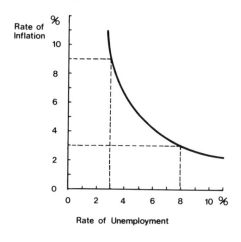

PHILLIPS CURVE

PICKETING   An attempt by an organized group to enlist the sympathy of third parties by notifying them of the existence of a dispute with handbills, placards, or signs carried by pickets walking to and fro near a site. In a labor dispute, union members may picket in front of the gates of a firm to persuade members of other unions, workers replacing those on strike, customers, and the general public that the firm is unfair to the picketing union and that people should cease doing business with the firm. Other kinds of disputes in which picketing is used include antiabortionists picketing a hospital where abortions are performed or conservationists picketing a firm they accuse of releasing toxic waste into the environment.

In peaceful picketing the number of pickets is few enough, the space between them long enough, and their other behavior nonthreatening enough that there is neither use of force nor threat of force against those who would cross the picket line. This sort of picketing is considered an exercise of free speech. When these conditions do not hold, the disputant being picketed may seek a court order to regulate the picketing so that it is peaceful or to prohibit the picketing where present and past behavior indicates that any picketing is threatening. See *Injunction.*

PIGOU EFFECT   In a situation of less than full employment, it is possible to achieve full employment by a severe enough decline in wages and prices. Ultimately, the increased purchasing power of dollar balances will encourage more spending and less saving out of current income. If the deflation proceeds far enough, there will be an increase in expenditure sufficient to provide full employment. Creditors are better off and debtors are worse off, but holders of money are better off in real terms and spend more. A. C. Pigou (1877–1959) identified the possibility as a theoretical answer to the less-than-full-employment equilibrium of J. M. Keynes (1883–1943) but did not endorse it as policy, for the deflation might well become draconian.

PLANNED ECONOMY   See *Centrally Planned Economy.*

POLL TAX   A tax levied at a flat rate on everyone. See *Head Tax* for more detail.

POOL   A loose federation of businesses to fix prices or control markets. See *Cartel.*

PORTAL-TO-PORTAL PAY   Pay for an hourly-rated employee which begins prior to the time that the employee reaches the actual work site and ends sometime after leaving the work site. For example, a miner covered by a portal-to-portal pay contract begins to receive pay upon arrival at the mine entrance (the "adit" to crossword puzzle buffs). The miner is paid for the time it takes to get from the adit to the vein, perhaps a mile or more into the mine shaft, plus the time it takes to get back to the adit, as well as for the time spent actually extracting the ore. Many of us experience portal-to-portal pay when we must pay an electrician or plumber for the time it takes to get from the shop to our house and back as well as for the time spent actually working on our problem.

PORTFOLIO BALANCE   The proportion of stocks of various kinds to bonds of various kinds to other financial holdings that will meet the goals of those holding the portfolio. For example, a portfolio emphasizing growth with some production of income and protection of principal will have a different mix (balance) of particular stocks, bonds, etc., than will a portfolio emphasizing current income.

POVERTY   The state of being poor, defined by low income and consequent low levels of consumption. The poverty line is the amount of
income that is necessary to provide the government's definition of
"bare necessities." Poverty income is any income below the poverty line. Official definitions of poverty income in the U.S. distinguish between rural and urban households because most rural families produce some real income, such as home-grown food, which
does not involve a market transaction. Poverty definitions also vary
according to household size because the average single man or
woman has lower consumption needs than a family of four consisting of father, mother, and two children. The poverty line for
each category is adjusted for changes in the consumer price index.
In 1988, the poverty line for a family of four in the U.S. was $12,091,
and in 1990 it was $12,675. Only a very few families of four in a
poor country such as Bangladesh would have earned the equivalent
of $12,000, and those would be considered rich, so poverty is a
concept whose quantification is relative to particular cultures. This
is not to deny the seriousness of poverty in the U.S. for those whose
incomes fall below the poverty line.

PREFERRED STOCK   Ownership shares of a corporation which guarantee a fixed percentage return if sufficient net corporate profit is
made to pay it. Preferred stock has a first claim against profit. After
this claim is met, holders of common stock own the remaining profit
(although some preferred stock may provide for participation in
the residual profit as well). Preferred stockholders, like common
stockholders, are owners rather than creditors of the corporation.
They stand behind bond holders and other creditors but ahead of
common shareholders in claim on assets in a dissolution of the firm.

PRESENT DISCOUNTED VALUE   See *Present Value*.

PRESENT VALUE   The value of an amount to be received in the
future, discounted to the present. One-hundred dollars in hand
today can earn interest over the coming year, so $100 to be received
a year from now is worth less than $100 available now. Present
value may be calculated for a single amount or for a flow of future
benefits. The formula for calculating the present discounted value
of a flow of future benefits is

$$PV = \frac{Y_t}{(1 + i)^t} + \frac{Y_{t+1}}{(1 + i)^{t+1}} + \frac{Y_{t+2}}{(1 + i)^{t+2}} + \frac{Y_{t+n}}{(1 + i)^{t+n}},$$

where PV = the present discounted value; Y = the income to be received at point t in time, point $t + 1$ in time, etc., and the income might vary from time to time; i = the rate of interest, usually expressed as an annual rate; and t = the future point in time, say, 1 year from the present date (it could be 1 day or 1 month with the appropriate adjustment of the interest rate).

To capitalize a *perpetual* income stream, divide the annual income by the annual interest rate (PV = Y/i). For example, an income in perpetuity of $1,000 with an interest rate of 8% produces the present discounted value of $12,500.

The benefits may be a flow of income to a person, the anticipated flow of income from a machine that a firm might purchase, a flow of recreational or flood-control benefits from a river dam, etc. See *Discounting, Cost–Benefit Analysis, Marginal Efficiency of Capital.*

PRICE The exchange value of one unit of a product or service, usually expressed in money units.

PRICE CONTROL Government price fixing. The term usually refers to price ceilings set by government to prevent prices from rising because of small supplies relative to large effective demand. Price ceilings prevent market prices from rationing the goods, i.e., ceilings prevent prices from rising as they otherwise would to eliminate some buyers when people want to buy more than is available.

When prices are prevented from rising to ration goods among buyers who are willing and able to pay, other rationing devices are needed. There is "first come, first served" rationing with long lines and empty-handed, disappointed people near the end of the lines. Or "rationing" may take the form of government distribution of ration cards or stamps on some equity principle, such as so many pounds of meat per person per month. When free-market prices are prevented from rationing goods, black markets often develop as an illegal underground economy to profit from the willingness to pay.

Price control usually starts with a price freeze. Relative prices of goods become distorted after a while as costs of production change and demand shifts. Government agencies are notoriously poor at adjusting prices in ways that will maintain production of the desired array of goods and services. These problems have dogged the government-controlled economies of eastern Europe and, after many decades of economic decline, they began to turn toward free-market economies in 1989 and 1990.

The U.S. has instituted price control in wartime to try to equalize the needed economic sacrifices. It tried peace-time price controls for a short time in the mid–1970s to try to control inflation but, as often happens, inflation was merely postponed. See *Rationing, Black Market.*

PRICE DISCRIMINATION   Selling identical units of a product or service at different prices to different buyers when there is no difference in supply costs. This price discrimination can occur only when there is no ability, or no incentive, for the low-price buyer to resell to the high-price buyer. Another form of price discrimination involves charging the same price to different buyers when there are different supply costs.

Price discrimination is illegal under the Robinson–Patman Act of 1936, unless there are proportional product or service differences; unless supply cost variations, if any, are proportional to the price differences; unless the price differences merely meet competitors' prices in good faith; or unless the price differences do not substantially lessen competition. See *Robinson–Patman Act, Basing-Point System.*

PRICE-EARNINGS RATIO (P/E)   The spot price of a share of common stock divided by the company's earnings per share as reported for the most recent four quarters. Extraordinary items affecting earnings usually are excluded. A high P/E means that the market participants judge the prospects for earnings growth to be good. A low P/E reflects the opposite. Investors are encouraged to sift through stocks with a low P/E in search of those that are undervalued—those whose profit prospects might be comparable to stocks with a higher P/E.

PRICE INDEX   A numerical time series that relates prices at different periods of time to the prices of a selected "benchmark," or base period. A price level is calculated for each time period and then converted into a percentage of the price level of the base period. Each price level is a summary number for all of the prices relevant to the particular index [consumer price index (CPI), producer price index (PPI), GNP deflator index, etc.].

It is complicated to develop the summary numbers, and judgment is required at several steps. What goods and services should be included? How should they be weighted so that rare, high-priced items (e.g., a luxury sports car) do not inappropriately overwhelm low-priced, large-volume items (e.g., bread)? How does one account for the same items selling for different prices at different locations and at different times of the quarter or year?

Once summary numbers are calculated, the one selected for the base period is placed equal to 100 (100%) and price levels for other time periods are expressed as a percentage of that price level, for example, falling to 70 or rising to 200 (percentage of the base period price level).

How does one account for the emergence of new products, the disappearance of other products, and a change in importance of some products over time? A new base year may be selected periodically to accommodate these changes, but then the new series will not be precisely comparable to the old. Comparisons over long sweeps of time are less meaningful because of these problems. See *Time Series, Consumer Price Index, Producer Price Index, Gross National Product Deflator, Constant Dollars*.

PRICE LEADERSHIP　A market situation in which one firm leads in making price changes and other firms follow. It occurs in oligopoly, where firms are closely interdependent and cartels or more informal agreements are illegal. Price leadership might occur in a market that consists of one large firm and several smaller ones. In a market of several firms of roughly comparable size, there might be tacit acceptance of one firm as price leader, or the leadership firm might change from time to time.

Price leadership refers to market activity of systematic price *increases* as well as price decreases. The result might be called collective monopoly because the leader will tend to raise price until profit is maximized for itself and most others, as though it were a collective decision rather than a pattern of individual actions. It suggests a tacit understanding. See *Parallel Pricing, Antitrust*.

PRICE SUPPORT　Government action to set a price above the free-market price. A price floor is established as a political decision to increase the revenues of the producers. Agricultural price supports to protect farmers' income commonly are found in the United States and the European Common Market, although protection more and more takes the form of subsidies.

Since the 1930s, the U.S. has provided price supports for basic crops such as corn, cotton, and wheat. When the support price is well above the market price, the government enters on the demand side, taking often huge amounts off the market to push the price up to the support level. The mechanism is nonrecourse loans offered on the crop by the Commodity Credit Corporation at the support price. When the support price stays above the market price, the farmers keep the loan money and the government gets the product that secured the loan. The surplus is held in government storage which is a cost added to the cost of the defaulted loans. The government would sell out of storage if the free-market price reaches the support price, but the huge government-owned surpluses hang over the market and tend to keep the market price below the support price. The government tries to hold surpluses in check by setting acreage allotments to qualify for the loan program, but the effort often fails when the support price is at a level that encourages greater labor, fertilizer, and machinery use per acre, as well as improved machinery and seed, for a greater output per acre.

A direct subsidy paid to support the farmers' income, such as deficiency payments based upon target prices, can avoid the government storage problem. But it still requires an effort to control production, depending on the basis for support payments. Subsidies, like support prices, distort production from what free markets would dictate, and they can be costly, depending upon the relationship between the target price and the market price.

Occasionally, free-market prices have risen above price support levels in the U.S. as a result of shifting world demand for U.S. crops. An example occurred in the 1970s when purchases from Japan, India, and especially the U.S.S.R. pushed the price of wheat up from $1.27 per bushel in June 1972 to $6.45 per bushel in February of 1974. The price fell to $3.00 by mid–1975. Much of the time, however, the free-market price has lain below the support price. See *Buffer Stock, Commodity Credit Corporation, Parity Price: Agriculture, Deficiency Payment, Subsidy.*

PRICE SYSTEM   An economic organization of society in which goods and services are freely produced and exchanged for money. Changes in money prices of goods and services and factors of production provide signals for changes in production and consumption. The term is used interchangeably with "market system," or *Market Economy.*

PRIMARY BOYCOTT   A concerted refusal to deal with a party (person, group, firm, or nation) with whom a disagreement exists. It contrasts with a secondary boycott, in which pressure is brought on a third party to induce the third party to bring pressure on a second party with whom one has a dispute. See *Blacklist, Boycott, Consumer Boycott, Labor Boycott, Secondary Boycott, Strike.*

PRIMARY PRODUCTS Raw materials such as ores, logs, and agricultural products. Products which have a high content of natural resources. Countries or regions which specialize in primary products usually find that the terms of trade with manufacturing countries or regions are disadvantageous.

PRIME RATE The interest rate charged by banks on loans to their most creditworthy (most financially sound) customers. When changed economic conditions, or anticipated changes, lead a major bank to change its prime rate, other banks tend to follow suit. Many other interest rates are related to the prime rate and change when the prime rate does.

PRIVATE ENTERPRISE The production and distribution of goods and services by private individuals and companies for profit, as distinguished from production and distribution by government. See *Free-Enterprise Economy, Capitalism.*

PRIVATE GOODS Generally, goods bought and sold in markets in the private sector of the economy, such as bicycles, bread, beer, washing machines, and wills. The producer can charge purchasers for the benefits of the product, and the price generally covers the producer's costs and sometimes the external costs to society. Most goods produced in the U.S. are private goods. Public goods are goods which are not easily marketable to individual purchasers so they are collectively consumed, such as national defense, police protection, and cloud seeding, or they are goods which involve large spillover (external) benefits or costs, such as education and river dams. See *Public Goods, External Benefits, External Costs.*

PRIVATE PROPERTY A type of control of land and other real property which provides the freedom to private persons to own, use, and abuse property and to transfer ownership of it as they choose. Private property has been predominant in the western world for several centuries with moderate amounts of restriction on the rights to use, abuse, and transfer. There has been growing social regulation of use and abuse as people have become more interdependent. Private property as a system of control differs from that in a socialist economy, where land and capital goods are publicly owned and controlled. See *Socialism, Mixed Economy.*

PRIVATE SECTOR That part of the economy consisting of households and business firms and excluding governmental units, which are the "public sector." See *Public Sector.*

PRODUCER PRICE INDEX (PPI)   The prices of goods and services that firms sell to other firms. The weighted average price of a selection of goods in wholesale markets, converted into a time series. The average weighted price of the base period is placed equal to 100 (percent) and the price levels of other time periods are related to it as a percentage of the base. Thus, a 30% increase of producer prices from the base year to the next year is shown as 130. The PPI used to be called the wholesale price index. It is produced by the Bureau of Labor Statistics in the U.S. Department of Labor. See *Price Index, Consumer Price Index, Time Series.*

PRODUCT DIFFERENTIATION   See *Differentiated Product.*

PRODUCTION FUNCTION   The functional relationship between the inputs of factors of production and output. It illustrates technological relationships of production, taking into account substitutability of factors of production as well as variations in the overall quantity of inputs relative to changes in output. See *Input–Output Relationship.*

PRODUCTION GAP   See *Deflationary Gap, Inflationary Gap.*

PRODUCTION POSSIBILITIES CURVE   A curve which illustrates the concept of scarcity and the consequent necessity to choose what to produce—one of the basic economic questions facing a society. Because resources of a society are insufficient to produce all that its members would like, choices must be made which entail sacrificing the production (and consumption) of some things if the production of others is to increase. The choice often is described as a choice between guns and butter.

The production possibilities curve simplifies a society's choices to two and illustrates the production *possibilities.* It assumes full employment of a given quantity and quality of resources, a given state of technological knowledge, and a given social framework.

Suppose that the choice is between military goods and civilian goods. In the illustration below, the quantity of military goods is measured on the vertical axis, and civilian goods on the horizontal axis. At one (unlikely) extreme the society might produce only military goods and can produce a maximum of OM. At the other extreme, the production of only civilian goods, OC quantity can be produced. With available natural resources, capital goods, labor, and techniques, all combinations of military and civilian goods that the economy can produce are shown as points on the curve MC. If the quantity or quality of resources increases (e.g., population growth or better training of labor), the curve would shift outward. Technological change is another major source of an outward shift in the curve. Such changes might cause the curve to shift to M_1C_1, illustrating an ability to produce more of both kinds of goods. If there is some amount of unemployment, as was true in 1940 in the U.S. (illustrated by point U), it would be possible to expand the production of both military and civilian goods until the production possibilities curve is reached. Then choice would be necessary once again.

The production possibilities curve is concave to the origin because of increasing costs. Costs of producing a product in one of the categories (say, military goods) will eventually increase as resources are successively shifted to it from production in the other category, because some resources are rather specialized and may be less efficient when shifted to produce the target product. For example, the production of food requires more land, while the production of a stealth bomber requires more electronic components. If resources were unspecialized and completely neutral, the production possibilities curve would be a straight line.

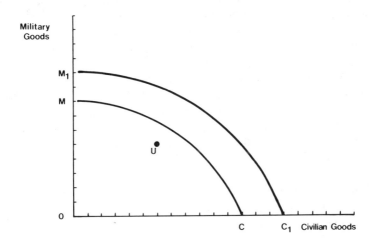

PRODUCTION POSSIBILITIES CURVE

PRODUCTIVITY The relation of output to input, usually measured as labor-hour output. Sometimes a combination of labor hours and dollars of capital is used in recognition of the role of both labor and capital in changes in output. Increases in productivity are caused by innovation and/or improvements in the quality of labor. If the measure is labor-hour output, an increase in the productivity measured may have occurred because of an increase in the *quantity* of existing kinds of capital as well as an improvement in the *quality* of capital or labor. See *Output per Labor Hour, Innovation.*

PROFIT   Total revenue minus total cost. 1. *As a business accounting concept,* profit, or net income, is a residual calculated by subtracting the total of costs paid out and owed, plus depreciation, from revenues received or receivable.

2. *As an economics concept,* profit again is total revenue minus total cost, but total cost may include more implicit costs than depreciation. For example, total cost would include the value of the rent of land even if it is owned by the firm, the interest cost of money even if it is "plowed back in" as retained earnings rather than borrowed from outsiders, and an imputed wage for an owner–manager of an unincorporated business.

Profit serves an important resource allocation function in the economy. When producers have the freedom to decide about the purchase of inputs and the amount of output, profit attracts resources into those activities which are most profitable, that is, production of those goods and services which are most desired by buyers who are ready and willing to pay for them. An economically efficient allocation of resources would call for consideration of implicit costs as well as explicit costs.

3. Profit may be considered as a functional return as well as a residual. In this sense, interest is carefully sorted out as a return for the use of money, whether it is called interest on bonds or dividends on stock. Profit, then, is the return to entrepreneurship for the creative introduction of change in the economy. See *Entrepreneurship, Innovation, Interest.*

PROGRAM TRADING   Buying and selling in financial markets that is directed by special computer programs. For example, a program would track the price of a share of stock of a company and automatically trigger a sell order when the price falls a specified number of points or reaches a specified lower level. It can also involve arbitrage between spot and futures markets. The severity of the stock market crash of 1988 was blamed, in part, on program trading which accelerated the fall of prices.

PROGRESSIVE TAX   1. A tax whose percentage rate increases as the tax base increases. The base might consist of such things as property, sales, or income. 2. A tax, regardless of base, which takes a *larger percentage of income* in taxes from high-income recipients than from the recipients of a low income. The U.S. federal personal income tax is progressive under the first meaning in that higher income increments are taxed at higher percentage rates. It may not be progressive in the second meaning if, despite the progressive tax-bracket rates, there are sufficient tax loopholes to permit those with high incomes actually to pay the same or a lower proportion of their incomes in taxes. Under the second meaning, a flat tax rate could be progressive if there are deductions that affect low-income recipients. See *Proportional Tax, Regressive Tax.*

PROPENSITY TO CONSUME   The relationship of household spending for goods and services to disposable personal income (DPY). The average propensity to consume (APC) is the amount of consumption out of income, or C/Y. The marginal propensity to consume (MPC) is the change in consumption resulting from a change in income, or dC/dY. Data and analysis may apply to patterns of consumption spending out of income for individual households or to patterns of consumption spending for the whole economy. See *Average Propensity to Consume, Marginal Propensity to Consume, Disposable Personal Income.*

PROPENSITY TO SAVE   The relationship of household saving to disposable personal income (DPY). The average propensity to save (APS) is the amount of saving out of income, or S/Y. The marginal propensity to save (MPS) is the change in saving associated with a change in income, or dS/dY. Saving is defined as that part of disposable personal income not spent for consumption. Data and analysis may apply to patterns of saving for individual households or to patterns of saving for the whole economy. See *Average Propensity to Save, Marginal Propensity to Save, Disposable Personal Income.*

PROPERTY TAX   A tax on things owned. The assets may be *real property* consisting of land and buildings (real estate) or *personal property* consisting of home furnishings, boats, securities such as stocks and bonds, etc.

PROPORTIONAL TAX   1. A tax whose percentage rate remains constant for all levels of the tax base (property, sales, income, etc.). A flat-rate tax with no deductions. A property tax, sales tax, or automobile excise tax might be examples of this meaning. 2. A tax which, regardless of base, takes a *proportional percentage of income* from taxpayers at each level of income. In this meaning, a taxpayer with higher income would pay a larger *amount* of tax but the same *percentage* of income as a taxpayer with a lower income. The constant rate for a property tax or sales tax would be *regressive* in this meaning of the concept. See *Progressive Tax, Regressive Tax*.

PROSPERITY   A phase of the economy characterized by a high rate of employment of people and capital goods. Typically, prosperity is accompanied by inflationary pressures caused by bottlenecks here and there in the economy. The opposite of recession or depression. See *Business Cycles, Depression, Recession, Recovery*.

PROTECTIONISM   The belief that domestic industry and jobs should be protected from foreign competition. Arguments for protection include the saving of jobs in industries which are weak competitors with foreign producers, the preservation of production which would be needed in wartime (today, that is virtually everything), provision for infant industries to grow to reach minimum long-run average costs, the counteracting of "unfair" competition from foreign countries which provide export subsidies, etc., and the pressuring of other countries which do not fully open their markets to imports. Methods of protection include tariffs, quotas, total prohibitions, and bureaucratic rules and processes such as unnecessary product specifications, inspections, and the like.

Critics of protectionism point to the general welfare improvement from free trade based on the principle of comparative advantage. See *Comparative Advantage, Free Trade, Infant Industry: Tariff Protection, Quota, Tariff*.

PROVEN RESERVES   Crude oil reserves that can be produced with current technology at today's prices.

PUBLIC GOODS   Goods and services which are not marketable to individual purchasers because the benefits flow to all in a group regardless of whether they all pay. Examples are national defense, river-channel dredging, and cloud seeding.

Public goods also may be goods which, though marketable, have substantial spillover benefits or spillover costs to those not purchasing them—there are lots of innocent bystanders affected. Where there are spillover benefits, less of these goods will be produced than is socially desirable if only the private market is relied upon. If there are spillover costs, more will be produced than is socially desirable. Examples of production with spillover benefits are education, sewage disposal, and fire protection. Examples of production with spillover costs are paper mills and meat-packing plants that do not fully control odor emission or waste disposal. If, in those cases, costs of full control were included, marginal cost would intersect marginal revenue at higher prices and lower quantity demanded. See *Private Goods, External Benefits, External Costs.*

PUBLIC SECTOR   That part of the economy consisting of federal, state, and local government, including subunits such as departments, agencies, commissions, school districts, water districts, etc. It excludes the private sector of households and businesses. See *Private Sector.*

PUBLIC UTILITY   A private firm that provides an important public good or service, e.g., natural gas, electricity, local telephone service, etc., usually under a government grant of monopoly. The monopoly is granted because rivalry among several firms in a locality would be highly inefficient. When the product or service is important to the public, government grants of monopoly are accompanied by government regulation, usually by a *public utility commission.* See *Natural Monopoly.*

PURCHASING-POWER PARITY   The price of one currency in terms of another that will maintain purchasing-power ratios between the countries. On the international gold standard parity prices were fixed by the relation of each currency to gold, hence to other currencies. When purchasing-power ratios changed, it was necessary for adjustments to be made internally in the price levels of the countries involved, or the gold price of the currency would have to change. A floating (flexible) exchange-rate system provides for the free movement of prices of currencies to adjust up or down as necessary, but purchasing-power parity may not be achieved if there are significant investment flows between the two countries under consideration.

PURE COMPETITION   A market in which there are so many buyers and sellers of a standardized product that no one person or group can influence price by withholding or dumping its product or withholding its purchases. Price is set impersonally by the interaction of buyers and sellers in the market, who buy and sell in reaction to that market price. An auction market such as the Chicago Board of Trade offers a setting for pure competition.

Three conditions are necessary for a market of pure competition: (1) The product of all firms must be a homogeneous product and recognized as such; (2) there must be a large enough number of participants that no one can influence price; and (3) there must be no restriction on the entry of participants into the market or their exit from it. Pure competition is perfect competition without perfect knowledge and instant adjustments. See *Competitive Market, Equilibrium of the Firm: Pure Competition, Equilibrium of the Market: Pure Competition, Homogeneous Product, Perfect Competition.*

PUT OPTION   A contract which permits the holder to sell ("put," or deliver) specified securities at a specified price during a specified time period, usually a few months or less. The option buyer pays a fee for the right to sell, a fee that the writer of the option receives for the obligation that he or she accepts to buy at the contracted price should the option be exercised. See *Options Trading, Call Option.*

PYRAMID SCHEME   A scheme in which investors are encouraged to leave both principal and interest untouched in an investment based on promised, unusually large interest rates. Investors who want either interest or principal returned are paid from funds received from new investors rather than earnings from what the scheme was supposed to invest in, earnings which often are insufficient or nonexistent. A fraudulent investment scheme.

QUANTITY THEORY OF MONEY   A theory that the level of prices in a country is determined by the quantity of money in circulation. It is expressed in an equation [developed by American economist Irving Fisher (1867–1947)] as $MV = PT$ (or, $P = MV/T$), where M is the quantity of money, V is the velocity of circulation of money, T is the volume of transactions for goods and services, and P is the price level. If V is constant and T changes very little over a short period of time, then the price level (P) depends upon the money supply (M). Others such as Alfred Marshall (1842–1924) and contemporary economist Milton Friedman have developed their particular versions of the quantity theory of money.

Critics argue that V is neither constant nor predictable and that T can change in critical amounts in short periods of time. Modern monetarists recognize that the relationship is complicated but continue to hold that the quantity of money is key to controlling the price level and the level of economic activity in the longer run. See *Monetarism, Monetary Policy*.

QUARTILE   A scale for classification of data into four parts. The first quartile marks the lowest quarter of the data. An income receiver at the third quartile of income receivers, ranked from lowest to highest income, receives more income than three-fourths of the income receivers. See *Decile, Percentile*.

QUASI-RENT   A rentlike return attributable to factors of production other than land arising from qualities of scarcity. It is a short-term surplus above the cost of producing a service or a capital good when the service or capital good is temporarily fixed in quantity. Quasi-rent is competed away over time when more of the capital good or service skill can be produced.

An example of quasi-rent is the amount of a wage that is higher than its opportunity cost (what can be earned in the next best occupation). This excess is a return on the unique skill of the wage earners which provides a perfectly inelastic supply curve for that labor in the short run, until more workers can be trained in the skill. The return, then, is similar to the rent return on land which is limited in supply.

The concept was developed by English economist Alfred Marshall (1842–1924). See *Rent*.

QUOTA A quantitative limit imposed upon transactions.

1. In international trade, it is a maximum quantity that may be imported into a country or exported from a country. As an import control a quota is an effective way to protect the sales of domestic producers. It may be more effective than a tariff, which increases the price of an imported product but permits those willing to pay the price to purchase the imports. A tariff that is not prohibitive will permit some importation and produce a duty income, while a quota will not produce any income.

2. In a cartel, quotas limit the amount that each member may produce and sell, in order to maintain a high income for the members as a group.

3. In business, a quota may be a minimum that must be sold in order to qualify for continued employment or to meet the requirements for bonus payments. Or, it is a production minimum imposed on a worker, a production team, or a factory. See *Cartel, Organization of Petroleum Exporting Countries, Tariff.*

RATIONAL EXPECTATIONS THEORY A theory that people develop expectations about the future course of events based upon recurring historical experience. When circumstances similar to the recent past arise, people anticipate and act upon expected government policies even before they are decided upon or announced. Thus, the policies themselves do not affect behavior—only unexpected, surprise policy changes will affect behavior. For example, the Federal Reserve Open-Market Committee (FOMC) has consistently placed control of inflation ahead of economic growth in its monetary policy actions over the decade of the 1980s. If successive months in 1991 were to show sharp increases in the consumer price index at the same time that GNP figures show sluggish growth, people would expect the FOMC to restrain growth in the money supply and increase interest rates. Even before the FOMC would meet to decide what to do, people would anticipate its action and sell bonds, and thereby cause interest rates to rise.

RATIONING The process by which goods and services are allocated among potential users. The price system is an allocating or rationing mechanism, given the distribution of purchasing power. Prices will tend to rise so long as people want to buy more than is available. Higher prices tend to drive out some would-be purchasers until those who remain are willing and able to buy just the amount that is available. The price system rations productive resources among producers as well as finished goods and services among consumers. When the price of a consumer product is bid up, the producers of it will try to expand production by buying more resources. Resource prices will tend to rise, and resources will be attracted to the industry whose goods are in short supply from other industries whose demand and product prices have not changed.

In situations of severe shortages, the price system may fail to work fairly. Other rationing processes may be adopted. During the oil shortage in the 1970s created by the OPEC cartel, gasoline often was rationed in the United States by service station operators on a *first come, first served* basis, until the supply was exhausted. Those at the end of the line received no gasoline no matter how much they were willing to pay.

In wartime, a major diversion of production from consumer goods to war material occurs in a relatively short time. As a matter of equity, countries tend to ration the remaining consumer goods on a *quantity-per-person basis* known as *non-price rationing* through a system of ration coupons superimposed upon the price system, usually accompanied by price control.

REAL INCOME   What income will buy; the goods and services that can be purchased with money income. The amount that can be purchased varies inversely with changes in the price level. Given a money income, the quantity of goods and services that can be purchased will decline with an increase in the price level and rise with a decrease in the price level. Real income, then, is money income corrected for changes in the price level. A time series of real income is calculated by dividing money income for each time period by the appropriate price index number for that period. The result shows the purchasing power of money income for each period compared to the base period. See *Money Income, Real versus Money Data, Real Wages, Deflation, Constant Dollars, Price Index.*

REAL RATE OF INTEREST   The nominal, or market, rate of interest corrected by subtracting the rate of inflation. If the nominal interest rate is 7.5% and the rate of inflation is 3.5%, the real interest rate is 4%. See *Real versus Money Data.*

REAL VERSUS MONEY DATA   Money data provides a measure of value in current prices, such as 1990 GNP in 1990 prices, 1980 GNP in 1980 prices, and 1970 GNP in 1970 prices. These gross national product figures fail to measure changes in real output over those decades because they include the influence of price inflation. Conversion to "real" data removes price inflation (or deflation) by dividing each GNP figure by an appropriate price index number for that year.

If the price index base is 1970 = 100, then use of the related index numbers for other years will express all of the GNP figures for other years in 1970 prices, and inflationary price changes will be removed. A special price index, the GNP deflator, has been developed which reflects the components of GNP. It is used to "deflate" GNP money data to measure real changes in output. Similarly, the consumer price index may be used to deflate disposable personal income money data to show real changes in consumer purchasing power. See *Real Income, Deflation, Money Prices, Price Index.*

REAL WAGES What wages will buy—the goods and services that can be purchased with money wages. Real wages are money wages actually received corrected for changes in the price level by dividing money wages by the consumer price index. The results show changes in real wages over time. See *Real Income, Real versus Money Data, Constant Dollars, Current Dollars, Price Index.*

RECESSION A decline in economic activity measured by falling GNP and rising unemployment. Officially a recession in the U.S. occurs when GNP falls for two consecutive quarters (6 months). A very deep and continuing recession is termed a depression.

In some historic theories of the business cycle, such as that of Joseph Schumpeter (1883–1950), recession was one of four stages of the business cycle, namely that stage from the peak down to the secular-trend line, where the depression stage began and continued down to the trough, or bottom of the cycle. The turning point from the trough upward to the secular-trend line was the recovery or revival stage, and the upsurge from there to the peak was the prosperity stage. Schumpeter argued that historical causation requires measuring cycles from equilibrium on the trend line, through the four phases, to the next equilibrium on the trend line. Others, such as the National Bureau of Economic Research, have measured cycles from trough to trough or peak to peak. See *Business Cycles, Depression.*

RECIPROCAL TRADE PROGRAMS Agreements under legislation which authorize the President of the U.S. to negotiate mutual tariff reductions with other nations to expand trade (including American exports, of course!). See *General Agreement on Tariffs and Trade.*

RECOVERY The phase of the business cycle that consists of an upturn in output, income, and employment after the economy "bottoms out," i.e., after the trough. Recovery is characterized by the expansion of spending in the private sector of the economy by consumers and businesses. See *Business Cycles, Depression, Prosperity, Recession.*

REDEEMABLE BONDS   See *Callable Bonds.*

REDISCOUNT RATE   The rate of interest charged by Federal Reserve Banks when they purchase commercial paper (short-term negotiable debt of businesses) from member banks. (The first discount rate is that charged by the member bank when it provided the issuer of the commercial paper with less than the face value of the paper.) Change in the rediscount rate is one of the tools used by the Fed to affect the reserves of member banks, the supply of bank credit, and thus the money supply. An increase in the rate makes it more costly for a commercial bank to sell some of these short-term assets to the Fed to increase reserves. A decrease in the rediscount rate, on the other hand, can encourage banks to sell commercial paper to the Fed. Payment is made by the Fed into the reserve accounts kept by the commercial banks at their regional Federal Reserve Bank. Commercial bank reserves are increased, hence their ability to make new loans.

The rediscount rate is different from another policy tool of the Fed, its discount rate. The *rediscount rate* is the rate of interest charged by the Fed to purchase commercial paper held as assets by commercial banks, while the *federal discount rate* is the interest rate the Fed charges for loans made by the Fed to commercial banks, loans that are debt obligations of the commercial banks. See *Discounting, Discount Rate, Deposit Multiplier.*

REDLINING   A practice by some banks and thrifts of denying loans to people of certain characteristics, such as race or gender, or to anyone in neighborhoods composed of certain racial or income groups, without an individual determination of the soundness of a loan to an individual applicant. The practice is illegal under the Community Reinvestment Act of 1977, which requires mortgage lenders to collect and report data on the race, gender, and income level of loan applicants and loan recipients in order to police lending practices. See *Community Reinvestment Act.*

REGRESSIVE TAX   1. A tax which takes a larger percentage of low income than of high income.

2. A tax whose percentage rate decreases for higher levels of the tax base.

A sales tax is a flat-rate tax and is a proportional tax, not a regressive tax under the second meaning above. But a sales tax is regressive in the first and most common usage because it taxes the sales of consumer goods and services, which constitute a larger share of income for low-income recipients than for high-income recipients. The exemption of food and prescription drugs from the sales tax in some states reduces but does not eliminate the regressive character of the sales tax in the first sense. See *Progressive Tax, Proportional Tax.*

REGULATORY AGENCIES   Agencies created to regulate the behavior of firms and persons in the public interest where market competition fails to do so. Some agencies, such as the Federal Trade Commission, attempt to prevent practices which reduce competition and create market control. They serve to enforce federal antitrust policy. Other agencies, such as state public utility commissions, try to simulate competitive market results in situations of natural monopoly by fixing rates and prices, enforcing maximum rates of return, and/or allotting markets. Still others, such as the Food and Drug Administration, attempt to protect consumers from fraud in advertising, materials, or workmanship.

Regulation sometimes fails when experts from the regulated industry are selected to staff an agency and they proceed to regulate in the interest of the industry rather than the public. On the other hand, appointment of regulators who have no knowledge of the industry can result in problems for the public as well. They can be overwhelmed by the expert attorneys representing the regulated industry. Some economists believe that regulation has served to reduce competition and increase prices; they point to the competition and price effects in the trucking industry following deregulation in 1980 as partial support for that position.

Other examples of federal regulatory agencies are the Interstate Commerce Commission, the Federal Reserve Board of Governors, the Federal Energy Regulatory Commission, the Federal Aviation Agency, and the Federal Communications Commission. Additional examples of state and local regulatory agencies are environmental quality agencies, barber examination boards, and local building inspection agencies. See *Antitrust.*

REINSURANCE   A sharing of the risk when an insurer of a particular risk in turn buys insurance from other insurers to cover part of it. For example, an insurance company might provide health insurance to a firm covering specified employee expenses up to $1 million per person and then try to protect itself by turning to another insurance company to insure that portion of the risk that is above $25,000 per person.

RELATIVE INCOME HYPOTHESIS   A hypothesis advanced by contemporary American economist James Duesenberry that consumption expenditure of a household is influenced by the income and expenditure of other households with which its members associate. Thus, if a household under study lives in a neighborhood in which the incomes of other households are higher, that household will tend to spend like its neighbors, and it will have a higher propensity to consume than would be expected from just focusing on that household's income level. Social circles and professional ties may have the same effect as neighborhoods in influencing the propensity to consume. See *Propensity to Consume, Absolute Income Hypothesis, Permanent Income Hypothesis.*

RENT   1. Economic rent is a payment above the supply price or opportunity cost for the use of a resource that is fixed in supply. The payment, therefore, is above the minimum amount necessary to assure the continued supply of that factor of production. Economic rent as a return to fixed factors other than land is called *quasi-rent.* See *Economic Rent, Quasi-Rent, Marginal Land.*
  2. Rent, in common usage, is a contractual payment per unit of time by a renter to an owner for the use of land or any other durable object which gives off its services over time. Unlike economic rent, it may include an allocated cost of production as well as a surplus above that amount due to temporary fixed supply.

REPURCHASE AGREEMENT (REPO)   An agreement to repurchase a negotiable security at a specified future date at the same price for which it was sold plus accumulated interest at the rate specified in the sale agreement. The sale of repos is commonly used by banks and other depository institutions as a supplemental source of funds for short periods of time.

REQUIRED RESERVES   Reserves against deposits which are required by law for all depository institutions (commercial banks, mutual savings banks, savings and loan associations, credit unions, agencies and branches of foreign banks, and Edge corporations). Required reserves must be held as deposits with Federal Reserve Banks or as vault cash. Most reserves are held on deposit in Federal Reserve Banks. Depository institutions which are not members of the Federal Reserve System (the Fed) may maintain their reserve balances indirectly with certain approved institutions which in turn hold deposits with a Federal Reserve Bank. The percentage of deposits required to be kept as reserves varies with the type of deposit, the volume of deposits and, for time deposits, the original maturity. The principal reason for requiring reserves against deposits is to provide a mechanism for the Fed to control the money supply, the bulk of which is checking deposits in banks and thrifts. Current reserve requirements may be found in the monthly Federal Reserve Bulletin. See *Bank Reserves, Excess Reserves, Monetary Policy, Deposit Multiplier, Edge Act Corporations, Money Stock.*

RESALE PRICE MAINTENANCE AGREEMENTS Agreements that permit a manufacturer to set the resale prices charged by firms that are distributors of its products. The agreements reflect a manufacturer's desire to prevent its products from being used as "loss leaders" to get customers into a store or to prevent cut-rate distributors from setting prices that generally establish a lower retail price "norm" in the minds of customers than the manufacturer desires. Resale price maintenance also protects small, full-price distributors from competition from price cutters and encourages promotion of the protected products, which have larger mark-ups.

Courts found such agreements illegal under antitrust law, so some manufacturers supported "fair-trade" laws to permit the practice. A number of states passed fair-trade laws but found that courts restricted their enforcement. The Miller–Tydings Act was passed by Congress in 1937 to give exemption from the Sherman Antitrust Act to manufacturers in states which had enacted fair-trade statutes, but the law was repealed in 1967 after decades of unsympathetic treatment in the courts.

RESET SECURITIES Bonds or notes which provide for resetting the interest rate periodically to restore a low market price to a price close to the face value. The provision is designed to attract buyers for the securities by providing some protection from loss in the value of their investments. Sometimes a reset clause is used in junk bonds to make them more attractive.

The reset concept works best when the market price has not dropped very far below the face value of the security. Suppose that a $1000 bond carries an interest rate of 12% but is trading at $500. A reset interest rate of 24% should restore the trading price to close to the $1000 face value. This example illustrates that when debt is trading at prices sharply below face value, a nearly impossible cost burden is created to set an interest rate high enough to restore the price to its original-issue value. To avoid such a burden, a company would try to raise new money to buy back the affected issue before the reset date arrives.

RESOLUTION FUNDING CORPORATION (RFC) An off-budget agency created by the Financial Institutions Reform, Recovery and Enforcement Act of 1989 (FIRREA) to sell to the public $30 billion in 30-year bonds to pay part of the cost of closing insolvent thrifts. The principal is not guaranteed by the federal government, rather it will be repaid by the purchase of low-cost zero-coupon bonds that mature at the same time as the bonds sold by the RFC. The cost of the zero-coupon bonds will be met in part by retained earnings and future annual earnings of the regional Federal Home Loan Banks, by continuing deposit insurance premiums paid by thrifts, and by the proceeds from the sale of the assets of failed thrifts. The Treasury will pay a major share of the cost of "bailing out" the thrift industry, a cost that in 1991 is expected to be a multiple of the $30 billion provided in the FIRREA.

RESOLUTION TRUST CORPORATION (RTC)   A federal agency created by the Financial Institutions Reform, Recovery and Enforcement Act of 1989 (FIRREA) to manage and dispose of the assets of insolvent thrifts after the Office of Thrift Supervision has taken possession of them. The law calls for the automatic termination of the RTC when it has completed its task and not later than December 31, 1996. After the termination of the RTC, the Savings Association Insurance Fund would handle the occasional insolvent thrift.

Most observers consider this an unrealistically early date to resolve the huge thrift bailout problem. Because of the large number and size of failed thrifts, the RTC has to move cautiously in trying to dispose of their assets to avoid serious disturbance to real estate markets and junk-bond markets.

The RTC is overseen by a board consisting of the Chairman of the Federal Reserve Board of Governors, the Secretary of the Department of Housing and Urban Development, two private citizens with experience in real estate or finance who are appointed by the President for 3-year terms and confirmed by the U.S. Senate, and the Secretary of the Treasury as chairman. The Board of Directors of the Federal Deposit Insurance Corporation is the Board of Directors for the RTC.

RETAINED EARNINGS   Undistributed profits. Corporate profit that is not paid out to stockholders as dividends. Companies retain earnings to finance an increase in the size of the business, i.e., to acquire more inventories, buy new equipment, or build new plant; or, they retain earnings as reserves against possible future weak markets; or, they retain earnings as a fund to purchase some of the outstanding shares of stock, etc.

In national income accounting, "retained earnings" is one of the categories that must be subtracted from national income to arrive at personal income.

REVENUE BONDS Certificates of indebtedness issued by government agencies which are backed by revenues from the specific project identified on the face of the bond, such as a sewage disposal system, a new water line, a toll bridge, or a toll road. Revenue bonds differ from *general-obligation bonds,* which are issued against the general taxing powers of the governmental unit issuing them. See *General Obligation Bonds, Government Bonds.*

REVENUE SHARING Revenue collected by one political entity which is shared with other levels of government. Some examples are gasoline taxes collected by the federal government that are allocated to states for highway construction and maintenance; or state gasoline taxes collected by states, a portion of which are allocated to counties and cities; or property taxes collected by counties which are shared with school districts, local TV reflector districts, etc. Some of the proceeds may be designated for particular uses such as schools, public assistance, or roads, and some shared revenue may not be designated, such as that distributed to state and local governments by the federal government during the 1970s.

The practice of revenue sharing may reflect the broader and more flexible taxing capability at one level of government relative to another. Or, it may arise from the desire to provide some minimum level of service regardless of the recipient government's ability to pay. See *Apportioned Tax.*

REVERSE ANNUITY MORTGAGE (RAM) A mortgage loan which provides periodic payments to homeowners based on the equity they have accumulated in their homes. The loans are designed primarily to permit senior citizens who need a larger flow of income to receive it from their home equities without having to sell their homes. This type of loan helps seniors who are physically able to remain in their homes to do so, and it helps others to keep their homes despite growing health-care expenses for their spouses.

Each payment received reduces the homeowner's equity until it is exhausted and the lender owns the home. Short of that, a senior who comes upon better financial times or an heir who inherits the home can stop receiving the reverse annuity mortgage payments and proceed to buy back equity in the home. If the home is sold, the homeowner and the lender share the proceeds according to current equity shares, just as with an ordinary mortgage.

REVOCABLE TRUST   A "living trust" agreement whose terms may be changed or voided at any time by the creator of the trust. See *Trust, Irrevocable Trust.*

RIGHT-TO-WORK LAWS   Laws that make it illegal to require union membership as a condition of employment. Right-to-work laws are directed at the *union shop,* which is a provision in a collective bargaining contract between union and employer that requires newly hired employees to join the union within a specified time in order to continue employment. The *closed shop,* which requires union membership before a person can be employed, was outlawed by the Taft–Hartley Act of 1947, but it has survived in the maritime and construction industries, where it provides a service to employers as well as workers. See *Closed Shop, Union Shop, Open Shop.*

RISK   The possibility of an untoward outcome because of the lack of perfect certainty in the real world. Some risks can be reduced or eliminated by hedging or by insurance, while other risks cannot be avoided—they constitute a pure form of uncertainty. Some risks, while unavoidable, might have their impact reduced by diversification of products, of assets in a portfolio, and so on.

Risk is associated with the purchase of financial instruments such as bonds, stocks, and mutual fund shares. The degree of risk tends to be reflected in the rate of return or interest rate. There is the risk that the firm will not pay dividends or interest, or not even repay the principal; there is the risk that inflation will reduce the purchasing power of the dollars paid out to the securities holders relative to the value of the dollars when the securities were purchased; and there is the risk that the market value of the securities will fall so that the purchaser will suffer a loss upon sale of the securities in the future. The higher these risks, the higher the interest rate that is required to induce possible purchasers to run the risk. See *Hedging, Insurance, Profit, Speculation, Uncertainty.*

ROBINSON–PATMAN ACT   A law passed in 1936 which amends the Clayton Antitrust Act of 1914 in order to limit price discrimination with more precise prohibitions. It was enacted primarily to protect small firms from the rapidly spreading chain stores. The Robinson–Patman Act prohibits brokerage allowances to buying firms. (Brokers are independent agents representing a number of sellers.) The Act permits advertising allowances only if they are provided to all buyers on a proportional basis. It prohibits price discrimination by a seller among buyers unless the seller can show that costs differ in proportion to the price differentials or that the goods differ in their grade or quality. The seller also may defend against a charge of price discrimination by showing that the prices only met competitors' prices in good faith, or did not substantially lessen competition. See *Antitrust, Clayton Antitrust Act, Sherman Antitrust Act.*

RUN ON THE DOLLAR   A substantial increase in the dollars offered for sale in international currency markets as people rapidly try to convert dollar holdings into other currencies because of a sudden decline in confidence in the exchange value of the dollar. It may be feared that the dollar will not serve well as a unit of deferred payment. A run on the dollar compares to a run on a bank in which depositors scramble to convert their deposits into cash because they have lost confidence in the bank. See *Money.*

SALARY Compensation for services, paid to a person in fixed amounts at regular intervals, most often monthly. Compensation paid to executives and supervisors that is unrelated to hours worked or pieces produced (the bases for calculating wages paid to manual workers and clerical workers). See *Wage*.

SAVING 1. Household abstention from present consumption out of current income. People save for a variety of reasons: to buy a high-priced item (for example, an automobile or a home) sometime in the future by gradually accumulating enough for a down payment; to pay for the children's education in the future; to provide for expenditure in one's old age; to provide an inheritance for one's heirs. Savings may be held in a variety of forms such as currency, checking accounts, savings deposits, securities, real estate, and other assets.

Some saving is forced rather than being an individual decision to abstain from present consumption. An example of saving forced on individuals is the retained earnings of corporations, which are not available to the shareholders but increase the firm's assets in which they hold a share.

2. In national income analysis, saving is that part of disposable personal income not spent for consumption. $S = DPY - C$. For society as a whole, saving releases resources from the production of consumer goods to be used instead to create capital equipment (investment), which permits larger consumption in the future. Increased saving may at times only reduce consumption without any

counterbalancing decisions by businesses to invest. The result may be falling national income and growing unemployment. Or, if investment exceeds saving in the economy, the result maybe inflation. See *Paradox of Thrift*.

SAVINGS AND LOAN ASSOCIATION A state or federally chartered financial organization which was authorized in 1932 under legislation creating the Federal Home Loan Bank System in the (imperfect) image of the Federal Reserve System. The banking crisis of the Great Depression led to a separation of financial powers among more narrowly conceived groups of institutions. Savings and loan associations were assigned savings deposit and home mortgage functions similar to those that had been performed previously by building and loan associations. They were mutual associations rather than stock corporations until recent years. In 1980, S & L's were given broadly expanded asset and liability powers that moved them in the direction of commercial bank powers. The broadened powers attracted the unscrupulous and confused the unwitting in the industry, with the resulting S & L fiasco that involved a large minority of S & L's at the end of that decade. See *Federal Home Loan Bank System, Savings Association Insurance Fund.*

SAVINGS ASSOCIATION INSURANCE FUND (SAIF) A federal fund that insures depositors in member savings institutions for up to $100,000 of their deposits. Details of the insurance coverage are presented under *Federal Deposit Insurance Corporation.* All federally chartered savings institutions must participate, and state-chartered ones may belong. The fund is built up by premiums paid by members based upon their covered deposit liabilities. It is used to pay depositors of failed thrifts when the sale of assets is insufficient to cover insured deposit liabilities.

Some states permit state-chartered banks, thrifts, and credit unions to insure their deposits with private insurance companies. The number of such insured institutions usually is too small to spread the risks properly, so that one or a few bank failures will cause the insurance company to fail, leaving depositors in the other banking institutions uncovered. This problem arose in Maryland and Ohio in the 1980s and in Rhode Island at the beginning of 1991. See *Deposit Insurance.*

SAIF was created by the transfer of funds and responsibilities to it from the Federal Savings and Loan Insurance Corporation (FSLIC) under the Financial Institutions Reform, Recovery and Enforcement Act of 1989 (FIRREA). The FSLIC was then disbanded. SAIF is under the direction of the FDIC, whose commercial bank insurance fund is now managed by a subsidiary parallel to SAIF named the Bank Insurance Fund (BIF).

In 1989 it was clear that the FSLIC held only a small fraction of the funds necessary to cover the deposit insurance liabilities in failed thrifts, let alone those in thrifts on the margin of failure. The FIRREA provided for the transfusion of $30 billion through the specially created Resolution Funding Corporation (RFC or Ref-Corp), an amount that turns out to be a fraction of the amount that finally will be needed. Another agency, the Resolution Trust Corporation (RTC), was created to manage and dispose of thrifts that become insolvent between 1989 and 1993, after which, it was hoped, the thrift debacle would be over and SAIF could manage thrift insolvencies under the direction of the FDIC. In addition to trying to resolve the thrift industry crisis, FIRREA is notable for adding a substantial number of new acronyms to the federal alphabet soup. See *Bank Insurance Fund, Federal Deposit Insurance Corporation, Federal Savings and Loan Insurance Corporation.*

SAVINGS BANK   A financial institution which accepted only savings and time deposits and made small personal loans and mortgage loans prior to the enactment of the Depository Institutions Deregulation and Monetary Control Act of 1980 (DIDMCA). It can be a mutual or a stock bank chartered by a state or by the federal government. The DIDMCA authorizes savings banks to offer interest-bearing transaction accounts called negotiable orders of withdrawal (NOW accounts), to make commercial, corporate, and business loans consisting of no more than 5% of their assets, and to accept demand deposits in connection with that business. They also were permitted to invest up to 20% of their assets in consumer loans, commercial paper, and corporate debt securities.

The Financial Institutions Reform, Recovery and Enforcement Act of 1989 (FIRREA) reined in some of the activities of thrifts that had been expanded. For example, commercial real estate loans that had been authorized up to 40% of a federally chartered thrift's loan portfolio are now restricted to four times its capital, affecting the lending powers of a majority of thrifts. And thrifts are now prohibited from investing in below-investment-grade bonds (junk bonds).

SAVINGS DEPOSIT   A non-negotiable interest-earning deposit, also known as a *passbook account.* Savings deposits are offered by savings banks, savings and loan associations, and commercial banks. Unlike time deposits, which have a maturity date and penalty for early withdrawal, the withdrawal of funds from a savings deposit can be made at any time the bank is open. (Some savings deposits provide for notice, often 30 days, prior to withdrawal, but the provision seldom is enforced.) Savings deposits are included in the Federal Reserve's money supply category known as M2. See *Time Deposit, Checking Account, Negotiable Order of Withdrawal, Share-Draft Account.*

SAY'S LAW   The "law of markets" developed by French economist Jean Baptiste Say (1767–1832) which holds that supply creates its own demand. While *some* goods may be in oversupply, a *general* glut or overproduction cannot occur because the production of goods and services creates sufficient income to purchase them. English economist John Maynard Keynes (1883–1946) published *The General Theory of Employment, Interest, and Money* in 1936 in which he tried to show that there *could* be a general glut and that there could be an equilibrium of the economy at less than full employment. Keynes credited Thomas Malthus (1776–1834) with being the first to recognize that Say's Law might be invalid.

SCAB   A person who goes to work for a company replacing employees who are out on strike. An epithet directed at such people when they cross a union picket line to enter the workplace.

SCARCITY   Too few resources in a society, relative to needs. Scarcity exists even in a so-called affluent society. Scarcity means that everything desired cannot be had; choices must be made by households whether to use limited income to consume this product or that service, or to save for the future; choices must be made by firms whether to use this combination of factors of production or that; choices must be made by society regarding whether to provide more day-care centers or devote more to national defense. A particular good or service is scarce if, when the price is zero, there is not enough of it to fill the demand for it. Scarcity is a basic concept of economics, which is the study of how society organizes to make the choices which scarcity requires.

S CORPORATION   A corporation that is taxed in very much the same way as a partnership. The firm usually is not subject to corporate income tax; instead, the firm's income is taxed directly to the shareholder. Since the top corporate income tax rates are higher than top personal income tax rates, an S Corporation status is advantageous when corporate profits are high. The advantage when there are "negative profits" is that corporate losses can be deducted by shareholders on their individual income tax returns up to their basis in the stock plus their loans to the corporation.

An S Corporation avoids the so-called ''double taxation'' imposed by the corporate income tax. The double taxation label arises from the same corporate income being taxed once under the corporate income tax and a second time as personal income when the shareholders receive the income as dividends. Of course, a corporation may retain all of its earnings for investment in assets. Shareholders then pay no individual tax on it until the shares are sold, hopefully at higher than the purchase price if the market reflects the higher asset value. At that time a capital gains tax would be owed on the increased value of the shares.

SEASONAL CYCLES (OR VARIATIONS)   Patterns which occur in a number of business activities over the course of a year and recur year after year. Some seasonal cycles are caused by nature, e.g., seasonal weather-related patterns in agriculture involving growing seasons, or in clothing styles reflecting the need for alternating warm and cool materials and design. Some seasonal cycles are artificial and are caused by the coincidence of business decisions, e.g., automobile production patterns related to the annual introduction of new models each September. Seasonal patterns can be identified and removed statistically to avoid confusing ''normal'' increases and decreases that occur within each year with those that may signal longer-run shifts in business activity. See *Business Cycles*.

SECONDARY BOYCOTT   Pressure brought by a first party against a neutral third party in order to win assistance in affecting the behavior of a second party with whom the first party has a dispute. For example, a union in a contract dispute with an employer may picket a key supplier of the employer, even though the union has no dispute with the supplier, to try to reduce the supplier's business and force the supplier to stop doing business with the employer. If successful, that would put economic pressure on the employer to agree to the union's position. Here the union is the first party, the employer is the second party, and the supplier is the third party. Secondary boycotts are outlawed under the Taft–Hartley Act of 1947.

Peaceful picketing of the second party to enlist the sympathy of third parties by informing them of the dispute is not a secondary boycott under the law. It has been judged an exercise of free speech when peaceful. See *Picketing*.

SECULAR STAGNATION   A hypothesis that economies mature and that there are forces at work which cause a long-run decline in the rate of growth of an economy. It becomes difficult for businesses continually to create sufficient jobs to employ all those seeking work. Forces that supposedly lead to secular stagnation have been identified as the reaching of the last frontier, a decline in population growth, a shift from capital-using to capital-saving inventions, etc. Secular stagnation was held to exist by many in the late 1930s and by many again in the early 1960s. Each time the concept has begun to achieve wide acceptance, clusters of new products and processes have emerged to stimulate prolonged economic growth.

SECULAR TREND   The trend of economic activity over the decades, illustrated by a time series from which seasonal variations and business cycles have been removed statistically. The secular growth in gross national product from 1860 to the present is estimated at about 3.2% per year.

SECURITIZATION   Conversion of different kinds of borrowing into securities that can be marketed. An example is the packaging of home mortgages with similar characteristics into groups or pools of mortgages, each pool being a bundle of assets against which securities then are sold. See *Government National Mortgage Association.*

SELLING SHORT   See *Short Sale.*

SENIORITY   A system for selecting individuals in which those with the longest service are selected first. Seniority might be used for promotion, for retention during layoffs, for rehiring after layoffs, or for a particularly desirable position or committee membership. Seniority may be calculated according to length of service in the job classification, in the plant, or in the firm, with the probability of a different seniority position in each grouping. Critics of seniority argue that selection should be based upon merit, so that it will be worthwhile for people to acquire skills and attitudes that increase their productivity. They argue that seniority stifles inventiveness and efforts to improve productivity. It discriminates against individuals in groups that have recently become upward mobile such as blacks and women. Defenders of seniority argue that, in many jobs, output and quality are determined by the machines used once a basic skill is mastered, so that a merit system merely opens the door to favoritism and discrimination. They argue that long service represents loyalty to the organization that is valuable and should be rewarded.

SHARE-DRAFT ACCOUNT An interest-bearing transaction account at a credit union, authorized by the Depository Institutions Deregulation and Monetary Control Act of 1980. It is included among "other checkable deposits" (OCDs) in the Federal Reserve's definition of M1, a money supply category. See *Credit Union.*

SHERMAN ANTITRUST ACT An antitrust law passed in 1890 to prohibit agreements by competitors which restrain competition, such as price fixing or market sharing, and to prohibit acts which are meant to create or maintain monopoly. It is enforced primarily by the U.S. Justice Department through prosecution in federal courts. See *Antitrust.*

SHORT RUN A period of time which is short enough that some variables are fixed, i.e., they do not have time to change in response to a change in an independent variable. For example, for the study of a firm, the short run may be a period of time in which at least one input of the firm, such as plant size, remains fixed in amount. For the study of a market, it may be a period short enough that new firms cannot enter nor can old firms leave the market. Or it might be a time period that would permit a change in the number of firms, but one short enough that market demand, technology, etc., do not change. For the economy, the short run may be a period of time in which major adaptations to a policy change (e.g., the full amount of bank deposit expansion following adoption of a policy to permit more rapid growth in the money supply) do not have time to occur. See *Long Run, Fixed Cost, Equilibrium of the Market.*

SHORT SALE The sale of commodities or securities which one does not now own, but rather borrows for immediate sale. The short seller hopes to profit by replacing the borrowed shares with the purchase of cheaper ones by the date set for future delivery. If the price falls between the time of the sale and the date at which the purchase is made to cover the delivery, the seller makes money; if not, the seller loses at least the cost of the transaction.

A short sale may be made to balance a comparable current purchase of shares in order to hedge against a decline in the price of the purchased shares, or a short sale may be made to make money on the speculation that the price of the item will fall. See *Hedging, Bear.*

SHORT INTEREST The number of shares in short-sale contracts that have not yet been purchased by short sellers for return to the lenders. See *Short Sale.*

SILENT PARTNER One who provides capital to a partnership but takes no active role in its management. Also known as "limited partner." See *Partnership, Limited Partnership.*

SILVER CERTIFICATE Currency which is "backed" by silver holdings of the Treasury and carries the promise to pay silver to the bearer on demand. Many dollar bills in circulation prior to 1963 were silver certificates. They were discontinued by Congressional action when the market price of silver was rising and it became profitable for the bearer to exchange the certificates at the treasury for silver. At the same time, the Treasury stopped buying silver for reserves against certificates. Silver certificates have been replaced as currency by Federal Reserve notes of the same denominations.

SINGLE PROPRIETORSHIP Also known as individual proprietorship. A privately owned business organization in which the owner is manager and risk taker and receives all of the profits, but also is liable for the debts of the business to the full extent of his or her personal wealth (with some limitations, such as the exemption of all or some of the equity in the person's home under some state bankruptcy laws). The business organization dies with the owner in the sense that, even though the assets may be transferred to others, creditors can claim full settlement before the transfer, which could seriously interrupt the flow of business. The new owner then would have to be identified and would become fully liable. See *Corporation, Partnership.*

SIT-DOWN STRIKE A concerted refusal to work by employees who "sit down" at the job site, stopping production. A type of strike that occurred in the mid-1930s as unions were attempting to organize the tire industry, the automobile industry, etc. As with other strikes, the purpose is to put pressure on the employer to win union recognition, improve wages and working conditions in a collective bargaining contract, resolve a grievance, or some similar goal. By occupying the work place, the strikers prevent the employer from replacing them with scabs, a great advantage over a walkout. They were especially effective during the Great Depression in situations where a lot of jobs were semiskilled and droves of unemployed were ready to take the strikers' jobs. Eventually courts held sit-down strikes to be an unlawful occupation of private property and issued injunctions to expel the strikers. In factories employing thousands of workers it was difficult to dislodge them and sometimes violence erupted in clashes with police. At other times the strikers attracted widespread attention to their cause by filing out of the plants peacefully, with flags waving and bands playing. See *Strike*.

SLOWDOWN   A concerted action by a group of employees to slow down the rate of production to pressure their employer to change wages or working conditions or to resolve a grievance. It is an action short of a strike that permits the employer to continue sales and the employees to continue to receive pay, but it does tend to raise unit costs. The opposite of "speed-up," which is instigated by the employer.

SOCIAL COSTS   Costs of production or consumption that are borne by society, including noneconomic as well as economic costs. Often the term is restricted to social costs that do not enter the cost calculations of producers or consumers unless forced upon them as costs by collective bargaining or governmental intervention. Examples are black-lung disease contracted by coal miners, air pollution caused by factory smoke stacks or consumer use of automobiles, and water pollution caused by dumping waste materials into streams and lakes. See *Costs: Accounting versus Economic, External Costs*.

SOCIALISM   An economy in which capital goods and natural resources are owned and managed by government rather than by private persons. Income from these sources (rent, interest, and profit) goes to the government for public use.

Before Karl Marx (1818–1883) socialism differed from communism on the basis of principles of income distribution: to each according to one's contribution versus to each according to one's need. Since Marx, the distinction between communism and socialism has become blurred as many of his followers in eastern Europe have used the terms interchangeably. Non-Marxist socialists generally believe that a socialist society can be achieved peacefully and can be democratic. Since Karl Marx, communists generally believe in the inevitability of violent revolution to achieve a communist society, and that dictatorship is necessary prior to achieving the final goals.

Many countries today have some degree of public ownership and operation of enterprise. Countries such as Sweden have mixed economies that fall more toward the socialist end of the spectrum, while the U.S. today has a mixed economy which is close to the capitalist end. The socialist countries of eastern Europe faced economic failure toward the end of the 1980s and began to turn toward market systems and democracy. See *Communism, Capitalism*.

SOCIAL-OVERHEAD CAPITAL   Capital which provides broad social benefit because it is basic to economic development. It is basic to the effective use of the modern industrial plant. Examples of social-overhead capital are highways, waterways, railways, communications systems, power systems, and education and training of the labor force. Social-overhead capital is characterized by combinations of some of the following elements: indivisibility, increasing returns, natural monopoly, huge investment of resources, and passage of some time between completion of the capital and full development of markets for its services.

SOFT LOAN   A loan providing lower interest or other easier terms for repayment than is provided in the regular market for funds. Soft loans are provided by government agencies as domestic subsidies and as loans to foreigners for developmental or military purposes. Sometimes a regular loan is converted to a soft loan, as happens when a foreign loan might otherwise go into default with zero repayment.

SOFT MONEY   1. A national currency which is hard hit by inflation so that foreigners receiving it in international trade have little confidence in it and want to convert it quickly into another currency. 2. Historically, paper money without 100% backing in gold or silver coin, as opposed to "hard" money in the form of gold and silver coins of intrinsic value as metal.

SPECIAL DRAWING RIGHTS (SDRs)   Created reserves for member nations in the International Monetary Fund which serve as a supplement to gold and reserve currencies, such as the dollar, for transactions in international trade. They may be created by an 85% majority vote of the members based upon the membership quotas and are then allocated according to the membership quotas. (The U.S., for example, has a quota amounting to 20% of the total IMF.) SDRs are a beginning in the development of an international medium of exchange other than gold. They have been used primarily as reserves, drawn on and paid to other countries to meet deficits in the balance of payments.

SPECIALIZATION   Concentration of a firm on the production of one good or service, or concentration of a worker or work crew on one part of a good or service because of the increase in productivity associated with it. As a production process is divided into its many constituent parts and motions, labor becomes more proficient as it is specialized to each step, and possibilities for mechanization become more evident. The increased productivity from specialization and division of labor becomes the basis for mutually advantageous exchange with other people and trade with other regions and nations. See *Comparative Advantage*.

SPECIFIC TAX   A tax that is calculated as a flat amount of money per unit rather than as a percentage of value, e.g., a tax of $0.50 per pack of cigarettes or $1.00 per liter of wine. "Specific duty" is a synonym often used in reference to import and export taxes (customs duties). The amount collected by a specific tax only varies with the number of units because it is an absolute amount per unit, while the revenue from an *ad valorem* tax varies with changes in price as well as changes in number of units. See *Ad Valorem Tax*.

SPECULATION   The purchase or sale of commodities, securities, futures contracts, or options with the hope of making a profit from a favorable price change. Speculation is a form of gambling (on the future course of prices) which may have positive social consequences as well as negative ones. In agricultural commodities markets, speculators may buy in expectation of rising prices between harvest and the period just prior to the next harvest. They add to demand at a time of glut on the market and help to buoy up low prices. In the spring, before the new harvest, they sell at what they believe to be the peak of prices, so they add to supply and help to moderate high prices. Speculation thus contributes to a dampening of seasonal price fluctuations and to greater price stability for consumers. In addition to reducing seasonal price swings, speculators in futures markets provide producers with a way to avoid risks of inventory-value loss by hedging. Favorable results occur when speculators buy low and sell high, helping to stabilize a market.

Speculation may have adverse consequences when it magnifies price swings rather than reduces them, as happens when speculators enter markets on the upswing and sell on the downswing, as sometimes happens in commodities markets, securities markets, and international money markets. See *Hedging*.

SPEED-UP   Increasing the rate of output per hour by, for example, speeding up an assembly-line track or increasing the speed of individual machines. On a piece-rate pay system, it occurs as an increase in the base number of units that must be produced per hour or per shift to earn the base piece-rate of pay. It reduces the firm's cost of production when output per unit of labor increases without a corresponding increase in employee pay.

SPILLOVER BENEFITS See *External Benefits*.

SPILLOVER COSTS See *External Costs*.

SPOT MARKETS Markets for securities, currency, and commodities in which sales are for immediate delivery. In contrast, sales in futures markets (or forward markets) provide for delivery in the future as specified in the contracts, and contracts sold in options markets provide for future delivery if the option is exercised. Examples of spot markets are the New York Stock Exchange and the "wheat pit" at the Chicago Board of Trade.

SPOT PRICE The price at which a security, a currency, or a commodity is sold on a spot market. The current market price for immediate delivery of the item. Also known as "cash price."

STABILIZATION FUND Under the charter of the International Monetary Fund (IMF) each nation has established a stabilization fund used to intervene in the foreign exchange markets to stabilize the exchange rate for its currency. Originally, under the international gold standard adopted after World War II, the funds were used to stabilize exchange rates between other nations' currencies and the dollar. This stabilized their currencies relative to gold for nations with little or no gold, because the U.S. agreed to buy and sell gold to all official holders (central banks and treasuries) at $35 per ounce.

With the shift to a flexible exchange-rate system in the 1970s, the stabilization funds can be used to stabilize any exchange rate, but often that of another currency with the dollar, which has continued to serve as an international currency used by many countries for payments in trade between them.

STAGFLATION A combination of inflation with slow economic growth (or even recession) and high levels of unemployment. Normally, a low or negative rate of economic growth is accompanied by price stability or *de*flationary pressures. Stagflation is the result of a supply shock, i.e., the sharp reduction of the supply of some basic product such as oil, causing an upward spiral of prices in the face of a high level of unemployed resources. The two OPEC oil price increases in the 1970s caused stagflation during that decade.

STANDARD OF LIVING 1. The typical level of consumption of necessities and luxuries by households in a particular country. Its essence is the real consumption of goods and services, but it is necessary to use money-value figures for summary numbers and comparisons. For comparative purposes the average or median income of other countries is translated into the money of the country for which the comparison is made. For example, income in yen, pounds, and francs in Japan, Great Britain, and France is converted into dollar figures to compare the standard of living in those countries to that in the United States.

Distortion in the comparison of standards of living may occur for many reasons. In some countries, particularly less economically developed ones, a larger percentage of goods and services is produced in the household than is the case in economically developed countries. Spinning, weaving, baking, vegetable gardening, etc., for home consumption are kinds of real income that are difficult to measure, and often they are not measured or are underrepresented in the money income data of less developed countries. In other, wealthier countries these goods and services, plus house cleaning, child care, elderly care, etc., very often are purchased with money income. Another kind of distortion may arise when the value of some desirable goods does not enter the calculations because they are not produced in a country and are not imported because of trade restrictions. Distortion also may occur because consumption is an imperfect measure of well-being. People in some countries are more ascetic in outlook while people in other countries are more driven to lavish consumption.

2. Standard of living sometimes refers to the level of consumption to which a society aspires and against which actual consumption is measured.

STATE BANKS Commercial banks which are chartered under the laws of individual states and are generally subject to state rather than federal regulation. However, many state banks are members of the Bank Insurance Fund (BIF) of the Federal Deposit Insurance Corporation (FDIC) and thus become subject to federal regulation. Also, the reserve requirements of state banks became subject to Federal Reserve determination under the Depository Institutions Deregulation and Monetary Control Act of 1980 in order to strengthen the Federal Reserve's control of the money supply of the U.S. The Financial Institutions Reform, Recovery and Enforcement Act of 1989 (FIRREA) further extended federal regulation of state banks by, among other things, prohibiting their investing in below-investment-grade bonds (junk bonds). See *National Bank*.

STOCK A certificate representing a share of ownership of an incorporated firm. See *Capital Stock, Common Stock, Preferred Stock*.

STOCK INDEX The average price of a selection of common stocks listed for each time period in a time series, or the average price converted into index numbers by showing the prices for identified time periods as a percentage of the average price in a base period. The most famous index of select stocks in the U.S. is the Dow Jones Industrial Average, followed by the Standard and Poor (S & P) 500 index. Dow Jones also produces transportation, utilities, composite, and equity market indexes, while S & P has four additional stock indexes. The principle stock markets also produce composite and specialized stock indexes. There are bond indexes as well. See *Stock-Index Futures*.

STOCK-INDEX FUTURES A type of futures contract, first introduced in February of 1982, that represents the value or some multiple of the value of a stock index, such as the Standard and Poor 500. The contracts are short-term and promise a future payment based upon the value of the index at the time that the contract is written. The seller expects the index to fall between the present and the specified future time, while the buyer expects the index to rise.

   Stock-index futures are used to hedge against stock transactions on the spot market or are used for arbitrage when the futures prices depart enough from spot prices. Stock-index futures are traded on the Chicago Board of Trade and the Chicago Mercantile Exchange. See *Futures Market, Stock Index, Stock-Index Options*.

STOCK-INDEX OPTIONS Options that are based on stock indexes such as Dow Jones Industrials, the Standard and Poor 500, and the New York Stock Exchange Composite Index. See *Options Trading*.

STOCK OPTION 1. A document providing the right, but not the obligation, to purchase shares of a company's stock directly from the company during a period extending into the future but at a presently guaranteed price. If the stock's price rises on the market, the option holder can purchase the permitted quantity directly from the company at the guaranteed price and sell it on the market for a profit. Stock options often are a part of executive compensation and sometimes are made available to others as well. A broad availability of stock options to employees and stockholders has been used as a strategy to make an unfriendly takeover more expensive.

   2. Stock options traded in stock options markets. The options may be "put" options or "call" options, giving the holder the right, but not the obligation, to sell stock in the first instance, or buy in

the second instance, at a fixed price during the time period established in the option. Stock options of many hundreds of companies are traded in options markets. See *Options Trading*.

STRIKE   A concerted refusal to work by a group of employees whose purpose is to place economic pressure on their employer to accede to their demands. Strikers do not resign from their employment; they consider themselves continuing employees who temporarily are not working. A primary boycott.

A *general strike* is a concerted refusal to work by employees of many (most?) employers in a community or country. Depending upon the cause, it may include employers who cease operations (close up the shop). A general strike is used to achieve political action. See *Collective Bargaining*.

STRIPPED BOND   A bond which has had one or more coupons stripped from it and sold separately so that the bond and the coupon are treated as separate debt instruments. A zero-coupon bond is one that effectively has had all coupons stripped from it. If issued that way it is the extreme of an *original-issue discount* bond. A stripped bond or stripped coupon can be a problem for an investor if there is a long time before maturity, because they react dramatically to changes in market interest rates. See *Original-Issue Discount Security*.

STRIPPED COUPON   See *Stripped Bond*.

STRUCTURAL UNEMPLOYMENT   Unemployment which results from deficiencies in the structure of society which block adjustment to change. Structural deficiencies include (1) the geographical immobility of labor or business, so that unemployed people and expanding businesses are not brought together; (2) a continuing lack of knowledge about job opportunities or about labor availability; (3) a lack of skill or training for jobs that are available; (4) monopolistic restraints on output, hence employment; (5) exclusion of persons from jobs because of race, national origin, sex, or other characteristics not related to ability to do the job; or, (6) exclusion of persons from jobs by action of a union or professional association in order to support the income of incumbent membership.

Structural unemployment is different from cyclical unemployment, which is characterized by periodic insufficient aggregate demand for goods and services (i.e., consumer demand, business investment demand for capital goods, government demand, and net exports). Another category, frictional unemployment, occurs because adjustments to change are not instantaneous, even when they are not prevented from happening by structural defects. The focus of policies to correct cyclical unemployment has been on the demand side, with attempts to affect the components of aggregate demand, while supply-side policies are needed to affect structural and frictional unemployment. See *Unemployment, Frictional Unemployment, Involuntary Unemployment.*

SUBSIDY 1. A payment to a business to help offset a low margin between costs of production and the market price. A subsidy is an alternative to setting a price floor higher than the free-market price, and it avoids the problem created by a price floor of what to do with the supply surplus. Subsidies often are found in agriculture to support domestic production and the income of farmers, who frequently are a politically powerful group. Subsidies also may be used to spur exports or to protect infant industries from foreign competition.

2. A payment to a household or on behalf of a household to provide greater consumption of a product than the market price would permit. Food stamps and subsidized housing are examples.

See *Countervailing Duties, Deficiency Payment, Price Support.*

SUBSTITUTE GOODS If two goods are substitutes, a change in the price of one, *cet. par.,* will cause the demand curve of the other to shift in the same direction. An increase in the price of *x* will result in a smaller quantity of *x* demanded and an increase in the entire demand curve for *y* as *y* is substituted for *x*. The cross-elasticity-of-demand coefficient is positive. Chicken and turkey are examples of very close substitutes, while chicken and pork are more distant substitutes. Some substitutes, such as beef and lentils, are not in the same food class; others, such as a fur coat and an automobile, may be in different general categories. See *Cross Elasticity, Complementary Goods.*

SUBSTITUTION EFFECT If the price of a product rises, *cet. par.,* the quantity demanded tends to decrease because it becomes more expensive relative to the whole array of other products that might be purchased instead.

There also may be an income effect from a price change. In so far as the product had been purchased regularly and some quantity will continue to be bought, the price increase is similar to an income reduction which would result in less of this product being purchased (and less of other products, too). See *Income Effect: Price Theory.*

SUPERMULTIPLIER A multiplier applied to GNP which combines
the responsiveness of investment expenditure to changes in GNP
with the responsiveness of consumption expenditure to changes in
GNP.

The simple multiplier shows that induced consumption expenditure (expressed as the marginal propensity to consume) will cause
growth of GNP by some multiple of an initial increase in GNP.

$$\text{Multiplier} = \frac{1}{1 - MPC} = \frac{1}{MPS}$$

where MPC is the marginal propensity to consume, MPS is the
marginal propensity to save, and $MPC + MPS = 1$.

Investment expenditure as a function of GNP is expressed as
the marginal propensity to invest, or MPI. Adding this to the simple
multiplier increases the multiplied effect.

$$\text{Supermultiplier} = \frac{1}{(1 - MPC) - MPI} = \frac{1}{MPS - MPI}$$

See *Gross National Product Multiplier*.

SUPER NOW ACCOUNTS Checking accounts that earn a higher
rate of interest than an ordinary NOW account and in return require
that a higher minimum amount be held on deposit. See *Negotiable
Order of Withdrawal*.

SUPPLY 1. In economics usage, the relationship between quantities
of a good or service willingly offered for sale by a firm or firms (or
by owners of factors of production) and prices of that good or
service. Supply usually is expressed as a schedule or curve relating
quantities supplied to various possible prices, other factors affecting
supply remaining unchanged. Supply is a series of possibilities, only
one of which may actually occur at one point in time as a quantity
supplied at a market price. A *change in supply* is represented as a
shift in the entire schedule or curve, while a *change in quantity
supplied* is shown as a move from one point to another on a supply
curve or schedule. Supply data is combined with demand data to
define the equilibrium output and price for a firm and a market.

2. In common usage, supply may mean a schedule or curve but
usually means the amount offered at the going price. See *Supply
Curve, Supply Schedule, Supply Function, Equilibrium of the Firm,
Equilibrium of the Market*.

SUPPLY CURVE A curve illustrating how quantity supplied changes
as price changes, *ceteris paribus*. A supply curve is illustrated in

panel A below. It shows a *change in quantity supplied* as a move from a to b along the supply curve following a change of price from P_1 to P_2. This curve slopes upward to the right, illustrating that higher prices bring forth larger quantities supplied. It could apply to a firm's supply of a product, or to a factor owner's supply of a productive factor, or to the whole market supply of either a product or a factor. See *Market Supply Curve*.

The curves in panel B illustrate a *change in supply*, i.e., a shift of the entire curve following some change in circumstances other than a change in price of the product, such as the introduction of a new, more efficient machine or a reduction in the price of a raw material.

In a market of pure competition, the firm's supply curve is its

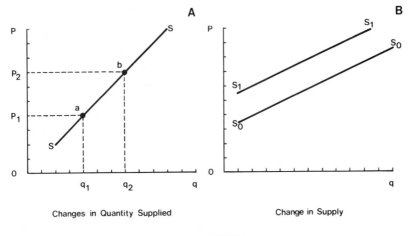

SUPPLY CURVES

marginal cost curve (MC), but only that portion of MC which is rising and lies above the average variable cost curve. If price should slightly more than cover the extra cost of producing another unit (its marginal cost), the firm will gain by producing it so long as the price at least covers the unit's variable cost. If price does not cover AVC, the firm is better off to shut down and absorb the fixed cost rather than having variable cost to absorb as well. The market supply curve in pure competition is the horizontal sum of the marginal cost curves of the firms in the market.

A monopolist firm does not have a supply curve because it sets price as well as quantity supplied. It will produce where marginal cost equals marginal revenue (MR), but marginal revenue does not equal price, so the intersection of MC with various possible MRs will not trace out a supply curve (which is a relation between P and Q, not MR and Q). See *Supply, Supply Function, Supply Schedule, Marginal Cost, Equilibrium of the Firm.*

SUPPLY FUNCTION 1. A mathematical expression relating quantities of a product supplied to those elements which affect quantity supplied.

$$S_x = f(P_x, I - O, P_F)$$

where x is the product, S is the quantity supplied, f is the functional relationship, $I - O$ is the technical relationship between the inputs of factor of production and output of the product, and P_F stands for the prices of the factors of production. A supply curve or schedule is projected on the assumption that $I - O$ and P_F do not change, so that S_x varies with changes in P_x, i.e., $S_x = f(P_x)$ *cet. par.*

2. A mathematical expression relating quantities of a factor of production supplied to those elements affecting the quantity supplied. For example, a supply function for labor might be stated as $S_l = f(W, Z, T, P_n)$ where S_l is the quantity of labor supplied, W is the price of labor (the wage), Z is the preference for leisure, T is the tastes and preferences for consumable goods and services, and P_n stands for the prices of consumable goods and services. A supply curve or schedule is projected on the assumption that preference for leisure and tastes for consumables and their prices do not change, so that $S_l = f(W)$ *cet. par.* See *Supply, Supply Curve, Supply Schedule.*

SUPPLY OF MONEY 1. The supply of money to hold; the money stock. It is determined by Federal Reserve policy, which causes the quantity of the money stock to expand or contract in accordance with the money multiplier. For definitions of the money stock, see *M, M1, M2, M3.* This is the concept of money supply used in Keynesian national income analysis considering the relationship between the supply of money and its price, the interest rate.

Under an international gold standard, the stock of money in a country will vary with the inflow and outflow of gold, unless the monetary authority pursues a monetary policy to counteract it.

2. The supply of money to use; the supply of loanable funds. It is determined by the willingness of lenders (households, businesses, insurance companies, pension funds, banks) to make their funds available to borrowers (households, businesses, governments). The willingness to lend, in turn, depends upon the interest rate (which is the price of money), expectations about future interest rates, the state of the economy, and government policy changes. The supply

of loanable funds and the demand for loanable funds determine the quantity of funds and the price (interest rate). See *Demand for Money, Money Multiplier, Money Stock, Loanable Funds Theory of Interest.*

SUPPLY SCHEDULE A numerical representation of the relationship between quantities supplied and prices per unit, *cet. par.* As explained under *Supply Function,* a supply schedule for goods assumes that the input–output relations of production and the prices of factors of production are given. A supply schedule for labor as a factor of production assumes that the preference for leisure remains constant and that the tastes and preferences for consumables and their prices do not change. The focus is on quantity supplied and price. An example of a supply schedule is as follows:

P	Q
$1	100
2	200
3	300
4	390
5	475

See *Supply, Supply Curve.*

SUPPLY-SIDE ECONOMICS A focus on variables that affect the supply of goods and services rather than on demand, in a search for policies to stabilize the economy. Supply-siders are particularly concerned with tax reforms, regulatory reforms, and other policies to stimulate supply by promoting savings, work effort, education and training, investment in plant and equipment, etc. Attention to the supply side is a reaction to what many consider to be an overemphasis on the demand side by Keynesians and neo-Keynesians.

The Laffer Curve, illustrating a particular relationship between tax revenue and tax rates, is a supply-side concept which some economists thought was relevant to the U.S. economy of the 1970s, while others scoffed (laffed?). See *Laffer Curve.*

SUPPORT PRICE A price floor for a product or service which is set above the market price. See *Price Support, Commodity Credit Corporation, Countervailing Duties, Nonrecourse Loan.*

SWEATSHOP A business that violates labor laws or health and safety codes. A firm that pays low wages, often on a piece-rate system that results in wages below the legal minimum wage, and or a firm that ignores fire hazards such as blocked fire exits or countenances illegal exposure to chemicals.

SYMPATHY STRIKE A strike by a union that does not have an immediate dispute with its employer but uses a strike against its employer to express "sympathy" to another union that is already out on strike.

TACIT COLLUSION Collusion among firms that are rivals in a market, based upon such things as a common understanding of the firms' interrelatedness and a common availability of data about the state of the market. Tacit collusion may involve holding prices rather than cutting them, or following a price increase by one firm, when rivalry might suggest opposite actions. It is as illegal as collusion based upon *overt* agreements to pursue a common policy, but much more difficult to prove. Individual firms in a market may act the same because the actions are sensible and logical responses to interdependence rather than because of tacit collusion.

TAKEOVER The act of taking complete control of a firm through the purchase of all outstanding stock. In the 1970s and 1980s, the group pursuing the takeover usually financed their purchases by issuing "junk bonds" with the help of brokerage firms such as Drexel Burnham Lambert and other takeover specialists. A takeover target may be a firm which is a "cash cow," i.e., a firm that generates large amounts of cash that could help the liquidity of another firm taking it over and make payment of interest on the junk bonds relatively easy. Another characteristic target is a firm whose stock is undervalued in terms of a low price/earnings ratio or undervalued relative to the net assets of the firm.

A friendly takeover is one initiated by incumbent management, with the takeover group consisting either of those current managers or a group friendly to them and their way of managing the company.

An unfriendly takeover involves an outside group that is critical of management and would throw the bums out.

The great takeover splurge of the 1980s has been criticized for creating excesses of indebtedness in firms taken over and for the wave of bankruptcies that began in 1990. Many of the takeover mergers made no economic sense but did create huge profits for the attorneys and the brokers that managed the takeovers. Some takeovers, however, have been praised for shaking up stodgy, overstaffed management and turning the companies into lean, competitive profit maximizers. See *Golden Parachute, Greenmail, Junk Bonds, Leveraged Buyout.*

TARGET PRICE   A price set periodically by the U.S. Department of Agriculture under Congressional direction for subsidized crops such as wheat, corn, rice, and cotton. If the average market price falls below the target price, a deficiency payment is made to each farmer enrolled in the program. Before each crop year, farmers must elect whether to enter the program and, if they do, each must adhere to acreage restrictions on the crop, restrictions on the use of set-aside acres, etc. Target prices are part of a subsidy program to protect farmers' income as opposed to a price-support program. See *Deficiency Payment, Price Support, Subsidy.*

TARIFF   A tax levied on a product when it is imported. The usual purpose of a tariff is to protect domestic producers from foreign competition, although in the nineteenth century tariffs were passed to provide a major source of income for the federal government. Protection and income are relatively incompatible goals because goods must be imported in order to produce tariff revenue. To reduce or eliminate imports the tax would need to be large enough to raise the effective price of the imported product above the price of a comparable domestic product. For the long run, the import price plus tariff would need to exceed domestic cost of production plus a normal return on capital investment or the domestic producers would go out of business.

Some argue that protective tariffs are needed in industries such as autos, steel, and textiles to prevent serious unemployment problems. It is true that, as domestic industries decline because of foreign competition, the unemployed resources may not quickly and easily shift to other employment. While specialized machines may sit and rust, and ownership shares lose value, the principal burden is borne by the workers who must be retrained and/or relocated to find alternative employment. Workers also bear substantial psychic costs in the loss of established relationships on the job, the loss of a market for one's skills and the prospect of starting over again at the bottom of the ladder and, if relocation is necessary, the loss of close contact with family, old neighbors, and familiar neighborhoods. When a large plant closes, myriad local service businesses also may fail as worker spending dries up. Since free trade provides a widespread economic benefit to society, it may properly be argued that when tariffs are reduced or eliminated, the economic cost of retraining and relocation should be borne broadly by society rather than just the unemployed workers and their communities.

Economists generally oppose protective tariffs as an interference with the efficient allocation of resources through mutually advantageous trade, although they do recognize that infant industries may need protection until they have time to achieve economies of scale. See *Quota, Peril-Point Tariff, Infant Industry: Tariff Protection.*

TAX INCIDENCE The place where the burden of a tax finally comes to rest after any forward shifting to customers or backward shifting to suppliers from the point at which the tax is levied. Identification of the incidence is complex. In the simplest example, if a per-unit

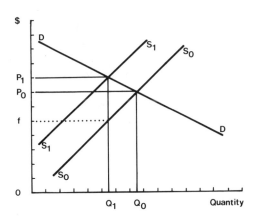

TAX INCIDENCE: A PER-UNIT TAX

excise tax is levied against the manufacturers of a product in pure competition, the market supply curve S_0S_0 in the accompanying figure will shift up vertically by the amount of the tax to S_1S_1. The amount of the tax is fP_1. The proportion of the tax burden on the sellers is fP_0, while the burden on buyers is the price increase, P_0P_1. Division of the incidence between seller and buyer depends upon the price elasticity of demand and the price elasticity of supply. The more *elastic* the demand, the greater the sales loss and the less the price increase, so the larger the portion of the tax that will be absorbed by sellers rather than passed on to buyers. Likewise, the more *inelastic* the initial supply curve, the more the incidence of the tax will fall on the sellers.

TAX MULTIPLIER   The amount by which one must multiply a change in taxes to determine the total resulting change in GNP. An increase in income taxes may cause a multiplied decrease in GNP, first because of the reduced consumption expenditure (C) as a percentage of the income taken away in taxes (according to the marginal propensity to consume, MPC), and then because of the continuing sequence of consumption expenditure reductions as the MPC works on successive reductions in income. The rationale is that a reduction in aggregate consumption expenditure following the tax increase will increase inventories and reduce orders for inventory replacement, which will reduce output and the income associated with that output, hence another reduction in consumption, and so on. An increase in excise taxes also reduces consumption expenditure by its effect on producers' income as well as buyers' income according to the incidence of the tax.

Unlike changes in investment expenditure or government expenditure, the initial effect on GNP will not be the entire amount of the tax because it occurs through the effect of the tax on income, thence on consumption according to the MPC, and the MPC is less than 1. (In contrast, the initial effect of a change in investment expenditure or government expenditure on GNP is the *entire* amount of that change because the entire amount was income generating.) An increase in taxes will decrease saving as well as consumption, and a reduction in taxes will increase saving as well as consumption. So the tax multiplier is not as potent as the investment multiplier or the government multiplier in its effect on GNP through consumer demand. (However, the effect of taxes on incentives may increase its potency on the supply side.) Note that in the equation below the numerator is not 1, as it would be for the I or G multiplier, but rather it is MPC, which is less than 1.

$$M_t = - MPC \times \frac{1}{1 - MPC} = - \frac{MPC}{MPS}$$

where M_t is the tax multiplier, *MPC* is the marginal propensity to consume, and *MPS* is the marginal propensity to save (which is $1 - MPC$). Note also that the tax multiplier is negative because an increase in taxes reduces GNP and a reduction in taxes increases GNP. See *Gross National Product Multiplier*.

TAX SHIFTING See *Tax Incidence*.

TECHNOLOGICAL CHANGE The introduction of new products, new kinds of machines, new arrangements of production such as the assembly line, and generally new ways of doing things in the economic process. It is the main driving force of economic growth. See *Entrepreneurship, Innovation, Technological Unemployment*.

TECHNOLOGICAL UNEMPLOYMENT Unemployment caused by technological change. A new technology may affect the relationship among factors of production and their output and, therefore, the demand for a factor. It may stimulate employment in the production of new products and new machines. An example is the development of assembly-line production that made labor more efficient and permitted Henry Ford to raise wages to attract more workers, while at the same time profits rose and the price of automobiles fell. Buggy-whip makers and farriers, however, lost employment with the advent of the railroad and the automobile.

A new machine may eliminate the demand for the skill of a group of workers, causing unemployment and reducing their wages when they are reemployed at a less skilled job. Employment will tend to expand in the industry that manufactures the new machines, and the price of the product or service may fall for consumers, but that is little consolation for those who lose employment and whose skill is no longer valuable.

Technological change usually is labor saving and may be capital saving. The problem is to speed the reallocation of resources from the old to the new with a minimum of pain. For workers from the replaced product or process, that means help to retrain or relocate them to take advantage of expanding employment opportunities where those exist. See *Unemployment, Frictional Unemployment, Structural Unemployment*.

TERMS OF TRADE The ratio of export prices to import prices. An improvement in the terms of trade occurs when export prices rise relative to import prices. When the price of oil on the world market went from $4 per barrel in 1973 to $24 in 1980, the terms of trade moved strongly in favor of the OPEC countries, because the world prices for OPEC country *imports* rose at a much slower pace.

A slump in export prices relative to import prices will turn the terms of trade unfavorable. However, in rare cases a country may be such an important buyer of a product in world trade that a shift in its demand curve will affect price. If so the importing country may gain by imposing a tariff on that product, which would affect total demand sufficiently to press down the product price. The import tax is shifted, at least in part, to the foreign producers. This discussion indicates that it is *change* in the terms of trade that counts, so the terms of trade often are shown in index number form. See *Exchange Rate*.

THRIFTS   Savings institutions such as mutual savings banks and savings and loan associations. Historically they have collected savings from the public in interest-bearing savings deposits and time deposits and made home mortgage loans. Savings banks have had somewhat broader asset authority than S & L's, including consumer loans as well as mortgages. Following deregulation in 1980, thrifts have been permitted to offer interest-bearing transactions accounts (checking accounts) that are called negotiable order of withdrawal (NOW) accounts and money market deposit accounts which have a limit on the number of checks that can be written and whose interest varies in proportion to changes in the federal money market rates. On the asset side, thrifts are now able to make construction loans to builders, a limited number of commercial loans, and a limited number of personal loans. By the end of the decade a very large number of thrifts (although a minority of the total) became insolvent because of mismanagement of their new powers. See *Savings and Loan Association, Savings Bank, Federal Home Loan Bank System*.

TIED AID   An arrangement in which one country makes gifts or loans to another country with the stipulation that some or all of the goods be purchased in the country offering the aid and that some or all be carried in the donor country's ships. If the donor country's prices were relatively low the purchases would be made there and tied aid would be unnecessary. When it is used, then, the clear implication is that the amount of aid is less because of relatively high donor prices. Domestic producers and shippers gain at the expense of those receiving the aid.

TIME DEPOSIT   Also known as certificate of deposit (CD). A deposit in a commercial bank, savings bank, or savings and loan association which is made for a specified time at an interest rate which varies with the term of the deposit and its size. There are penalties for early withdrawal of funds in the deposit. Most of these deposits (those under $100,000) are nonnegotiable. Those over $100,000 (usually over $1,000,000) may be negotiable. See *Certificate of Deposit, Savings Deposit.*

TIME SERIES A statistical sequence of numbers measuring a variable over time. When shown on a chart, the variable amounts are measured on the vertical axis and units of time are measured on the horizontal axis.

TOTAL COST (TC) 1. The sum of total fixed cost and total variable cost in a business enterprise. 2. In the long run there are no fixed costs—all are variable—so total cost equals total variable cost. Total cost is subtracted from total revenue to determine the profit of a firm for a period of time. 3. Economists will impute implicit costs of wages, interest, and rent (which a firm may not include in total cost) to produce a total cost figure which must be covered by total revenue if the firm is to maintain the flow of resources to it over the long run. See *Implicit Costs, Imputed Costs, Opportunity Cost, Total Fixed Cost, Total Variable Cost.*

TOTAL COST CURVE A curve illustrating how total cost changes as output of a firm changes. The curve below is a short-run curve because there are fixed costs.

In the figure, total cost is measured from zero on the vertical axis. That portion of total cost that consists of fixed cost is shown by the amount from zero vertically to the TFC line. Total fixed cost is the same for each level of output by definition. The total variable cost curve is then added vertically to total fixed cost to illustrate total cost.

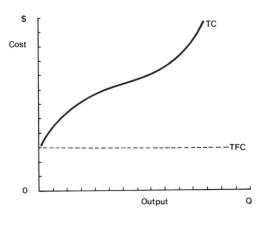

TOTAL COST CURVE

The shape of the total cost curve above the fixed cost portion is the shape of the total variable cost curve, which in turn draws its shape from the Law of Diminishing Returns. It has been added vertically to the total fixed cost curve. See *Total Variable Cost Curve, Total Fixed Cost, Diminishing Returns, Average Cost.*

TOTAL FIXED COST (TFC) The sum of all those costs that exist even if output is zero, and which do not vary with changes in output. Their existence defines the period under consideration as the short run. An example of fixed cost is the depreciation cost of a firm's factory building.

TOTAL FIXED COST CURVE A curve illustrating total fixed cost (TFC) as output changes. Since it exists when output is zero and does not change with output, the TFC curve is a straight horizontal line beginning on the vertical cost axis at the amount of TFC, as shown in the figure below.
See *Average Fixed Cost Curve, Total Cost.*

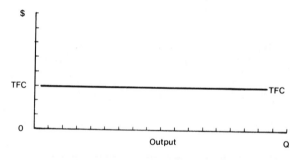

TOTAL FIXED COST CURVE

TOTAL PRODUCT (TP) CURVE A curve depicting how output changes as the quantity of variable inputs changes. In the long run all inputs are variable, while in the short run some inputs are fixed. The TP curve is a short-run concept and takes its shape from the Law of Diminishing Returns. As more and more units of a variable factor of production are added to a given quantity of fixed factors, a point will be reached where the addition to total output will begin to diminish. From that point on each additional unit of the variable factor will add less to output than the preceding unit did.

Prior to that point there may be increasing returns because the fixed factors will have very little of the variable factor to work with, and each added unit of the variable factor will add more to output than the previous unit as the proportion of variable to fixed factors becomes more productive.

Eventually, more units of the variable factor will cause output to decline, a situation of negative returns. One can readily imagine adding more and more pounds of fertilizer (the variable factor) to an acre of wheat and reaching the point where additions of fertilizer burn some of the wheat.

In the figure below, increasing returns occur as the quantity of the variable factor increases up to y_1 of the variable factor, after which additions of the variable factor produce diminishing returns. Point t on the curve identifies the transition from increasing returns to diminishing returns. The TP curve would turn down when the point of negative returns is reached. Total output declines when more of the variable factor is added.

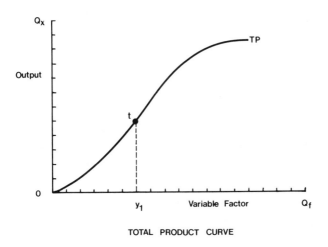

TOTAL PRODUCT CURVE

TOTAL REVENUE (TR) The quantity sold multiplied by price per unit of output. $TR = P \times Q$. See *Total Revenue Curve*.

TOTAL REVENUE CURVE A curve illustrating the possible total revenue (TR) of a firm for a range of outputs in a given demand situation. In pure competition the firm can sell all it can produce at the going market price, so the total revenue curve is a straight line from the origin. If nothing is sold, TR is zero, and each additional unit sold will increase total revenue by its price. This TR curve is illustrated in panel A below.

A firm that has market power in a market that is not purely competitive, such as monopoly, monopolistic competition, or oligopoly, will find that it has to reduce price in order to increase sales, so its TR curve will rise at a decreasing rate. The slope of the curve will become negative when, to sell another unit, the necessary price reduction on all previous units will total more than the new price of the additional unit. Such a TR curve is illustrated in panel B below.

See *Marginal Revenue Curve.*

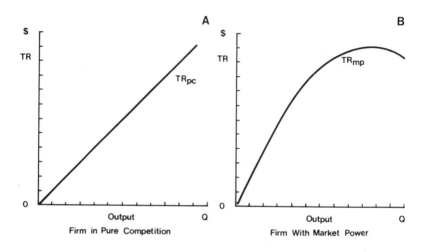

TOTAL REVENUE CURVES

TOTAL REVENUE PRODUCT (TRP) The total revenue from the output attributable to a particular quantity of a variable factor of production. To decide how much of a variable factor to employ, a firm wants to know what revenue can be attributed to each additional unit of the variable factor (its marginal revenue product, MRP) as well as its cost. MRP is the change in TRP when the quantity of the variable factor is changed by one unit. TRP is found by multiplying the *total product* for each quantity of the variable factor by the price per unit of the product. See *Total Product, Total Revenue Product Curve, Marginal Revenue Product.*

TOTAL REVENUE PRODUCT CURVE A curve illustrating how total revenue to the firm changes as the quantity of a variable factor of production changes. (The *total revenue curve*, on the other hand, shows how total revenue changes as the *quantity of output* changes.) The total revenue product curve resembles the total product curve because TRP is the product of TP times the price per unit of output.

In the figure below, TRP is measured on the vertical axis and the quantity of the variable factor of production is measured on the horizontal axis.

See *Total Product Curve, Marginal Revenue Product.*

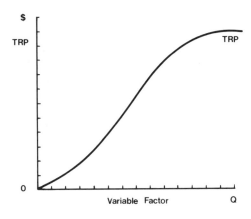

TOTAL REVENUE PRODUCT CURVE

TOTAL UTILITY The total satisfaction from the consumption of a quantity of a good in a given time period. Its role in economics is to serve as the base for developing the concept of marginal utility in the theory of consumer demand. See *Marginal Utility.*

TOTAL VARIABLE COST (TVC) The sum of all those costs which vary with changes in output. TVC is zero at zero output because a firm producing nothing would not employ any variable factors of production. Use of the term, total *variable* cost, implies that there are fixed costs as well, so this is a short-run concept. TVC is derived from the Total Product relationship between output and variable factor inputs, and it changes according to the Law of Diminishing Returns as output increases. See *Total Variable Cost Curve* for an illustrated explanation.

TOTAL VARIABLE COST CURVE A curve which illustrates how total variable cost changes as output changes. It is derived from the total product curve (TP) which illustrates how output changes as the quantity of variable factors changes. If we look at this relationship from a different angle by reversing the axes from those shown in Illustration 53 we would illustrate how the quantity of variable factors changes as output changes. Then we can multiply the quantity of variable factors at each particular level of output by the price per unit of the variable factors and arrive at total variable cost for each level of output.

In panel A below, the TP curve is shown with output on the horizontal axis rather than on the customary vertical axis (see the *Total Product Curve* entry), while the quantity of the variable factor is shown on the vertical axis. With this reversal of axes, the shape of the *Total Variable Cost* curve can be recognized in the *Total Product Curve*. In panel B below, TVC starts at the origin, increases at a diminishing rate up to point *t*, and then increases at an increasing rate as each added unit of the variable factors adds less to output than the previous unit. Diminishing returns translate into increasing costs as more of the variable factors are required per unit of output.

See *Total Product Curve, Average Variable Cost Curve, Total Cost*.

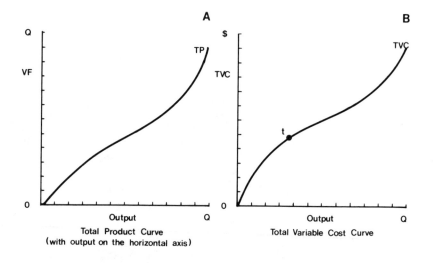

SOURCE OF A TOTAL VARIABLE COST CURVE

TRADE PROTECTION Discrimination against the importation of foreign goods in favor of domestic products. It may take the form of tariffs, quotas, exchange controls, or legal and administrative rules affecting imports such as elaborate and time-consuming inspections. See *Protectionism*.

TRADITION-DIRECTED SOCIETY A society whose economic choices of what to produce, how to produce it, and for whom are made by following patterns established by prior generations. The technology of a tradition-directed society is based on "rule of thumb," with skills passed on from father to son and mother to daughter. Economic relationships are closely intertwined with social relationships and subsidiary to them. Change occurs very slowly. Examples of tradition-directed societies are ancient China, ancient Greece, Medieval Europe, and the primitive societies studied by anthropologists.

TRANSACTION ACCOUNTS Checking accounts in depository institutions, excluding those which limit check writing to no more than three per month.

More precisely, "transaction accounts include all deposits on which the account holder is permitted to make withdrawals by negotiable or transferable instruments, payment orders of withdrawal, and telephone and preauthorized transfers in excess of three per month for the purpose of making payments to third persons or others. However, MMDAs and similar accounts subject to the rules that permit no more than six preauthorized, automatic, or other transfers per month of which no more than three can be checks, are not transaction accounts (such accounts are savings deposits)" (*Federal Reserve Bulletin,* January 1991, **77,** A8).

TRANSACTIONS VELOCITY OF THE CIRCULATION OF MONEY The rate at which the stock of money turns over per year to carry on transactions between buyers and sellers. It includes all GNP transactions plus all of the payments for intermediate goods that were eliminated in calculating the value of all *final* goods and services in the economy (GNP). $V_T = T/M$, where V_T is the transactions velocity, T is the volume of transactions, and M is the money stock. It is a concept used in some quantity theories of money and prices. See *Income Velocity of the Circulation of Money.*

TRANSFER PAYMENTS Payments which transfer income to people without there being a contribution to the current production of goods and services in return. They include such private payments as gifts and allowances where there is no *quid pro quo*. Government expenditures such as Social Security benefits, unemployment insurance payments to the unemployed, welfare payments, farm subsidies, and interest on the federal debt are all transfer payments. Some represent drawing down funds created by past contributions to production. But when trying to aggregate the value of transactions to arrive at the gross national product for a year, it is important *not* to count payments which merely transfer income from some to others to one side of the production process.

TREASURY BILLS (T BILLS)   Short-term marketable obligations of the U.S. Treasury with maturities of 13, 26, or 52 weeks from the date of issue. Treasury bills are sold at auction in minimum denominations of $10,000. See *Treasury Bonds, Treasury Notes, Treasury Securities.*

TREASURY BONDS   Long-term marketable certificates of indebtedness issued by the U. S. Treasury which mature in 30 years from the date of issue. (They have been issued at other times for shorter maturities such as 20 years.) Treasury bonds are sold at auction in minimum denominations of $10,000. See *Treasury Bills, Treasury Notes, Treasury Securities, Government Bonds.*

TREASURY NOTES   Intermediate-term marketable obligations of the U.S. Treasury which are issued to mature in from 2 to 10 years (currently 2, 3, 5, 7, and 10 years). Treasury notes are sold at auction in minimum denominations of $10,000. Treasury notes fall between Treasury bills and Treasury bonds in maturity. See *Treasury Bills, Treasury Bonds, Treasury Securities.*

TREASURY SECURITIES   Marketable obligations of the U.S. Treasury which include Treasury bills, notes, and bonds. Treasury obligations are safe investments in that the federal government can always pay them off, if not with funds from taxes, then by reborrowing (or even printing money since the national government controls the money supply). To pay off maturing securities, either taxing or borrowing will affect the nation's economy and the *current market value* of negotiable Treasury securities that are not maturing. However funded, the security holder will be paid in full at maturity. No other security carries such strong assurance against default.

Because negotiable Treasury obligations may experience a fall in market price prior to maturity, they do contain some risk if the need should arise to sell them before maturity. Another risk is that repayment at maturity may be in dollars whose purchasing power has declined because of inflation. If the inflation were anticipated by the market at the time the securities were issued, this risk would be compensated by a higher interest rate. See *Treasury Bills, Treasury Bonds, Treasury Notes, Government Bonds.*

TRUST   1. In general usage, a legal arrangement which provides for a *trustee* to hold assets provided by the creator of the trust for the benefit of another and to administer them according to the terms of the trust. See *Irrevocable Trust, Revocable Trust.* 2. In business, the allocation of asset control by two or more firms to a group of trustees who then would manage the affairs of the group to the advantage of the owners. Control typically would be provided by turning over a controlling amount of voting stock. A trust was a form of market control used in the nineteenth century to avoid common-law prohibitions of conspiracy in restraint of trade by two or more competitors. The word *trust* came to stand for any giant business or arrangement among firms involving substantial control of an industry. Antitrust legislation has been enacted to try to prohibit such arrangements. See *Antitrust*.

UNCERTAINTY A situation in which the statistical probabilities of outcomes cannot be predicted and therefore cannot be insured against (as opposed to *risk,* which is insurable). It is one of the considerations that leads people to prefer to have a sum of money (purchasing power) now rather than to receive it in the future. Consequently, it is one cause for the existence of interest, which is a payment for giving up present control over a sum of money in exchange for future repayment. See *Interest, Risk.*

UNDERDEVELOPED COUNTRIES See *Less Developed Countries.*

UNDERGROUND ECONOMY Neither a mining nor a science-fiction community, but rather the scope of economic activity that is unreported in GNP and other data, untaxed where taxable, and usually illegal. The illegal drug trade in the U.S. amounts to billions of dollars and is a major example of transactions in the underground economy of the United States. Black-market products exchanged outside of a rationing system are a common part of the underground economy of many countries and go unreported in official statistics. The sale of term papers to procrastinating college students is a small part of the underground economy that is unreported and unethical, if not illegal.

UNDERWRITER 1. An investment firm which, alone or in concert, undertakes the sale of new issues of stock by purchasing them for resale or by guaranteeing the price for an underwriter's fee.

2. An insurance firm acting as guarantor (insurer) for a risky venture.

UNEARNED INCOME Income other than compensation for one's labor, such as income in the form of rent, interest, dividends, or profits. Unearned income is an income distinction made by many social reformers who believe it should flow to the state, representing all citizens, rather than being paid to individual owners. It also is an income distinction made by the U.S. Internal Revenue Service (strange bedfellows!) in its income tax regulations. The designation makes supporters of the concept of private property irate because "unearned" appears to be synonymous with "undeserved." See *Earned Income*.

UNEMPLOYMENT Productive resources that are not being used. Land and capital goods standing idle and people out of work. Usually the term refers to *involuntary* unemployment of resources: idle land and capital goods which the owners would prefer to be used but are not, and people who are not at work but are actively seeking work. For official statistics measuring unemployment in the labor force, the unemployed are people who are 16 years of age or older, who are actively seeking work, and who are ready and willing to accept going wages on jobs for which they are qualified, but who cannot find jobs.

Voluntary unemployment of land and capital goods occurs when the owners decide to hold them off the market. Voluntary unemployment of people occurs when those 16 years of age or older are doing other things, such as being a student or a homemaker, which they prefer to being in the labor force. See *Full Employment, Labor Force*.

UNFAIR LABOR PRACTICES Specified actions of employers or unions that are prohibited as interference with the rights of workers, employers, and the public.

The National Labor Relations Act of 1935 (Wagner Act), Section 8, prohibits certain *employer* actions as unfair labor practices. It is an unfair labor practice for employers:

1. To interfere with, restrain, or coerce employees in the exercise of the rights guaranteed in Section 7, which states that "Employees shall have the right to self-organization, to form, join or assist labor organizations, to bargain collectively through representatives of their own choosing, and to engage in concerted activities, for the purpose of collective bargaining or other mutual aid or protection;"

2. To dominate or interfere with the formation or administration of any labor organization or to contribute financial or other support to it;

3. By discrimination in regard to hire or tenure of employment or any term or condition of employment to encourage or discourage membership in any labor organization;

4. To discharge or otherwise discriminate against an employee because he has filed charges or given testimony under the Act;

5. To refuse to bargain collectively with the duly designated representatives of his employees.

The Labor–Management Relations Act of 1947 (Taft–Hartley Act) amended Section 7 of the Wagner Act to add that employees "shall also have the right to refrain from any or all such activities except to the extent that such right may be affected by" a valid union security clause. The Act prohibits unfair labor practices on the part of *labor unions*. It is an unfair labor practice for a labor organization or its agents:

1. To restrain or coerce employees in the exercise of their rights in Section 7 of the Wagner Act as amended above; or to impair the right of an employer in the selection of *his* representatives for the purposes of collective bargaining or the adjustment of grievances.

2. To cause, or attempt to cause, an employer to discriminate against an employee for membership or nonmembership in a labor organization except where a valid union security clause is in effect. A valid union security clause can only be enforced against an employee for nonpayment of dues or initiation fees uniformly required as a condition of acquiring or retaining membership.

3. To refuse to bargain collectively with an employer, provided it is the duly certified representative of his employees.

4. To engage in, or to induce or encourage the employees of any employer to engage in, a strike or a concerted refusal to use, manufacture, process, transport, work, or handle goods where the object is:

   a. To force an employer or self-employed person to join any labor or employer organization,

   b. To force or require any person to cease dealing in the products of any other producer or doing business with any other person, or to force or require any other employer to recognize or bargain with an uncertified union.

   c. To force or require an employer to recognize or bargain with a particular labor organization as the representative of his employees if another union is the certified bargaining agent.

    d. To force or require an employer to assign particular work to employees in a particular labor organization or trade, craft, or class rather than to employees in another union, trade, craft, or class.

    5. To require employees covered by a union security clause to pay membership fees which the National Labor Relations Board finds excessive or discriminatory under all circumstances.

    6. To cause or attempt to cause an employer to pay or deliver or agree to pay or deliver any money or other thing of value, in the nature of an exaction, for services not performed or not to be performed. See *Featherbedding*.

UNFAVORABLE BALANCE OF TRADE A situation in which the value of a country's merchandise imports exceeds the value of its merchandise exports. It is a designation held over from mercantilist thought of the sixteenth and seventeenth centuries. A more neutral term is "trade deficit." See *Balance of Trade, Favorable Balance of Trade, Mercantilism*.

UNFRIENDLY TAKEOVER See *Takeover*.

UNION See *Labor Union*.

UNION SECURITY MEASURE Any clause in a collective bargaining contract that protects the position of the union, such as a union shop clause which requires newly hired employees to become union members shortly after being hired, or a union dues check-off clause which assures payment of union dues because the employer agrees to deduct union dues prior to payment of wages and transfers the amount to the union.

UNION SHOP A clause in a collective bargaining contract which provides that all employees covered by the agreement must belong to the union. New employees must join the union within a specified time after being hired (often 60–90 days) in order to continue being employed. A union shop clause is considered a union security or maintenance-of-membership measure. Right-to-work legislation enacted by a few states is directed at the union shop in particular. It seeks to establish a "right to work" without union membership being a requirement for continued employment. A union shop differs from a closed shop, which requires that a person belong to the union *before* being employed. See *Closed Shop, Agency Shop, Open Shop, Right-to-Work Laws*.

UNIT COST

UNIT COST Total cost divided by quantity produced. Also known as *average cost* or *average total cost*.

UNIT ELASTICITY An elasticity coefficient of 1, which indicates that the percentage change in quantity equals the percentage change in price when one is considering price elasticity of demand or price elasticity of supply. When the price elasticity of demand is 1, neither an increase nor a decrease in price will affect total revenue of the firm. Unit price elasticity of demand is illustrated by the midpoint of a straight-line demand curve and by a rectangular hyperbola where the elasticity is 1 at every point. Unit price elasticity of supply is represented by a supply curve which is a straight line from the origin. See *Elasticity*.

UNSECURED NOTE An obligation to pay a specified sum in the future which is not secured by any specified collateral. The general assets of an individual or of a corporation stand as the security behind the debt. See *Collateralized Bond Obligations*.

USE TAX A tax on the use of something such as an automobile or a mobile home. Often a use tax is companion to a state sales tax and permits the state to collect the equivalent of its sales tax on merchandise purchased in another state where sales taxes are lower or nonexistent.

USURY Interest in excess of the maximum allowed by law. In medieval times all interest was considered usurious (and immoral) because loans tended to be made by the rich to the poor for consumption of necessities. The concept of interest as synonymous with usury began to change as borrowing more frequently occurred to fund a production process that hopefully would show a net productivity over cost of production in the future. Eventually it became clear that interest could serve a useful purpose as one of the prices which governs the allocation of scarce resources to their most desired productive use. In a modern developed country, even most consumer borrowing is for capital-like goods, i.e., consumer durables such as automobiles, homes, refrigerators, personal computers, and the like, rather than for minimal consumption of food and shelter.

While interest no longer is a synonym for usury, many states in the U.S. continue to have usury laws to protect consumers by setting maximum interest rates for consumer loans. In periods when high interest rates are generated by capital markets and

304

federal economic policy, such as in the 1970s, some state usury laws have had the effect of cutting off access to borrowed funds by the very consumers whom the states are trying to protect.

UTILITY   1. The satisfaction derived from the consumption of a good or service. It is subjective and cannot be quantified objectively. See *Marginal Utility, Total Utility.*

2. A company which is a regulated natural monopoly such as a natural gas company, a telephone company, or an electricity distributing company. See *Natural Monopoly.*

VALUE-ADDED NATIONAL INCOME ACCOUNTING   The calculation of GNP by totaling the value that is added by each firm in the production sequence from raw material extraction to sale of finished products. Value added is measured by subtracting net changes in inventories and cost of goods purchased from gross sales. It is equal to the amount paid by each firm for wages, interest, rent, and profit. It should equal GNP calculated by adding up the value of all final goods produced, plus changes in inventories.

VALUE-ADDED TAX (VAT)   A tax on the value that is added by each firm in the production process. It taxes the difference between the sales price and the cost of materials in transactions at each stage of production and distribution. It is considered easy to collect because one firm's cost equals another firm's revenues, hence each transaction provides a record in each firm for calculating the tax. A value-added tax is imposed on firms, while a "sales tax" is imposed on consumers based on the value at the time of final sale. The incidence of the tax may not remain where it is initially imposed. See *Tax Incidence*.

VALUE OF THE MARGINAL PHYSICAL PRODUCT   The marginal physical product of a variable factor of production multiplied by the unit price for which the product can be sold. It equals *Marginal Revenue Product* if the product price does not change as more is produced. It is greater than marginal revenue product when the product price must be reduced in order to sell more. See *Marginal Physical Product, Marginal Revenue Product.*

VARIABLE ANNUITY   An annuity that pays amounts of money at regular intervals but which may change the amount paid from year to year depending upon changes in the rate of return and/or changes in the market value of the assets in an annuity fund. For example, shares of stock held in a fund may change in price or in the size of dividend payments. A fund's real estate values and/or rental returns may change. The net change in asset values and returns in a fund can cause a decrease or an increase in the size of the periodic annuity payments, depending on the direction of the net change. See *Annuity.*

VARIABLE COST   The cost of production which varies with output. Variable costs are zero when output is zero. See *Average Variable Cost, Total Variable Cost, Fixed Cost.*

VELOCITY OF CIRCULATION OF MONEY   The rate at which the stock of money is turned over per year to carry on all of the transactions between buyers and sellers is the transactions velocity of the circulation of money. The rate at which the stock of money is turned over per year for *income-generating* transactions is the income velocity of the circulation of money. The income velocity is measured by dividing GNP by the money stock: $V_y = GNP/M$.

The transactions velocity includes *all* transactions, including those not counted in GNP. It adds to GNP transfer payments and all of the payments for intermediate goods that were eliminated to avoid double counting in calculating the value of all *final* goods and services (GNP). The transaction velocity is measured by dividing the total of all transactions in the economy for the designated time by the money stock: $V_T = T/M$. The concepts are used in quantity theories of money and prices. See *Income Velocity of the Circulation of Money, Transactions Velocity of the Circulation of Money.*

VENTURE CAPITAL   Funds invested in new companies entering untried areas of production. The investments are characterized by high risk because of the unknown, but they also can produce very high returns if successful.

VERTICAL INTEGRATION   Consolidation of successive stages of production under the control of one firm. See *Vertical Merger.*

VERTICAL MERGER   Combination into one ownership of firms producing in successive stages of a production process. A vertical merger may be forward toward the finished goods market or backward toward raw material producers. See *Horizontal Merger, Conglomerate Merger*.

VOLUNTARY UNEMPLOYMENT The number of people 16 years of age and older who are neither at work nor actively seeking work; hence they are not counted in the labor force. A person is voluntarily unemployed if there are jobs available for which he or she is qualified, but the person decides against entering the labor force. Instead the person may be a student, a retiree, a homemaker (who may work hard but whose services are not exchanged in a labor market), or someone who just does not want to enter the labor force and can exist without employment. See *Involuntary Unemployment, Labor Force*.

WAGE 1. The return (income) to the labor factor of production for services rendered, including salaries and payments in kind. In this sense, wages are the aggregate amount paid for labor services, as opposed to returns to other factors of production such as rent paid for the use of land, interest paid for capital goods, and profit paid for entrepreneurship.

2. Compensation paid for labor services on an hourly or piece-rate basis to manual (blue-collar) workers, some clerical workers, and others on routine jobs. Contrasts with *salary,* which is paid as fixed compensation to executives and supervisors regardless of hours worked. See *Salary.*

WAGE GUIDEPOSTS A policy tool used by government to attempt to control inflation by publicizing wage-rate changes that are declared to be fair and consistent with the public interest. There is an implied threat to bring public pressure to bear against businesses and unions which exceed those guideposts. Wage guideposts constitute a type of incomes policy used with diminishing success by the Kennedy, Johnson, Nixon, and Carter administrations. See *Incomes Policy, Wage-Push Inflation.*

WAGE-PUSH INFLATION Inflation caused by an increase of wages beyond increases in productivity. Increases in wage costs may be added directly to prices in a relatively strong economy that is predominantly one of administered pricing rather than pure competition. Wage-push inflation focuses on union–management wage bargains and is a subcategory of cost-push inflation. Another type of cost-push inflation is generated by a sharp increase in the price of some basic, widely used resource, such as oil. Demand-pull inflation, on the other hand, is initiated by changes on the demand side of the market rather than on the cost/supply side. See *Cost-Push Inflation, Administered Price.*

WAGE RATE The price offered for human labor per hour, per day, per week, per month, or per year. For determination of the wage rate, see *Equilibrium of the Firm: Factor Market.*

WALKOUT A common term for a strike by employees who leave their work to try to halt production. They thereby hope to put economic pressure on their employer in an effort to achieve some change in the work relationship. A walkout might not halt production if the employer can hire other workers (often referred to as strike breakers or scabs), nor is a walkout effective if the employer would like to reduce output anyway. See *Strike, Sit-Down Strike.*

WELFARE ECONOMICS The study of conditions in an economy that will maximize general economic well-being, that is, achieve all of those changes that will make one or many people better off without making anyone worse off. (It is *not* the study of public welfare systems in support of the poor.) More precisely, maximization of economic welfare occurs when two conditions are achieved: (1) no further change in the economy is possible that could make one person better off without an adverse effect on another person, and (2) no further change is possible that can make one person better off and one worse off but yet provide sufficient gain to the former to fully compensate the latter and still leave some gain to the former.

These two conditions in welfare economics are an attempt to avoid consideration of shifts of resources that would require a value judgment. When an equilibrium is reached which conforms to these conditions, the economy is at what is known as a Pareto optimum [Alfredo Pareto (1848–1923)]. A value judgment, on the other hand, would hold that the condition of person x *ought* to be improved at the expense of y without full compensation to y.

WELFARE STATE A nation which uses political power to reduce economic inequality by redistribution of income or property. Redistribution often takes the form of taxation of the rich more than the poor with the proceeds used to provide public services for some designated segment of the population or for everyone. Sometimes the transfer is direct, using income and property tax revenues to provide food, clothing, and shelter for the poor.

Most modern countries are welfare states to some degree in that they provide public support for the poor in addition to private philanthropy. Some nations have carried the redistribution so far that they have affected incentives for productivity adversely. Some refer to Sweden as an example of a country where taxes are so high that economic incentives are negatively affected. Observers argue that economic incentives have been adversely affected in the U.S.S.R. and some eastern European countries, illustrated by the reluctance of many people in those countries to accept the rapid shift to market-directed economies which began in 1989. People are enthusiastic for political democracy but many do not appear eager to exercise initiative and competitiveness in economic activity; they are more comfortable with job guarantees regardless of efficiency and often fail to relate this to low living standards. They worry about unemployment when inefficient plants are closed and when jobs are required to meet Western efficiency standards.

WILDCAT STRIKE   A strike by unionized employees without authorization from the union. Some possible characteristics of a wildcat strike are (1) a strike by organized employees that is not permitted under a no-strike clause in a collective bargaining contract (so the union cannot openly support it); (2) a strike by members of a local union under local leadership without authorization by the national union under a constitution which requires national office approval; (3) a strike by a dissident faction in a union led by people who want to show aggressiveness to win support against incumbent union officers; (4) a strike which occurs although it is prohibited by law (so, again, union officers cannot condone it); (5) a walkout by a group of "hotheads" who are angry about the time it is taking to settle a grievance or who are unhappy with a grievance outcome. Several of these meanings may have applied at once when a coal miners' strike in the early 1950s was prohibited under the national emergency procedures of the Taft–Hartley Act. John L. Lewis, president of the United Mine Workers, urged the miners to return to work, yet they stayed out, assuming he really didn't mean it.

WINDFALL PROFIT   A profit that occurs because of some circumstance beyond the control of the firms involved, such as some of the profits earned by oil companies in the U.S. following the OPEC oil price increases in the 1970s. Sometimes the windfall is considered an unfair gain that arises from public policy but occurs at the expense of the public, such as unusual profits received by many producers of war material during World War II. An "excess profits" tax was imposed to take away those windfall profits.

WORLD BANK   See *International Bank for Reconstruction and Development.*

WRAP-AROUND MORTGAGE   A second mortgage which calls for the borrower to pay the total of both first and second mortgage payments to the holder of the second mortgage, who then makes payment on the first mortgage. This assures the holder of the second mortgage that the payments are kept up to date. Otherwise, foreclosure by the holder of the first mortgage could leave the holder of the second mortgage holding the bag.

XEROX An excellent example of success in nonprice competition, a company's name and brand being used as the common designation for a whole class of objects. In this case, any copy machine often is referred to as a Xerox machine, no matter what company manufactured it. Even more often, Xerox is used as a verb of general reference, the act of copying a document. It's every manufacturer's dream, and my opportunity to have an X entry. See *Nonprice Competition*.

YELLOW-DOG CONTRACT A contract which requires an employee to agree not to join a labor union as a condition of employment. The contract was made unenforceable under the Norris–LaGuardia Act of 1932. Prior to that time the contracts were enforced by means of court injunctions against unions for inducing employees to break their contracts and join the union. See *Injunction*.

YIELD CURVE A curve relating interest rates to notes and bonds of various maturities. A normal interest curve is positively sloped, illustrating higher interest yields on the face value of notes and bonds of similar rating the longer the time to maturity. This pattern occurs because the longer the period the greater the risk of loss through default, inflation, and alternative uses of the funds foregone. A negative, or inverted, curve sometimes occurs when there is a very strong short-term demand for funds and short-term interest rates rise above long-term rates. In the figure below, interest rates are measured on the vertical axis and maturities are measured on the horizontal axis.

See *Inverted Yield Curve.*

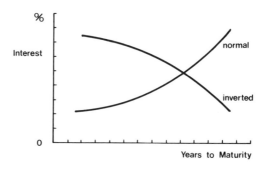

YIELD CURVES

ZERO-COUPON BOND   A bond which is sold at a price which represents the present discounted value of the maturity price of the bond. An original-issue discount bond. The interest return is not paid or payable periodically, but rather accrues in value as the bond approaches maturity. Before the 1980s, the increase in value generally could be treated as a capital gain at maturity rather than as ordinary interest. Because there is no annual or semiannual interest payment, there was no yearly income tax obligation while the bond was held. When the bond was sold or matured, there was a capital gain that was taxed at capital gains rates, which were lower than the top tax rate for ordinary income. Today the annual increase in value of a zero-coupon bond generally is treated as ordinary interest income and taxed annually even though it is not received annually.

A U.S. Series E bond Savings Bond illustrates a zero-coupon bond in that a person may pay, for example, $500 for a bond whose maturity value is $1000 in 10 years, for an effective compound interest rate of 7.18%. There is no annual interest payment; the interest takes the form of accumulated value of the bond. The bond is an exception to the general tax treatment of original-issue discount securities (OIDs) in that there is no income tax liability until the bond is submitted for redemption. A Series E bond is not negotiable, but it may be cashed in early for less than the maturity value. Upon redemption, the accumulated interest is treated as ordinary income, not capital gains. See *Coupon, Original-Issue Discount Security, Deep-Discount Bond.*